AUSTRALIAN SCREEN SERIES

General Editor: Sylvia Lawson

The Screening of Australia:
Anatomy of a National Cinema
Volume 2

THE SCREENING OF AUSTRALIA

Volume 2

ANATOMY OF A NATIONAL CINEMA

SUSAN DERMODY

ELIZABETH JACKA

CURRENCY PRESS • SYDNEY

First published in 1988
by Currency Press Pty Ltd,
PO Box 452 Paddington
N.S.W. 2021, Australia

Copyright© Susan Dermody and Elizabeth Jacka 1988

This book is copyright. Apart from any fair dealing for the purpose of private study, research or review as permitted under the Copyright Act, no part may be reproduced by any process without written permission. Inquiries should be addressed to the publishers.

National Library of Australia
Cataloguing-in-Publication data
Dermody, Susan
    The screening of Australia. Volume two, Anatomy of a national cinema.

Bibliography.
Includes index.
ISBN 0868191876

1. Australian Film Commission. 2. Moving-picture Industry — Australia — History. I. Jacka, Elizabeth. II. Title: III. Anatomy of a national cinema. (Series: Australian screen).

384'.8'0994

Mad Max 2 cover photo featuring Bruce Spence as the Gyro Captain, reproduced by kind permission of Kennedy-Miller.

Published with the assistance of the Australian Film Commission.

In memory of Bill Bonney
(Associate Head of the Faculty of Humanities, NSWIT,
from 1975 until his death in 1985).

Acknowledgements

Photos reprinted with the kind permission of; Kennedy-Miller, *Mad Max*, *Mad Max 2*, *Mad Max 3*, *The Dismissal*; Seven Keys, *Return of Captain Invincible*; Samson Film Services, *Odd Angry Shot*; Don McLennan, *Hard Knocks*; Anthony Ginnane, *Snapshot*, *Dead Kids*; Bob Weis, *Pure Shit*; Fringe Dwellers Productions, *Fringe Dwellers*; South Australian Film Corporation, *Sunday Too Far Away*; Inma Productions, *Wrong Side of the Road*; Anthony Buckley, *Caddie*; Margaret Fink Films, *My Brilliant Career*; Phillip Adams, *The Adventures of Barry McKenzie*; Hexagon Productions, *Alvin Purple*; Palm Beach Pictures, *Newsfront*, *Starstruck*; Storm Productions, *In Search of Anna*; Chris Fitchett/John Ruane, *Queensland*; Smiley Productions, *Stir*; McElroy and McElroy, *The Last Wave*; Anthony Buckley, *The Night the Prowler*; Film House Australia, *The Chant of Jimmie Blacksmith*; Limelight Productions, *Puberty Blues*; South Australian Film Corporation, *Breaker Morant*; Pavilion Films, *Monkey Grip*; Syme International Productions, *Careful He Might Hear You*; Illumination Films, *Man of Flowers*; Phillip Adams, *We of the Never Never*; Limelight Productions, *Silver City*; Seon Films, *Plains of Heaven*; John Sexton and Michael Edgeley International, *The Man from Snowy River*; TRM Productions, *Strikebound*; John Hughes, *Traps*; Anthony Buckley, *Bliss*; Rimfire Films, *Crocodile Dundee*; Seon Films, *Wrong World*; Associated R+R Films, *Gallipoli*; Henry Crawford Productions, *A Town Like Alice*.

Contents

Acknowledgements	6
PART ONE	
1. The Second Cinema: A Doubled Industry	11
2. The Aesthetic Force-Field	28
PART TWO	
3. The First Phase (1970-75): The Prototypes Emerge	77
4. Transition 1 (1975): Touchstone Successes	97
5. The Second Phase (1976-80): Seemly Respectability	110
6. Transition 2 (1980-81): A Tentative Maturity	151
7. The Third Phase (1981-): Middle-Aged Spread?	179
8. Epilogue: Famous Last Words	231
Notes	247
A Select Filmography	252
Index	273

PART ONE

1

The Second Cinema: A Doubled Industry

In the Bicentennial year of 1988 the 'new Australian cinema' celebrates its twentieth anniversary, if we count its birthdate, symbolically from the setting-up in 1968 of the Film and Television Committee of the Australian Council for the Arts. This committee produced the blueprint for the film industry in the seventies, an industry born in a moment of desire for a 'national culture' in opposition to British and American cultural dominance, but never free either of the dominance nor of the problems that riddle the question of national culture — especially in a second world state like Australia.

In Volume One of *The Screening of Australia*, subtitled *Anatomy of a Film Industry*, we traced the economic, political, cultural and bureaucratic forces which brought this new cinema into being, and strongly determined its character, after a virtual halt to commercial feature production since the late thirties. We examined the imprint upon the industry of the project of cultural nationalism which flourished in the late sixties and returned in waves throughout the subsequent years to the present, affecting not only the agenda for government-assisted feature production, but also resurgences of local theatre, visual arts and literature, as well as politics, fashion, advertising, tourism and so forth. However, unlike these other cultural forms, film is suspended between culture (and cultural debates) and industry (and the discourses of employment, profitability, the language money 'speaks').

As we have seen, the history of Australian cinema is in part the history of the fluctuations in the balance of these two influences.

The picture is confused, however, by the contradiction inherent in government assistance to commercial interests on cultural grounds. In this volume, analysis of the films themselves illustrates the way that contradictory requirements of two different desires has tended to limit the types of films that can be made in Australia. The industry has a sense that it must compromise between the dutifully bland and 'cultural' and the dutifully commercial. This compromise tends to overwhelm the moments of genuine richness that should be fully explored and acknowledged.

We have also seen how throughout the seventies the feature industry was largely a creation of government policy, especially responsive to inner and outward agendas of the main film body, the Australian Film Commission (AFC). The task of the AFC and of its predecessor, the AFDC, was to foster the development of an Australian cinema that was cultural enough and Australian enough to justify its direct subsidy; but it was also charged with steering the industry towards eventual financial viability. By the late seventies, the irreconcilable nature of these two ambitions was becoming apparent as film budgets rose beyond the commercial scope of the local marketplace, and pressure increased within the industry for a kind of 'privatisation' of government funding for the industry. The eighties have mainly been the era of a much expanded indirect subsidy to the industry through various stages of change to amendment 10B(A) to the Taxation Act, permitting (decreasingly) generous 'write-offs' of tax liability to tax-payers investing in feature films. The AFC has correspondingly retreated to a supporting role, only gradually returning to its former gate-keeping status as it has had to increase both its investment in non-deductible areas of budget and its assistance in script development.

In the seventies, the culture-industry 'couple' turned out to be an opposition, and this has been amplified in the eighties by the rise of the film-financing sub-industry. It has, however, also been modulated by a new, intensely commercial version of 'nationalness' that we see at work in *The Man From Snowy River* and *Crocodile Dundee*. Nevertheless, it is probably still true to say that the history of the industry has been a history of mainly deadlocked contest — with many small shifts and mutual accommodations — between the claims of the commercial, the cultural and the national. The two reasonably distinct faces of a doubled industry that we identified in the previous volume as 'Industry-1' and 'Industry-2', emerging from the early tax-incentive period, are still recognisable today. Even though 'Australianness' is now probably far from the simple object for contempt that it once was for Industry-2, it is still true that Industry-1 has a less consciously opportunistic attitude towards the question of representing Australia.

More by the coincidence of all of these factors, than by deliberate aesthetic design on the part of the government film instrumentalities, certain kinds of films dominated the directly-funded cinema of the seventies. The pattern of filmmaking was touched on in Chapters 1 and 3, and also in the concluding chapter of Volume One. The dominant groupings are defined in detail in Chapter 2 of this volume, and then elaborated across the various phases of the Australian cinema, through to their surprisingly late persistence in the eighties, in subsequent chapters.

The Australian industry, like those of other 'second world' countries, exists in an environment strongly conditioned and even regulated by the norms established by Hollywood during seven decades of economic and aesthetic dominance. For more than sixty years, the local distribution and exhibition chains were owned or controlled by the American majors, and it has been only in the last few years that realignments in the international industry itself have led to the transfer of the local exhibition majors to local hands. However, regardless of the fine details of ownership connections, Australian screens (film and television) continue to be dominated by American product. Locally-produced films have had to compete both at home and abroad within a set of viewing expectations that is American, or formed by American culture abroad. At the same time they must display sufficient distinction from American product to permit differentiation in the marketplace, both here and overseas. Again we feel how bound the films have been to a narrow, and essentially contradictory, set of choices. And again, government, while willing to intervene at the production level, has never been willing to intervene in the marketplace of distribution and exhibition; and the deregulatory environment of the late eighties makes this possibility seem ever more remote.

Of course, the precarious position of the Australian industry in a situation so dominated by Hollywood intensifies commercial pressures — on the one hand, to find a sufficient (but unthreatening) difference; on the other hand, to introduce elements intended to make the films more universally commercial, in Hollywood's own terms. One answer to foreign domination has been to package carefully selected and marketable commonplaces of Australian 'national type' and 'colourful locale' for comfortable consumption, at home or in America, or even Japan, or of providing down-home varieties of Hollywood. *Crocodile Dundee* has given the second, 'sophisticated' variant of this strategy some extremely good press. However, it is difficult to imagine endlessly repeatable success for this formula, with or without Paul Hogan. *Crocodile Dundee* itself began to exhaust its own small territory even before the film was over.

The other place where market competitiveness has been sought is in the notion of making Australian films more 'international', by effacing the Australian character of their setting, story and actors, and searching limbo for good 'universal' stories and genre elements abstracted from their cultural origins, and securing overseas 'stars' (affordable ones) to enhance the commercial prospects of the films. The host of films produced under this regime have no outstanding success to vindicate their strategy, unless the third *Mad Max (Beyond Thunderdome)* is asked to stand in here. In fact, few have any kind of theatrical exhibition life in their country of origin.

Industry-1 and Industry-2 have in one sense, formed around these two quite different answers to the problem of Hollywood. The place where their differences have articulated themselves has been the various struggles over Australian content that have been present since the earliest days of revival and continue into the present. In chapter 5 of the previous volume we described how measures to safeguard the Australian nature of the films that received government subsidy were built into the enabling legislation of both the AFDC and AFC, and how later, when the 10B(A) tax provisions for film were introduced in 1981, these safeguards were embodied in their administration. Nevertheless there has always been pressure, muted during the seventies, but increasingly vociferous in the eighties, to 'deregulate' Australian content. The argument from many producers has been that if we are to have a successful and financially viable industry, we must sell in the lucrative American market; and the use of overseas stars in particular is seen as a prerequisite for likely success in this market, and even more importantly, for securing pre-sales.

The union representing Australian actors, Actors' Equity, has maintained a militant stand against the wholesale importation of overseas personnel; and at times when government policy might have weakened on this issue has managed to exert enough industrial muscle to hold back a potential flood of overseas actors. This consistent stand, along with the persistence of Industry-1 values within some mileux (and genres) of the industry, despite 10B(A), has retarded the tendency for Australia to seem a conveniently cheap and exotic outpost of Hollywood — a Canada of the South Pacific, perhaps.

But if we have escaped the fate of endless *Porkys* and *Police Academies*, so far, Queensland is now to be a new home away from home for Dino de Laurentiis, promising to produce five 'Australian' features by the end of 1988 with average budgets of $5-$10 million. The cheap local facilities (in current U.S. dollar exchange terms) are also proving attractive to other U.S. producer/distributors, such as New World Pictures. Industry passivity towards these significant on-shore moves of American 'minor majors' is a desolate sign of the times: Australians in the late eighties are still in thrall to righteously greedy and illiberal politics of the Right, and 'dollars and sense' talk effortlessly prevails. Even though it represents import replacement of some considerable commercial importance, national culturalism simply has no 'push' at present. With Australia, as an economic entity, all but dissolved in the wash of the international money market, national culturalism has rarely looked more impotent, fragile or anachronistic.

National cinema, national psyche

If this has been a doubled industry developed among the conflicting influences of culture, commerce and nationalism, as Volume One argued, how far has the corresponding national cinema also been caught up in the bounds of contradictory desires? National cinema studies always attempt to read national 'psyches' from the cinemas in question, even if they go no further than tacking on some generalising observations to a simple accretion of director-based career studies. Such studies frequently assume a fairly unproblematic, reflectionist relationship between the film output of a country and its social history, ignoring the specific conditions of production and circulation in the local industry, and the nature of the aesthetic field it creates for itself.[1]

Perhaps the classic of this is Siegfried Kracauer's *From Caligari to Hitler* (1947), which reads an unconscious premonitory history of the German nation in films from the Weimar Republic to the rise of Hitler, as though reading a patient's past dreams to uncover the roots of a pathology. Despite all the problems of teleological fallacy in this procedure, and of the assumption that there is a national psyche or inner soul of a people to be located (rather than constructed), Kracauer's reading of Weimar cinema as deep premonition is compelling. It tells a good story in classic terms — a case history in which a torn and tortured being struggles to articulate a livable identity within a family battleground of desire and law. The cinema is seen as the place where the nation's personal demons are projected, only to be finally empowered, rather than exorcised, in a hopeless choice beteween tyranny and chaos.

However, Kracauer's theory of a national inner soul is romantic and fatalistic, like the national cinema/national soul that he describes, in its slippage from one ontological category to another, from effect to cause, from imaginary to real. The notion that national identity is a constructed and usually conservative set of meanings endowed momentarily with a measure of consensual approval, was nowhere in sight. Kracauer was dealing in souls and ghosts, a rich demonology.

Other writers have worked productively in this territory. Thomas Elsaesser's attempt to find an intermediary term between history and psychoanalysis in his work of national cinemas (in particular, German cinema of the Weimar period, and post-war film, especially the films of Fassbinder) is appealing and instructive in the Australian context, as Stuart Cunningham has pointed out.[2]

Elsaesser's work starts from more sophisticated notions of both history and the constructed (if partly unconscious) nature of the 'social imaginary' (as he calls the intermediary term between national/cultural history and a psychoanalytic reading of the texts of a national cinema).[3] The influence of Foucault's theory of history-writing, as a radically sceptical examination of the way past discursive structures 'think' us in the present, can be felt in the way he analyses the perceptual set in which Weimar period films were made and seen. Instead of reading the inexorable procession of Germany into fascism, he looks for wider historical processes, including the particular balance of technology and the arts in Germany under the stress of rapid industrialisation, and the resultant foregrounding of demonic, Faustian overreachers, mad scientists, and doppelgangers. Pushing forward and overrating the visual is one effect of this same struggle between discrepant discourses — and German fascism is another. Filmmaking was a way of participating in the power, brutality and terror of industrialisation — a participation in the discourse of Frankenstein, perhaps. But the films are full of the anti-technological, conservative ideology of late Romanticism grounded in the new psychology of the unconcious, which Elsaesser sees as an attempt to formulate a response to the pity and terror inspired by the spectacle of industrialisation.[4]

So they express (and place the spectator within) a split in the process of representation; the spectator is placed as the filmmaker is placed, in the position of the double, watching himself.[5] Elsaesser sees the visual pleasure of the films as inseparable from German anxiety about having or losing power and control; in particular, he examines the use of the point-of-view shot as the strategy that allows the spectator sufficient control to enjoy, rather than masochistically suffer, the perception of anxiety. In other words, he brings the notion of 'social imaginary' to the point of defining characteristic optical or specular strategies in the German body of film.

A 'social imaginary' in this sense, has more to do with a textual mode of address and historical process, than with *zeitgeist* and content. At risk of over-simplifying Elsaesser's complex and subtle argument, it is possible to describe his crucial mediating term as something between an historically shaped and specified perceptual mode or set, and its symptomatic set of practices and pleasures. As such, the notion of a 'social imaginary' is productive as a middle term, since it belongs to a genuine middle ground between two estranged impulses in film theory. It is at once a kind of back door for history into a psychoanalytic framework, and a backdoor for the unconscious into an historic framework.

Characterising an Australian 'social imaginary'

The German cinema, both pre and post-war, offers particularly fertile ground for the uncovering of buried memory, and the recurrent processes that both betray and enact it. Is Australia a suitable case for treatment? Can we expect to find a 'social imaginary' of such powerful consistency pushing to the surface all or most of the 'discursive entities' associated with the film industry of this country? Certainly, Australia has not been a 'ground zero' of twentieth century history in the way that Germany has. The second world capitalist dominion status of Australia, like that of Canada and New Zealand, has shielded it from much of the major trauma of direct warfare and economic attrition that has shaped many other histories in the recent past.[6]

Like the physical continent itself, the economic 'zone' we inhabit is temperate, but subject to a far more erratic 'rainfall' (coincidentally benign local effects of larger external economic interests) than we realise. It is a peripheral economy, with minimal sovereignty, dominated before World War I by the needs of British capital, and changing between the wars but especially in the post World War II period to a primary economic and political domination by the United States, with a secondary domination by the trade and investment interests of Japan and the Common Market countries. Our manufacturing and mineral sector, which probably determines the real limits to our declared sovereignty, is dominated by branches of American Japanese and European multi-national corporations. The industrial base, shrinking rather than expanding since the late sixties, is protected by tariffs and largely confined within national borders, with an exceptional minority of companies establishing themselves outside the borders as multi-nationals.

Politically, Australia, Canada and New Zealand share a similar history as self-governing white dominions within the British Empire. In each case, the indigenous populations at the time of European overseas expansion, commencing in the late fifteenth century, were sufficiently sparse to be subjected to genocide, paternalist assimilation or effective banishment to the hinterlands of the new settler colonies. British institutions were adopted as if there were no distinction to be drawn between colonial and metropolitan experience, history and interests. Australia has been notoriously slow to dismantle the legal apparatus of dependency, long after the economic patterns that dictated dependency were altered beyond recognition.[7] The geographical and political separation of six original colonies has persisted jealously in many forms since federation in 1900; and contributed inertia and conservatism to the political system as a whole.

While these broad geo-political factors have assigned Australia to a relatively quiet and obedient place in twentieth-century world history, it is also precisely these which have produced a particularly inward national drama. This should be the starting point for any structuring 'social imaginary' belonging to a national entity, 'Australia'.

The discussion that follows is prefaced by the idea, already implied, that culture and cultural identity are at times constructed in national terms, or involve a construction of that which is 'nationally Australian'. But Australianness is a construction, dependent for its meaning and recognition on particular contexts and uses, and dependent for its plausibility on its appeal for various publics. And it is, at any given time, only one of several terms like class, race, gender and region, from which an essentially historical identity can be constructed. To some extent, its viability is always dependent on the partial suppression of these other, more specific terms which give our present the context of a history.

As Sylvia Lawson has argued, the problem for Australia is that it is post-colonial without being post-revolutionary.[8] In the economic and political terms explored above, dominion capitalism has allowed Australia a comfortable semblance of independent economic development, and has until recently maintained high living standards relative to those of other industrialised capitalist (or, 'first- world') countries. Identification with the metropolitan centre of colonial days has remained remarkably strong, blurring and dislocating local identity. The fact that we were a settler colony — anxious to put aside, but never bury, the confusing factor of our early penal-settlement status — also blurs the political boundaries of identity for white Australians. Meanwhile, for Aboriginal Australia, the other side of the frontier presents a history of invasion, near genocide and cultural obliteration. But the white settlement of Australia has never been sufficiently discomfited by its dependent status, economic or political, to develop even remotely revolutionary tendencies. And so the problem of decolonising the Australian mentality is both severe and subtle. There is little agitation for systematic or profound decolonisation in this sense; but the generalised, rather melancholy desire for an Australian identity has been at times widely felt and expressed.⁹ It was on the back of such desire, beginning to intrude into public agendas again in the late sixties, that the demand for 'a film industry' was raised and carried forward, and eventually acted upon by government.

A more dominating and repressive colonial regime might have produced a sharper focus both for the desire and its popular analysis. Instead, from this ambiguity comes a self-imposed inhibition that operates around desire: a double bind, or series of double binds. Are we the lost child, pathetically obscured from the parent, or the rejected child, loudly asserting its difference, if not independence? We are fixed in a series of positions of radically unequal economic and cultural exchange with Britain and the U.S. which we cannot afford to change for something else.

The 'second world' we inhabit is bound to reproduce the first world, yet needs to assert a measure of independence, of product differentiation, to market or circulate our reproductions. The third world absorbs and internalises first world values too, in a way which, according to dependency theory, forces those countries into a 'systematic development of underdevelopment'[10]. Second-world underdevelopment is less apparent economically; it is most striking at the cultural level. Second-world countries like Canada and Australia are riddled with post-colonial ambiguity and anxieties. They feel second best within their own markets and culture, forced to second guess what their authentic indigenous culture should be.

In this situation in which we do and do not have a parent to make decisions for us, who creates our imaginary and live relations to the world according to interests not necessarily coincidental to our own, our identity becomes both clamorous and permanently obscure; a riddle from an implacable sphinx. For where do 'we' end and the 'other' begin? Who is the other by which we define our difference, ensuring 'us'? Britain? America? How are 'they' to be satisfactorily disentangled from what we have internalised and hybridised from them? Our film industry proclaims its central role in revealing an identity we don't know we have until we recognise it: we are forced by it to eternally enact a ritual of recognition, to know again what we need to 'know'. Can we afford to know too much, to recognise real differences, or the real point of difference? Can we ever financially afford to end our adolescent dependence?

In the simplest sense, it is precisely the entire preoccupation with national 'identity' that organises the social imaginary of the films under scrutiny here, and that runs through many wider cultural spaces. 'Identity' exists within coordinates of time (names, generations, family histories, national stories, accretions around the name 'Australia', etcetera) and space (the soil, the land, landscape, maps, borders, coastlines and heartlands): history and place.

On the one hand, the motif or 'burden' of the Australian place is endlessly manifest in films, painting and literature. One version describes our anguish about the uninterpreted nature of the place: we are several generations of European settlers, with relatively little history, without a white Australian mythos: lone figures, lost in a landscape. Ross Gibson argues that it is possible to write a detailed history of European (and white explorer and settler) literary projections on to the 'blank' landscape, empty space, dead 'centre'.[11] Bernard Smith's path-making work on European vision projected on to the South Pacific region in Australian painting logically precedes it.[12] Analyses like these emphasise the estrangement of 'our' culture from its place, and give us enough distance to make the process at last recognisable.

Closely related to the 'figure in the landscape' is the personal sense of inhabiting either a second-rate culture 'of our own', disdained by the metropolitan centre, of which we are an urbanised periphery, or a second-hand culture not quite our own, imported across the lamentable distances that separate us from the source. If anguish marks the first, discontent marks the second. There is no 'authenticity' to a situation so defined; so it becomes an urgent lack, although every approach has proven that 'authenticity' is never there when you get there. Authenticity is, instead, the result of authoritative and sensitive discourse, of a construction that taps enough current desires and fears to enter successfully the currency of ways of seeing.

The perennial melancholy around which we organise our national stories is related more perhaps to problems of time than space: the inevitable, honourable loss of our 'best' causes, the myths of the underdog, stories that unify us in defeat. And who defeats us? The tyrants are usually overt or covert British or American interests or individuals, the power against which we can't afford to win. We lost 'our best' at Anzac Cove because of the brutal and rigid self interest of British generals, rather than the Turkish enemy. We lost our great Les Darcy and Phar Lap to dark conspiracies of the American crime and business worlds. Ned Kelly went down to Queen's men with pommy accents, Whitlam to Queen's men with Australian ones. We savour the delicious and honourable melancholy of our perpetual defeat. Even an odd reversal, like the 1984 America's Cup win, while it occasions intense national pleasure, cannot upset the deep pattern.

In fact, the occasional win merely shows the strength of the competitive undercurrent in most Australian stories: the 'other', the foe 'we' embrace, can be the continent, landscape, emptiness; the mother country, great and powerful friend, patron; the bosses, generals, wardens; the feminine. The contest is mournfully predestined to be lost, in most cases; 'winning' versions such as the America's Cup and *The Man From Snowy River* are rarely put forward, but do great business when they coincide with a high point in the oscillating wave of desire for a proud 'identity'. It is not surprising that the signs of positive desire are always picked up and amplified first by advertising, while film picks up the clues a beat or so later, in the seventies and early eighties. If, in the films, the process of feeling and knowing one's self as 'Australian' is marketed as content, so, even more nakedly, in particular cycles and genres of television advertising 'Australianness' is used to sell products or evoke a communal 'we' receptive to the idea or service. (See Volume One, Chapter 1, on the 'humanity ads'.)

We can observe essentially the same blurring of the distinction between desire for identity and product differentiation in the migration of particular aspects of film industry output into official culture. So, for example, in 1985 a major retrospective of Heidelberg School Australian landscape painting was mounted in Sydney and later in other capitals under the title 'Golden Summers'. The exhibition had a huge advertising budget and circulated as an 'event', like the earlier Monet exhibition which drew bigger crowds than a football grand final. As the crowds gathered and queued past, Sotheby's in London prepared to auction Australian impressionist works at record prices, past the one million pound mark for the first time. The most striking visual coincidence, made clearer by the gathering of this hallmark collection of Australian official culture, was the one between the rediscovery of those paintings and the AFC[13] genre of soft period films. (See Chapter 2.) Suddenly it was familiar all over again; the AFC genre recirculated the imagery of Edwardian figures in the suddenly dazzlingly beautiful Australian landscape — bush, trees, sandstone and yellow light. Now Golden Summers recirculated the Heidelberg School originals on currents of familiarity strengthened by the film genre, and the honour accorded to the official culture became ever more 'natural', beyond analysis.

It is worth risking accusations of vulgar Marxism for a moment to comment that we can glimpse in this process a romantic bourgeois dream of authenticity, the construction of a self-aware, bourgeois culture as a backdrop to the oscillations between pleasure and embarrassment around the question of national identity. At the same moment, of course, we glimpse the effacement of the curators, investors, stockpilers, 'owners' of this official culture: those who have these romantic desires are never present. Rather a bourgeoisie and its official culture are part of the process itself, as the objects of their desire and their status are mythologised and naturalised at one and the same moment.

The Double Bind

These are examples of the double bind that simultaneously excites and denies a desire to establish or 'recognise' national identity within an economic and political posture that, both implicitly and explicitly, accepts dependence. The deep ambiguity about the difference also plays itself out in the establishment of a film industry or national cinema. Solanas and Gettino's thesis, formed in Argentina, called for a 'third cinema' in opposition to the internalised 'first cinema' of Hollywood and the neocolonial 'second cinema' that consciously and unconsciously strives to reproduce the Hollywood models of production and circulation, counterfeiting the local sense of historical reality.

The implicit and sometimes explicit aim of a second cinema, even if it is never achieved, is to make films that succeed in Hollywood's terms, in the U.S. market. At the same time, it is necessary to assert difference if there is to be any marketable aspect to these films outside the borders of their country. Indeed, since 'the movies' is generally collapsed into 'Hollywood' within the overseas territories of that cultural empire, marketable difference is necessary in the home marketplace as well. In both markets the distinguishing feature is national identity, national flavour; ironically, this has the sense of an exoticism at home as well as abroad, but that may have as much to do with the manufacture of nationalism in any product (Australiana or Americana for instance) as with neocolonial alienation from 'that which is our own'. If a film industry can manifest a social imaginary in its discourse, then for a second cinema like that of Australia, it will include a powerful set of desires about Hollywood, that institution of American cinema. Whether the industry is protesting its viability or clamouring for subsidy on the ground that it is essential to Australian identity, the phantom of Hollywood hovers over the proceedings.

On the textual level, too, insofar as there is a form that can be identified or recognised as 'Hollywood', it is the structuring absence; it is to be replicated either as far as possible, or as far as a modest degree of conscious difference will allow. Very few films have consciously and directly addressed the 'Hollywood' problematic as critical subject: *Newsfront, Starstruck, Goodbye Paradise*, and to some extent all the consciously eccentric films.[14] It must also be noted that two other formal systems, or subsystems, not completely discrepant with the dominant system, help determine the shape of the aesthetic force-field in these films: British 'quality' television drama and documentary, or social realist drama which directly flows from the Grierson school of government documentary production.[15]

But the important point here is that a second cinema, with its national-cinema base, will tend neither to compromise the projection of a likeable self-image, nor test the supposed inability of Americans to understand much outside their own culture. A second cinema may be expected to present some evidence of resistance, but primarily it will accommodate the dominant stylistic paradigm of Hollywood film.[16] Its most aesthetically interesting films are probably those that to a degree refuse to play this game, or that produce conscious mutations; its least interesting, those that attempt to pass themselves off as 'the real thing', erasing all signs of their local production. In other words, as long as Hollywood continues to homogenise world cinema, both economically and stylistically, indigenous cinemas will be 'second', secondary, and therefore will speak only their specific relationship to it. The only exceptions are in countries with their own dominant

The Second Cinema: A Doubled Industry 25

home industries, such as Hindi cinema in India, or Chinese cinema in Hong Kong.

For all its problems, the notion of the social imaginary is useful. It points out the need to imagine a way in which both the major conflicting desires of recent film theory — history and the unconscious — can make sense of each other and of an entity like an Australian film industry or national cinema. It offers a way of making the notions of form and textual practice in a definable family grouping of films, like that of national cinema, historically specific. Furthermore, there is a ready congruence between social and cultural history, the national, the familial, the social imaginary and the construction of the subject in psychoanalytic terms; and in this set of relations, 'social imaginary' is a helpful mediating term.

But if there is a social imaginary that can be reliably theorised and observed at play in recent Australian film, then it is one caught up in the very problem of a perpetual sense of loss over who we are and how we should be, and declare ourselves as, Australian. The problem, that is, of endlessly trying to recognise and remember a social imaginary that might be Australian, and then of presenting and examining the movement of that process into content, into thematic display. In view of our second-world/second-cinema status, the deep ontological uncertainties of any national construction of Australianness produce a peculiar tension that encourages stagnation in Australian film: it is caught in one double bind in asserting and also withdrawing from an identity that can never be taken for granted while it remains in accommodating dependence. It is also caught in another double bind, asserting and withdrawing from a sufficient 'difference' from Hollywood. These double binds become, effectively, the social imaginary of our cinema: it is a social imaginary caught out by the very problem of what might take place in its own space, because that cinema is attempting to project a national identity of such uncertain and self-conscious status.

There is also the perpetual danger, created both by the films and the way they are marketed, of taking national identity unproblematically, consenting to the perpetual construction of meaning announced as natural, historical, inevitable, true — and adequate — in each fresh articulation of the familiar. So there is a double problem: to examine a body of films in terms of a social imaginary that constantly threatens to collapse into the self-conscious content of the films; and to constantly question 'national' as a construct, remaining alert to other more critical, less compliant articulations of national histories, and to the other histories which are obscured by a national focus.

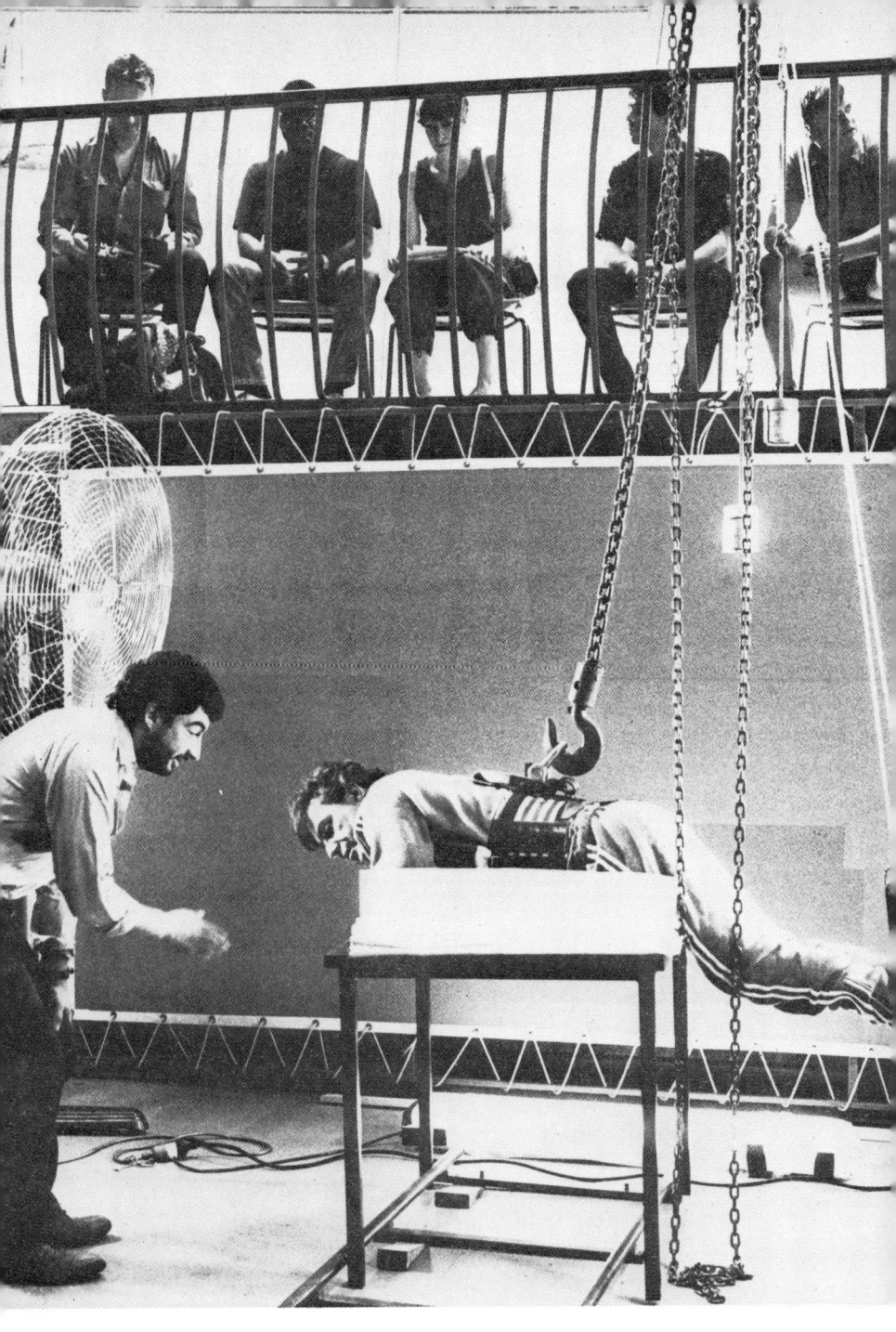

Big-budget schlock: the creaky machinery of the trans-national genre pic. Director Phillipe Mora instructs Alan Arkin, in *The Return of Captain Invincible*.

2

The Aesthetic Force-Field

In this chapter we attempt to uncover an anatomy of Australian film as it has grown since 1970 to try and see its parts, tendencies, specialisations, limitation and desires. We look at the pattern of aesthetic decisions that have been consistently repeated, creating identifiable styles which have persisted until other styles have been formulated in response; we look at the ways in which they are themselves responses to the dominant industry positions (Industry-1 and Industry-2) which we identified in Volume One. We are also concerned to examine the use of actors as iconic registers: ways of speaking Australianness; particularly in view of the continuing project of presenting national life on film, countering the imported culture that has always been the norm in this country. The industry desire to speak Australianness has continued to organise the force-field of feature production, to a greater or lesser extent, in accord with, or reaction to, this project. In the five chapters which follow, we trace in detail the way Australianness has been articulated in each of the three main phases of the industry since 1970.

The Aesthetic Field

The AFC Genre
(* denotes children's film; parentheses indicate a partial influence.)

1973 *Libido: The Child
    Lost in the Bush*

1974 *(Between Wars)*
1975 *Picnic at Hanging Rock*
1976 *Caddie*
   Break of Day
   *Let the Balloon Go**
   (The Devil's Playground)
   (Mad Dog Morgan)
1977 *The Getting of Wisdom*
   The Mango Tree
   Picture Show Man
1978 *The Irishman*
   Weekend of Shadows
   (The Chant of Jimmy Blacksmith)
1979 *My Brilliant Career*
   (Tim)
   (Dawn!)
1980 *Breaker Morant*
   Manganinnie
   *Fatty Finn**
1981 *Gallipoli*
   (The Killing of Angel Street)
1982 *The Man From Snowy River*
   Ginger Meggs
   Kitty and the Bagman
   Squizzy Taylor
   We of the Never Never
1983 *Careful, He Might Hear You*
   (Molly)
   Phar Lap
   Undercover
   Winds of Jarrah
1984 *Silver City*
   *Tail of a Tiger**
1985 *(The Boy Who Had Everything)*
   Emma's War
   (Rebel)
1986 *Burke and Wills*
   For Love Alone
   Kangaroo
1987 *The Place at the Coast*
   The Umbrella Woman

The respectable and slightly sanitised quality of the AFC genre compromises the bite of *Caddie's* social criticism. Helen Morse and Jacki Weaver.

Slow pans across the surfaces of period objects and decor: decoration replaces expression. Judy Davis in *My Brilliant Career*.

The most obvious aesthetic grouping among the films since 1970 is the picturesque period film formed in the wake of the success in 1975 of *Picnic at Hanging Rock*. This is not necessarily the largest nor the most commercially successful group, but these film have tended to be the most 'citable', the ones deemed worthy of international showcasing and that have earned honourable mention, if not glory, for Australia as a fledgling film culture. The phase in which these films dominated was the middle one, 1975 to 1980/1, when the Australian Film Commission and its preferences dominated local production and strongly influenced the way Australian film came to be officially thought and talked of.

Picnic was in fact developed by the Australian Film Development Corportion, and the investment transferred to the AFC on changeover in 1975. Although it is the obvious film of the group because of its critical and financial success, it is not especially typical. It is primarily a period thriller organised around fantasy and enigma, and only secondly a film that borrows its sensibility, languor and 'good taste' from its class-conscious Edwardian dress, decorum and art design. Nor was it the first film of the revival to exhibit some of the AFC genre's characteristics. *The Child* segment of *Libido*, in 1973, foreshadowed them very clearly, as is made clear in the next chapter.

The staple AFC-genre films were supported by bodies other than the AFC. For example, *My Brilliant Career* was funded by the New South Wales Film Corporation. But gradually the AFC-genre came to characterise worthy investment by the AFC, films 'we could be proud of'.

'Genre films', in a looser sense than we have been using it here, are films whose identity responds primarily to genres perennial in some echelons of the international marketplace; for instance they appear among lower-budget U.S. cinema and telemovies, cable- and video-fodder. These films acquire a marketplace identity and attempt to trade from it. Australian cinema tends not to be genre-based, in this sense, although there have been 'genre' films in production from the earliest point at which money could legally be invested or written off in their name at a reasonable profit. (The first truly profitable exception is the huge box office success of *Mad Max*.) The number of projects developed and publicised as genre films increased after the 1981 tax incentives, but even in this phase they have remained a small part of the aesthetic field. This looser category of genre films, with minimal interest in, or address to, their local client culture, will be explored separately. At this point it is worth noting that the category has an inverse relationship to the AFC genre's project of positively projecting a middle-brow cultural worthiness to the world. Their existence could be seen partly as a reaction against both the critical 'citability' and limited economic viability of the AFC genre.

The phenomenon of the AFC genre was noted from time to time in the late seventies as a persistent tendency of Australian cinema to fall back on pretty 'period', 'nostalgia' or 'history' films when it should be addressing the not-so-pretty 'real', contemporary, Australian world. Despite growing critical impatience, *My Brilliant Career* crowned the seventies' cycle of these films with a second resounding commercial and critical success in 1979. Period films were given a new lease on pride after *Breaker Morant* (1980) turned the genre towards the rich commercial possibilities of declared nationalism and male Australianness expressed as heroes or, better yet, martyrs. This in turn gave rise to a distinct and enduring species of television mini-series that includes *The Dismissal, The Last Bastion, Bodyline* and *Anzacs*. It has continued to show traces of the blend of AFC genre and the 'male ensemble' film that appeared with *Breaker Morant* and *Gallipoli*. But the beautiful AFC-genre 'quality' period film, frequently organised about a strong female character, has survived well into the eighties; for example, *We of the Never Never, Silver City, Emma's War* and *For Love Alone*.

The term 'genre' for this category of films seems justified because of the way it acquired, from 1975-9, a recognisable marketplace identity and a thematic and stylistic coherence. What are its defining characteristics?

The films have a literariness that can usually be tracked back to their origins in middle-brow fiction; but even those few not based on novels (*The Picture Show Man, Let the Balloon Go* and *Kitty and the Bagman*) have a literary feeling. This seems to inhere in their gently descriptive and evocative creation of period, and even more plainly in their character- rather than action-based narratives. The stories feel relatively unshaped, motivated by character, interested in 'sensibility' in the tradition of the novel rather than the moral choice and action of the more plotted melodrama. (Compare, for instance, *The Irishman* with *The Man from Snowy River*). Frequently the literariness is second hand, mediated by the conventions and expectations of originally British 'quality' dramatised literature on television.

It is striking how morally inoffensive and bland the characters tend to be, as though in the hope of wooing a broad general audience, including aunts and the occasional uncle. Commentators like Phillip Adams were wont to point out that 'Australian films' (that is, AFC-genre films, so often conflated with Australian films at large) centre on strong, assertive women verging, as in *My Brilliant Career* on the larrikin. Meanwhile, the male characters are recessive, sensitive in temperament and doomed to failure (including failure at the box office). There is a sense of withdrawal in these 'tasteful' films from the comically offensive masculinity of the ocker comedies. Perhaps this also needs to be thought of as part of a more pervasive split in Australian fiction generally between the low-life and popular in which larrikin and even ocker masculinity is allowed free range, and, on the other hand, middle-class 'cultivated' fiction where circumspect, vulnerable men lose ground constantly to assertive women who belie the myth of the relentless masculinism of this society.

Characterisation within the AFC genre has often been as curiously innocent of history as the stories, despite the period settings. The exact historic shadings of class, sex, place and race are rarely there. Perhaps the only real exception is *Newsfront*, whose archival devices and script give it some of the force of a genuine history film. The others are mainly period films with aspirations to 'timeless' concerns. History does not provide the narrative drive but is rather a source of imagery, details for the art design and a rationale for slowed pacing, all of which ensure the 'quality' effect. If the deliberately vulgar, often R-rated ocker comedies first attracted audiences to the odd idea of going out to see 'Australia' on the big screen, after *Picnic at Hanging Rock* the attraction was that of quality film, distinctly different from the general look and concerns of locally produced television drama. What mobilised an audience for *Picnic* was the astonishing rumour that it was a ravishing art movie, a bit along the lines of *Elvira Madigan*, just as good, and set in the suddenly, startlingly photogenic bush and intense light of Australia.

These films have unshaped narratives, nearly always short of an ending and sometimes just petering out in explanatory titles, which follow essentially safe characters along a few twists of unfolding sensibility. It is not surprising therefore that they have tended to be limited in their exploration of *mise en scene* and editing. The cinematography is dedicated to the glories of

Australian light, landform and vegetation, often with clear traces of a romantic, even charm-school, Australian post-impressionism. The approach of the camera is functional rather than expressive. The closest thing to *mise en scene* are lyrical pans across picturesque landscape or beautifully dressed interiors, giving brief, rapturous play to cinematography's recognition of what is our own. This includes not only distinctly beautiful place, but space, history and cultural traditions. It is as though cinematically conscious *mise en scene* was thought to be intrusive, potentially alienating or unsettling; audiences were to be wooed, reassured, invited to a safe place where no demands would be made beyond feeling with the character, and feeling proudly at home in the setting. Similarly, editing is generally subjugated to a gently paced television-drama notion of the functional, with few passages of action.

The unconscious, the subjective, the marvellous, the disturbing, the cinematically literate: these are all off-limits to this tasteful, rather old-fashioned film storytelling. 'Innocence' and 'freshness' were qualities detected in the films screened overseas that fairly quickly became calculated — but some of the effect of an 'innocent' filmmaking may derive from an unconsciousness towards film traditions. Despite all-Australian settings, its blood lines were revealed in 'quality' British television rather than the traditions of film. The AFC genre engages 'history' as a way of marketing a safe product, inviting gentle nostalgia for a moment seen passing harmlessly under glass. It does not engage with history as a process with repetitions, repercussions, incompletions and possibilities, nor with any element likely to disturb our sense of the present.

The prominence of the AFC genre on the list of 'proud' or 'citable' Australian films — and occasionally on the list of box office successes — has clearly had a powerful influence on the aesthetic field. The other main groups of films have tended to complement or oppose this politically privileged group of films. What does it mean for Australian cinema to have had such unexceptionable, 'nice', even bland films at the centre of its field of possibilities? Our survey of other goupings below, and the remaining chapters of the book, are really our venture into the possible answers to that question; but some points can be made here.

The AFC genre is generally unproblematic as regards the local content requirements of the Australian Film Commission Act. Our cinema and its administrative history reveal a dearth of coherent notions about locality, regionalism and the shadings of

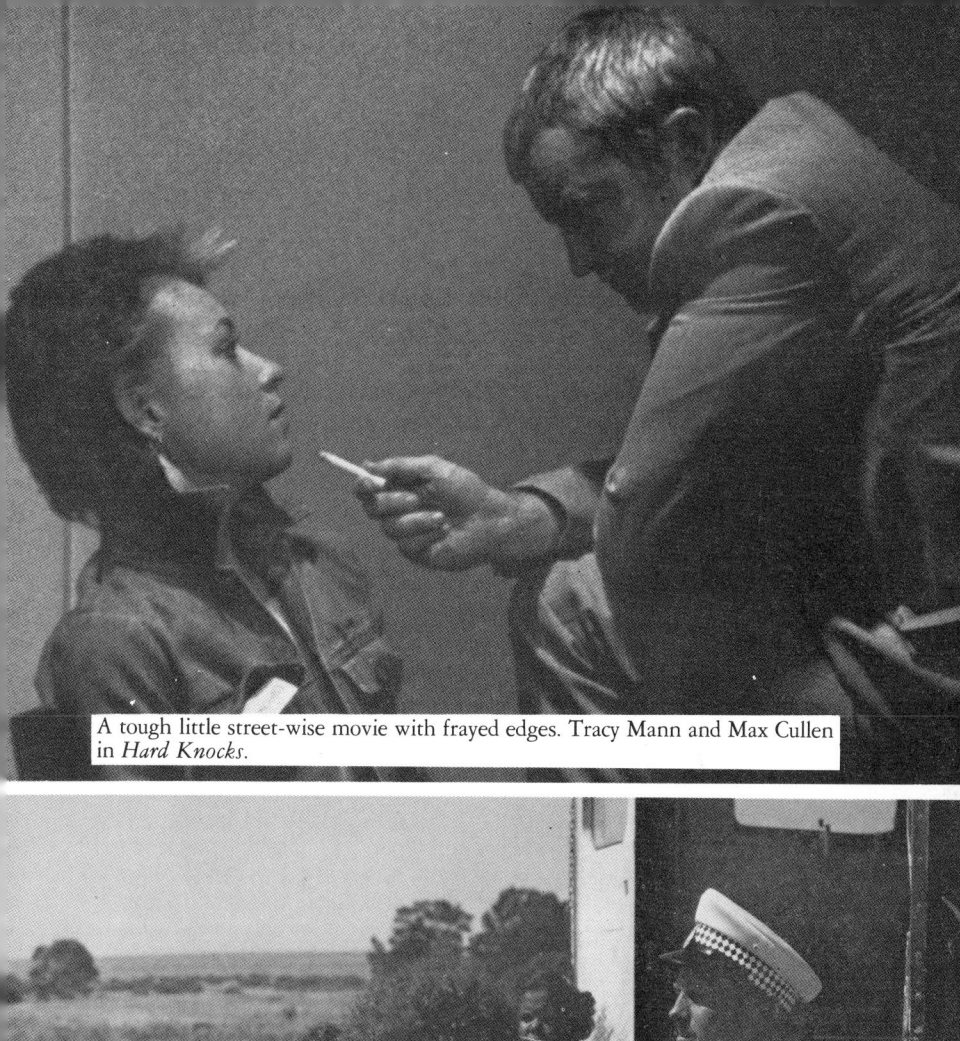

A tough little street-wise movie with frayed edges. Tracy Mann and Max Cullen in *Hard Knocks*.

Wrong Side of the Road: a social realist film with an 'inside' sense of the subject. The band, Us Mob, and Chris Haywood.

cultural difference that might help it escape the conservative, generalising impulses of nationalism. In this situation, the film crammed with museum pieces (touchstones of the past, *ergo* a culture) and embellished with lyrical passages of landscape (touchstones of a distinctive geography, *ergo* a homeland) is somehow certified as authentically but tastefully Australian. It is clear, in examining the history of the AFC, that this local breed of 'quality' film often pushed aside projects with quite different, and perhaps more dangerous, notions of Australianness. For example, *Mad Max*, the unproduced *The Unknown Industrial Prisoner*, and a number of features which were relegated to the ultra-low budgets of the Creative Development Branch, like *Hard Knocks*, *Palm Beach*, *Wrong Side of the Road* and *Going Down*.

Secondly, the conspicuous, rather than numerous, presence of these films has provided a preserve for a slightly romantic Australianness that was simple and conservative. It was a mode of Australianness that proved itself very amenable to the boyish heroics of *Breaker Morant*, *Gallipoli*, *The Man From Snowy River*, *Phar Lap* and the veritable flood of mini-series which came after them. It proved to be fertile ground, at last, for an easily marketable nationalist Australianness that was at home in stories of winners (or those who lose winningly); and this crowded out other possibilities that were more genuinely local, difficult, qualified or historic. The AFC genre and its permutations had a diffident beginning with such films as *Break of Day*, *Weekend of Shadows* and *The Irishman*. Nevertheless, as its confidence increased, it constructed a 'we' that is white, middle-class, comfortable, unharried by history, aware of its luck in living in a huge and beautiful place, able to declare its beauty, contented with its relaxed social arrangements, and glad not to be 'poms'. A 'we' of the 'Never-Never', perhaps?

But it must be mentioned that the conspicuousness of this genre of Australian film, complete with what Pauline Kael called 'The Seal of Good House-Keeping', has offered an important protection to the Australian industry. A comparison with the Canadian film industry yields strong contrasts which illustrate the protective effect offered by the development of an often studiously 'innocent' Australianness, marked 'Quality — For Home Consumption and Official Export'. While the AFC genre circulated overseas as English-speaking art film, refreshingly different to staple American fare, Canada concentrated on developing Hollywood North, fearful that it has no special 'otherness' to sell. Obviously, ten thousand miles of Pacific Ocean also helps to insulate Australia from some of the worst effects of 'Canadianisation', or the process by which a revived Canadian national cinema became, with the exception of the French-Canadian preserve, an appendage of Hollywood, providing profitable financial deals and snow scenes. Australia also has the advantage of a distinctive and immediate 'otherness' that Canada either does not have or does not succeed in identifying on film. The Canadian industry seems to have internalised completely the American belief that Canada is a poor, pale copy of itself; it seems that there are more dismal forms of the cultural 'Never-Never' than the one in which the AFC genre has cocooned the Australian cinema.

It is also possible that the cocoon spun for the industry by the officially blessed AFC genre has ensured the survival of Industry-1 in the face of Industry-2, since the introduction of tax-incentive-based film investment. Whether this has preserved aesthetic leeway and variety against the onslaught of commercial values from the cultural limbo of the film finance industry, or merely prolonged the life of an aesthetically exhausted impulse well past its moment, is open to debate. But it seemed in 1982 that the threat of 'Canadianisation' was at least partly held back by the existence of a respectable, well-established (if neither profound not challenging) canon of worthy, 'quality' Australian films. The AFC genre is at the heart of that canon, and Industry-1, while neither fixed nor a completely discrete milieu, contained an identifiable group of people whose track records have been dignified by some association with the genre.

To make the point a little more generously, it does seem that the central existence of this genre has established a level of 'niceness' in the industry that has permitted the safe passage of a number of films which are interestingly eccentric to any of the main groupings: *Shirley Thompson Versus the Aliens, Backroads, Third Person Plural, Newsfront, Going Down, Winter of Our Dreams, Lonely Hearts, Monkey Grip, Goodbye Paradise.* These situate themselves as Australian without anxiety or nationalist gestures, because the central ground was occupied by a safe, benign genre.

The Fringe Dwellers sails close to the wind, with its uncertain mixture of social realism and comic stereotype; almost a black version of *Dad and Dave*. Kristina Nehm and Justine Saunders.

The Social Realist Film

Social Realism
(Parentheses indicate a partial influence.)

1970 *Three to Go*
    (Jack and Jill: a Postscript)
1972 *(The Office Picnic)*
1973 *(Libido: The Family Man)*
    27A
1975 *The Golden Cage*
    The Promised Woman
    (Sunday Too Far Away)
1976 *(The Fourth Wish)*
    Queensland
1977 *Backroads*
    F.J. Holden
    Temperament Unsuited
    Summer City
1978 *Mouth to Mouth*
1979 *Cathy's Child*
    (Dawn!)
    (Just Out of Reach)
    (Kostas)
    (Palm Beach)
1980 *(Blood Money)*
    Hard Knocks
    Stir!
1981 *Hoodwink*
    Wrong Side of the Road
1982 *The Clinic*
    (The City's Edge)
    Fighting Back
    (Freedom)
    (Monkey Grip)
    Moving Out
    Sweet Dreams
1983 *(Puberty Blues)*
1984 *Annie's Coming Out*
    Fast Talking

Street Hero
(On Guard)
1985 *Fran*
On the Loose
A Street to Die
1986 *The Fringe Dwellers*
Backlash
Shortchanged
The Still Point
1987 *(High Tide)*

The AFC genre has not been the only conscientious aesthetic category within the larger body of Australian films. There has been another, less showcased centre of 'worthiness' which has helped to preserve a ground of established values against the cold logic of quickly-turned profit: the 'social realist' or 'social problem' group of films, strongly influenced by the tradition and ethos of Film Australia/Commonwealth Film Unit documentary. Here too we can identify concerns that have helped to hold back the threatened slide into Canadianisation.

This grouping does not have a marketplace identity — indeed, the films have never been marketplace performers. They have almost always been low-budget, strongly influenced by the Creative Development Branch side of the tracks of Australian Film Commission funding, with close cousins among the social documentaries funded by CDB or Film Australia. There are traces of a politically radical impulse and values generally absent from the almost offensively inoffensive AFC genre, though convergence of the two can be sensed in films that are not quite members of either — like *The Killing of Angel Street, Kostas, Cathy's Child, Dawn!, Sweet Dreamers, Annie's Coming Out, One Night Stand*. In its lower-budget, social-problem reaches, the genre shares an ideology of 'independence' as an unquestioned and self-evident value: taking up issues and displaying concern are seen as aesthetic and political credentials in themselves. It is in this group of features more than any other (except, perhaps, the small cycle of 'Australian Gothic') that links between the feature and low-budget 'independent' sectors of Australian film culture are evident and on display. Many of the feature film makers who have come from the low-budget sector (for example, Richard Brennan, John

Duigan, Tom Cowan, Ken Cameron) have continued to exercise influence in the low-budget feature area in opposition to more overtly commercial values.

The defining characteristic of the group is the choice of subject-matter and the relatively plain, dramatised documentary treatment thought proper for such subject matter. The subject is usually an oppressed, socially-marginalised, urban individual or group, and the oppression is seen as a result of social pressures on that individual or group. Favoured groups are migrants (*Three to Go, Promised Woman, Kostas, Moving Out, Cathy's Child*), blacks (*Backroads, Wrong Side of the Road, Women of the Sun*), the working class (*Queensland, Love Letters from Teralba Road, F.J. Holden, Blood Money, Fighting Back*), youth (*F.J. Holden, Mouth to Mouth, Hard Knocks, City's Edge*), derelicts (*27A, Queensland, Listen to the Lion, I'll Be Home for Christmas*), prisoners (*Stir!, Hoodwink*).

The treatment of social issues tends to be instructive and didactic, much in the liberal humanist style of Film Australia: 'Pay attention, be moved, become aware, feel concern, pity and perhaps anger'. The films validate their presentation of contemporary, urban 'reality' through a style which ranges from 'documentary' - hand-held camera, untidy framing, following action as if without premeditation, loose editing, direct and variably focused sound, — to well constructed television-style realism. *Hard Knocks* and *Wrong Side of the Road* are at one end of this continuum, and *Cathy's Child, Hoodwink* and *Fighting Back* at the other.

The mode of address within these socially concerned, 'problem' films varies — and sometimes wavers painfully — between an 'outside' and 'inside' sense of the subject. The first involves a 'social work' position toward the 'client' subject — and, by extension, toward the 'client' audience. It is most uncomfortable to detect the signs of distance, otherness, even contempt towards the subject which surface at times in the best-intentioned films. *Fighting Back*, for example, was frequently reviewed in these terms. The 'inside' sense of the subject involves a careful and loving observation of a sub-culture, with enough confidence to risk the making of jokes, and with the do-gooding impulse kept well at bay. *Going Down, Wrong Side of the Road, Puberty Blues, Fast Talking, Queensland*, much of *Mouth to Mouth*, and *Stir* more or less fit this description, though *Going Down* and *Puberty Blues*, like *Palm Beach*, only partly fit the 'social realist' grouping. *F.J. Holden* shifts disconcertingly between the two registers, seeming at times to patronise and impoverish lives to which it otherwise accords a sense of abundance and fascination.

The more relaxed, less didactic, 'inside' films tend to be those that play with genre, or else treat a social group for whom a kind of film sub-genre already exists, like the youth culture film (*Hard Knocks, Pure Shit, Mouth to Mouth, Fast Talking, Going Down*), the rock musical (*Wrong Side of the Road, Hard Knocks*, the ABC television series *Sweet and Sour*), the road movie (*Backroads, F.J. Holden, Wrong Side of the Road*), and so on. The youth culture film, of which the road movie and rock musical examples here are really variants, in its Australian manifestation can afford to be both socially critical and *of* the group, because it is speaking directly to the group through the genre that belongs to it. Perhaps it is the spirit of social criticism and radicalism, stemming partly from the social realist tradition, that has kept the Australian youth culture film at some distance from the 'exploitation' end of the range seen in imported examples like *Class of '84* or the *Porky's* films. It is also interesting, in passing, that the most uncertain example in this sub-group is probably *Street Hero*, which has also been the biggest-budget and most outwardly market-conscious of social realist films to date. Its uncertainty lies not so much in the way it slips between outside and inside modes of address, as in the compromise between its social issue and conscious (if not always deft) packaging for the youth market. The other examples are, by comparison, poor cinema, lacking the budgetary scope to exploit a market.

The process of finding sub-genres within this grouping, and of locating social realist aspects or passages in films not listed here, is almost endless. This points to the comparative lack of uniformity of generic identity among this grouping compared with the AFC genre. It is perhaps best seen as a cluster of films with some aesthetic similarities stemming chiefly from a social realist or social problem drive within the narrative. That may steer the film towards the case study with the danger of offensively 'social working' the audience and the subject; or it may, more gently, permit some affectionate recognition of a sub-cultural or marginal *milieu*.

But the two tendencies — AFC genre and social realist — are linked by more than their sense of worthiness. The social realist school of film answers the period film with an emphatically urban, contemporary social conscience, and a lean, even mean, anti-lyrical, documentary style. Here we find a sense of delegated responsibilities. It repeats across the whole aesthetic field of Australian film, and finds echoes in its supporting institutional structures. This is especially true of the division, in the Australian Film Commission, between mainstream and independent, which permits the Creative Development Branch to delegate to Project Branch questions of audience and viability, and the Project Branch to delegate to the CDB questions of innovation, experimentation, aesthetic risk. It is also perceivable in the early history of producers versus obdurate distributor and exhibitor interests; this has been replaced by the opposition of Industry-1 and Industry-2. In this process, everyone is relieved of the difficult task of attempting to find an aesthetic centre, a whole view, a non-reactive position.

With such an arrangement of unspoken but complicit mutually delegated responsibilities, we find blandness, staleness and repetition on the cultural and aesthetic level; on the political level (how the industry responds to change and formulates its will and personality), blandness, staleness and paralysis also reign, even if all the talk is of struggle and opposition.

Thus there is 'quality' period film but virtually no history film; there are small essays of social 'problems' and sub-cultures, but a virtual embargo on aesthetic risk. As we will see, there is also expressly commercial film, piously constructing itself within a cinematic and cultural limbo, in reaction to the very worthiness of the first two groups with their tenets of 'quality', 'Australianness' and 'relevance'. There are, of course, exceptions to these rules, and the exceptions tend to make up the relatively small category (considered separately below) of 'eccentrics'.

An Aesthetic of Commercialism

Purely Commercial
(* indicates a film especially chilled by commercial or exploitationist motives.)

1970 *The Naked Bunyip*
 Alvin Purple
 (The Adventures of Barry McKenzie)

1973 *Essay in Pornography*
     (Libido: The Husband)
     *Alvin Rides Again**
1975 *The Man from Hong Kong*
     *Inn of the Damned**
     *Plugg**
     *Scobie Malone**
     *Australia After Dark**
     *The Love Epidemic**
     (The True Story of Eskimo Nell)
1976 *Deathcheaters*
     *(Barney)**
     *Fantasm**
1977 *Raw Deal*
     *Fantasm Comes Again**
1978 *Patrick*
     *ABC of Love and Sex — Australian Style**
1979 *Felicity**
     *Snapshot**
     *Thirst**
     (The Money Movers)
     (Tim)
1980 *The Earthling**
     *Final Cut**
     *Harlequin**
     (Touch and Go)
1981 *Roadgames**
     *The Survivor**
     (The Race for the Yankee Zephyr)
     *Centrespread**
     *Nightmares**
     *Pacific Banana**
1982 *(Attack Force Z)*
     Dead Easy
     *Dead Kids**
     *The Dark Room**
     *Desolation Angels/Killing Time**
     *Early Frost**
     Lady Stay Dead
     (Next of Kin)

Sexploitation: Sigrid Thornton and Robert Bruning in *Snapshot*.

The splatter end of exploitation. *Dead Kids*.

(*Midnite Spares*)
(*Runnin' on Empty*)
Norman Loves Rose
The Pirate Movie*
The Return of Captain Invincible
Turkey Shoot*
Slice of Life
1983 *Hostage**
Now and Forever*
Breakfast in Paris*
Stanley
1984 *Razorback*
Run Chrissie Run*
(*Coolangatta Gold*)
1985 *Charley's Web*
(*The Empty Beach*)
Jenny Kissed Me
The Naked Country
Son of Alvin

As if in complete rejection of the period 'quality' and social conscience alternatives, there is a third, clearly related aesthetic tendency: the drive towards an avowedly pure commercial notion of 'product' and film industry. There is no mention here of 'cinema', nothing so conceptualised, so long-term nor so beside the point of profit. The tendency is not recent; it has been part of the aesthetic field right from the beginning, although it acquired a powerful new respectability in the early days of financing under section 10B(A) of the Taxation Act. Witness the upsurge of numbers in 1982. On the whole, the films that belong here have been far less conspicuous, with virtually no diplomatic showcasing. It is doubtful, though, that they have, overall, achieved any greater share of commercial success than less single-mindedly commercial films.

There are, perhaps, two categories of film involved here. The first, soft porn, can be dispensed with quickly; it needs little comment in this context because it is a staple of all film industries. The only interesting aspects are, firstly, a degree of overlap between this category and another group of films, discussed below, which deal with sexual mores and repression. At their core lies Tim

Burstall's work. The second interesting point is that direct pornography is not a prolific part of the aesthetic field, even though more than one eminent male spokesperson for the industry has argued that their regular production could give a reasonable financial base to the industry at large, such that for instance a production company might make one or two *Emmanuelle*s in order to finance a quality, citable film. The early porn, or at least, titillation films, masqueraded coyly as documentaries on Australian sexual attitudes, or night life (*Naked Bunyip, Essay in Pornography, Australia After Dark*). Later, they simply modelled themselves on overseas soft-core successes (the *Fantasm* films, *Felicity*).

The second category is less simply described. On the whole, it comprises films derived from loosely-formed and lightly-held notions of 'genre' from outside the culture of origin, conceived in terms of market exploitation categories, including home video and cable television. The pertinent distinction here is between this cinematically illiterate, market-based view of genre, in a cinema which is not genre-based, nor nearly prolific enough to be so, and on the other hand the rare examples of home-grown genre formed in response to cinema history, with a sensitivity to local cultural inflections. The AFC genre developed as a tacit genre with considerable representative authority, to the point where outsiders could mistake its films for Australian cinema itself. The *Mad Max* films developed an Australian-made car-crash genre, partly out of 'Australian Gothic' (discussed below), and for the rest, out of a bizarre and original convergence of such action genres as the western, science fiction, fantasy, and samurai films. And a small number of other films, mainly 'eccentrics', have used genre in order to talk about the local, the regional and the culturally specific, without seeming too baldly to do so (*Palm Beach, Heatwave, Puberty Blues, Goodbye Paradise, Starstruck*).

Within the group of limbo-like 'genre' films, one can identify several which are especially cold-hearted towards their audience. This must be a subjective list, and open to debate. At a critical level, the argument has never begun; the cold films are generally ignored, although their close analysis might yield much richer insights into the desires and dealings of Industry-2, and the schizophrenic tendencies of the industry as a whole, than any reiteration of the failures of Industry-1. It must also be admitted that the list could be reorganised into sub-types, especially sexploitation/horror (*Snapshot, Final Cut, Roadgames, Turkey Shoot, Killing Time*), action/adventure (*The Man from Hong Kong, Raw Deal, The Money Movers*), and thrillers (*End Play, Summerfield, The Survivor, Patrick, Harlequin, The Dark Room, Next of Kin*). But there are others, that loom randomly and fade into unseen obscurity, with no relationship to any real known audience and its desires (*Raw Deal*, a meat-pie Western spin-off from television-land; *Thirst*, an awkward vampire film; *Winds of Jarrah* and *Breakfast in Paris*, both attempts to make killings on the light romance market).

Of course, the makers of these products conceive of them well outside the terms of this criticism. For Tony Ginnane, John Lamond, Terry Bourke, and the swarm of instant producers seen briefly in the 10B(A) boom year of 1981/2, their trans-national 'genre' films (often made with a sort of fabricated American identity), were products consciously designed for easy recognition in specific overseas markets. The packages were intended for marketing in terms easily understood by film-buyers from Argentina, Hong Kong, Turkey, Libya and the U.S. cable market. They had to be emptied of all reference and relationship to the site of production; they had to belong to a trans-national American-derived, moneyed cultural limbo — a sort of violent world of American Express.

Does it matter if films like this occupy a permanent niche — of varying size — in a small industry like this, with its relatively 'sweet' climate of government support? There is no consistent or defensible argument for their programmatic exclusion, not so long as the supportive and regulatory role of the state remains benevolent, indirect, and mediated by a rhetoric of free-market business and private profit. A State-owned industry (Phillip Adams' Czechoslavakia of the South Seas?) would not provide such a niche; but then such an industry might congeal even more stolidly around a tasteful, worthy set of possibilities, somewhere between the academicism of the AFC genre, the institutionalised conscience of social realist film, and the European art movie. In a completely bureaucratised industry, would the eccentrics and the home-grown genres get a look in at all?

It is hard to estimate precisely the effect of either the AFC genre, the conspicuous tip of the iceberg, or of the cold commercial mass below the waterline of public consciousness on the history and politics of the industry. The obvious tension, and complementarity, between them clearly sustains both; but the net effect does seem to be unfortunate. Some exceptions, some local effects, have squeezed by, as we shall see; but the distressing blandness of the output as a whole is the result of the circumscribing effect of middle-brow good intentions above and a culturally stupid 'commercialism' below. The distressing staleness of the pattern, maintained with little change for more than a decade, is also attributable to the entrenched notion that here is identifiable 'quality', and that it is the answer to the 'natural', ever-present threat of the carpetbagger mentality.

Meanwhile, the films in this category constantly signal the danger of which John Hinde warned: that local film industries are chancy, and often not very interesting affairs, to be launched almost anywhere by anyone with money, and that there is nothing intrinsically worthwhile in maintaining them at the expense of other, more pressing public needs. They amplify the irony of taxpayers' support, on grounds of public interest or culture, for activity that often serves private interests for whom cultural questions are remote. They display, like warning signs, the 'nothing' of so much advertising that progressively removes habitable, usable culture from the reach of our imagination. They lack the vitality of a genuinely 'inside' generic practice, like Roger Corman's New World, but even so, a closer scrutiny may yield interesting diagnostic insights into some of the more submerged currents and motivations of our culture — especially those organised around a fast buck.

What remain to be sorted out, after the three main groups that have pulled the aesthetic field into its current shape and held it there so long, are the interesting, shorter-lived or sometimes less prolific, but certainly influential, cycles of film, and the category we are naming the 'eccentrics', the films that go against the general grain and follow their own strong wills.

Australian Gothic

Australian Gothic

1970 *Jack and Jill: a Postscript*
1971 *Wake in Fright*
 Homesdale
1972 *(The Adventures of Barry McKenzie)*

Private Collection
1973 *The Office Picnic*
Shirley Thompson versus the Aliens
1974 *The Cars That Ate Paris*
1976 *Summer of Secrets*
1977 *The Night the Prowler*
The Plumber
1978 *(Long Weekend)*
1979 *Mad Max*
(Dimboola)
1981 *Mad Max 2*
1982 *(Runnin' on Empty)*
(Midnite Spares)
Going Down
Starstruck
1983 *Stanley*
Man of Flowers
(Razorback)
1985 *Bliss*
Emoh Ruo
1986 *Malcolm*
1987 *Those Dear Departed*

The earliest of these smaller cycles was the emergence of Australian Gothic as early as 1971 in Peter Weir's *Homesdale*, although some signs of it are evident in the anti-documentary aspects of *Jack and Jill: a postscript* (1970) and in the darker hyperbole of the Canadian co-production, *Wake in Fright* (1971). The cycle really came to fruition in Jim Sharman's *Shirley Thompson versus the Aliens* and *The Night the Prowler*, with less fortunate effect also upon his *Summer of Secrets*; and it flourished in Peter Weir's *The Cars That Ate Paris* and *The Plumber*, although it was sadly lost from sight in the more self-conscious mysticism of *Picnic at Hanging Rock* and *The Last Wave*, and buried completely by the romantic earnestness of *Gallipoli*. There are strong, subterranean influences of Australian Gothic detectable in the *Mad Max* films, and in their car crash successors like *Runnin' on Empty* and *Midnite Spares* in 1982. In general, however, the cycle lost strength in the mid-to-later-seventies, when the three main aesthetic influences described above held greatest sway, but there have been signs of a re-emergence in 1982-3 in films already cited, and in some aspects of *Going Down*, *Starstruck*, *The Return of Captain Invincible*, *Stanley*, *Man of Flowers*, *Bliss*, and (more tenuously) *Lonely Hearts* and *Razorback*.

The earlier Weirs and Sharmans best illustrate the cycle. They are in fact art films coming up into the feature category from the underground of experimental filmmaking, and from the sense of the marvellous in cartoon art, horror comics, and matinee serials (after *Fantomas*, *Flash Gordon* and *Zorro*). Their hallmark is dark, inward comedy, in strong contrast to the loud and outward ocker comedy of the contemporaneous *Barry McKenzie* films and the early David Williamson/Beresford/Burstall films, which will be explored separately below. 'Normality' — of the Australian suburban and small town strain — is the hunting-ground for Gothic/comic hypberboles and motifs: the mix master; the front yard; the car, and the car crash; and the other things that litter the landscape of contained insanity. The normal is revealed as having a stubborn bias towards the perverse, the grotesque, the malevolent. Characterisation is born, in these films, out of deliberately pathological — rather than social or psychological — kinds of stereotype. Few 'sane' protagonists escape normality with their lives or sanity completely intact. And the stereotypes themselves are strongly flavoured with memories of popular trash culture.

Visual style is strong, deliberately distorted by wide-angled, staring lenses and enriched by fantasy art-design — spike-encrusted VWs, suburban houses that are veritable museums of Australian household kitsch, 'found' locations like the now dismantled *papier-mache* underworlds of the Luna Park River Caves attraction in Sydney, or the horror-comix details of the Hummungus tribe in *Mad Max 2*. And the sources 'quoted' in this visual style are deliberately *mixed*; the best examples of Australian Gothic are intuitive and bizarre mixtures of B-grade genres, as the exploration of examples in the next three chapters reveals.

The impulse is sceptical and poetic — very different, obviously, from the impulses of conscientiousness, worthiness, 'quality' or social value of the more 'official' and citable areas of the AFC genre and social realism. There is kinship to the horror film, hybridised by the generic mix which may include action, western, rock musical, sci-fi fantasy, teen film, bikie film. The horror film, however, depending on how remote it is from tongue-in-cheek self-consciousness and an ambiguous urge to laughter, tends to be a conservative form — however amenable it may be to private viewer subversion. The blackness of Australian Gothic invites a wry, knowing, surreal self-mockery which generally steers it away from conservatism.

Its origins lie in the university-based, libertarian, satirical tradition expressed in *Oz*, *Private Eye*, Martin Sharp's and Richard Neville's work in *Honi Soit* and *Tharunka*, university stage revues, Barry Humphrey's closely-related one-man theatre, and television work like *The Mavis Bramston Show*, as much as in underground films. This tradition was itself a loud, late camp-follower of older avant-gardes like surrealism, dada and Italian futurism. This places the ocker comedy, *The Adventures of Barry McKenzie*, at least partly within the constellation of Australian Gothic; another part of its influence is clearly registered in the next group of films to be considered, which deals with stereotypes of Australian sexual behaviour, and its important sub-cycle, the male ensemble film.

The Sexual Mores Film and the Male Ensemble Film

Sexual Mores/Sexual Difference
(* denotes sex comedies; ** denotes romantic comedies.)

1968 *2000 Weeks* (Burstall)
    (Three to Go: Michael)
1971 *Stork* (Burstall/Williamson)
    Demonstrator
1972 *(The Adventures of Barry McKenzie)* (Beresford)
1973 *Libido: The Husband; The Family Man* (Williamson)
    Alvin Purple (Beresford)
    The Office Picnic
1974 *Petersen* (Burstall/Williamson)
    Alvin Rides Again*
    (No. 96)*
1975 *(The Box)**
    End Play (Burstall)
    The Great MacArthy
1976 *Don's Party* (Beresford/Williamson)
    Eliza Fraser* (Burstall/Williamson)

       (The Devil's Playground)
1977 *(F.J. Holden)*
       (Journey Among Women)
       (Summerfield)
       The Singer and the Dancer
1979 *The Journalist*
       The Last of the Knucklemen (Burstall)
       Just Out of Reach
1980 *Maybe This Time*
1981 *(Puberty Blues)* (Beresford)
1982 *(The Dark Room)*
       Duet for Four (Burstall)
       (Monkey Grip)
       The Best of Friends**
       Norman Loves Rose**
       Breakfast in Paris**
       Sweet Dreams
1983 *The City's Edge*
1984 *Fantasy Man*
       (My First Wife)
1985 *(The Naked Country)*
       Relatives
       (Jenny Kissed Me)
       (Unfinished Business)
1986 *The More Things Change*
1987 *Shadows of the Peacock*
       (Warm Nights on a Slow-Moving Train)

A much looser conjunction, yet one that displays considerable stylistic kinship and definite sub-cycles, could be loosely termed 'sexual mores' films. Generally, those that seem to belong here would not invite inclusion amongst the social-issue/social realist films, even though there is a kind of pop-sociology to the way sexuality and repression are examined in them. The sexual mores group is geared more towards titillation than to social conscience. If both categories correspond to genres of journalism and gestures towards social documentation, this one is distinguished by its treatment of sexuality. Like those surveys of sexual behaviour and custom published from time to time in the tabloids — even the classier weekly ones — the films are designed to arouse curiosity of a voyeuristic, sensational kind, and to cater equally for audiences or readerships professing sexual prurience *or* license.

From early days, Australian films were quick to exploit the possibilities of the R-certificate, introduced in 1972; generally by making ribald sex-comedies like *Stork, Alvin Purple, The True Story of Eskimo Nell, Eliza Fraser*, and in a kind of four letter word breakout, that echoed the one that had led the liberalisation of theatre censorship in the sixties. By the mid-seventies, R-certificate violence was wedded with sex in the 'cold films' of the purely commercial group. They rarely contained four letter language, partly because of a predilection for settings of wealth and socially cold behaviour signifying the moneyed class, but mainly because they eschewed idiomatic and vernacular speech and behaviour for fear the product might be contaminated by local identity.

So there is a distinction to be drawn between the 'cold' films, which often pose women as natural victims of violence and fear (although sometimes men are also victims) and the sexual mores films, where outbreaks of violence are usually between men, and part of an exploration of male group behaviour. The sexual mores films are dedicated to the local — its sexual stereotypes, aberrations, customs — in the most general, sociological of terms. But within this field of interest, the sexual mores films and their sub-cycles have richly cultivated the domain of expressive Australian idiomatic language, using it as a primary sign of Australianness and cultural difference, especially in the work of David Williamson and the distinct and influential 'male ensemble' film (these last two strongly overlap). The question of the articulation of Australianness through vernacular speech is taken up further below in the section on actors and iconography, and its process is traced in detail throughout this volume.

The earliest examples of the social mores group is the work of Tim Burstall and Bruce Beresford as directors, with David Williamson as writer: *Stork* (Burstall/Williamson), *Petersen* (Burstall/Williamson), *Don's Party* (Beresford/Williamson). The early sex comedies (*Stork, Alvin Purple, Eliza Fraser*), the television spin-offs (*The Box, No. 96*), and the early ocker-comedies (*Stork, The Adventures of Barry McKenzie, Petersen, Don's Party*), partly overlap with the straight sexual mores group, which rarely excluded comedy or ocker exaggerations of male Australian behaviour. They can be thought of as generic sub-types of the larger family group. For example, the family relationship between the ocker comedy and the male ensemble film — even in its later, AFC-genre-influenced serious forms like *Breaker Morant* and *Gallipoli* — is clear, mediated by films like *Don's Party*, *The Club* and *The Odd Angry Shot*.

The range of the sexual mores films is from ribald, even grotesque exaggeration through to a kind of kitchen-sink school of realism — from *Stork* and *'Bazza'*, through *Petersen* to *Don's Party*, *F.J. Holden* and much later examples like *Maybe This Time*, *Puberty Blues*, and some aspects of *Monkey Grip*. Generally, aesthetic energy is directed towards the knowledge, fleshing out and manipulation of social and sexual stereotypes; men can be both social and sexual in their stereotyping in these films, women are generally limited to stereotyping of sexual response. It is not directed very much to visual style, complexities of mise en scene or of sound track; style is functional and familiar, reminiscent of television drama. What is thought to make these feature-film material rather than television drama, seems to be the ambition to probe sexuality explicitly and provocatively, looking at different behaviours, and forms of repression.

Films dealing almost obsessively with Australian sexual repression, the legacy of male-female segregation accompanied by a relentless belittling of the 'place' and restricted role of women, the hostility between the sexes that turns their encounters into brief skirmishes which spill over into violence — these are needed and should be welcomed as a highly creative centre within the 'aesthetic field'. But with few exceptions, and from the earliest Burstall and Beresford films, the sexual mores film cycle has been curiously limited in its expressive and intellectual power. Admittedly, films like *Journey Among Women* and *Puberty Blues* — in very different ways — have proposed a female view of a bleak and blighted sexual landscape. It must be said that Burstall, as well as Beresford, has sought to put women on the screen and let them speak their bitter piece on the matter; from David Baker's *Family Man* segment of *Libido*, through *Don's Party* and *Petersen* to *Duet for Four* and *Maybe this Time*, films of the sexual mores group have let the disgusted silences or angry outbreaks of women speak for themselves. But the point of view, and mode of address, of these films has still been persistently that of the old-fashioned male. The questioning of traditional roles and relations between the sexes — and of their cinematic representations — which marked the late sixties and the seventies is not registered here.

Furthermore — as their close kinship with ocker and sexploitation comedies and male ensemble films suggests — these films frequently allow more than a touch of ockerdom into their address, as if it overflows irresistably from the ocker subject matter. They employ and invite complicity, or at least momentarily complicit laughter, as they display the crassness or grossness of male behaviour. Sexism is admitted 'as a joke'; it is expected that an audience will laugh when, for example, 'as a joke', a woman in a bus in *Alvin Purple* wears a T-shirt that reads, across her breasts, 'Women should be obscene and not heard'; the woman herself has permitted the laugh, surely?

For the majority of films in this cycle, comedy is present in particular scenes and dialogue exchanges without turning the films into comedies, the exceptions being the sub-groups of sex comedy and lighter, romantic comedy. But the traditional force of comedy is usually there, placing women as the butt of archaic sexual jokes engendered somewhere in male fear of female sexuality. This persists into the spin-off male ensemble group of films; most sharply in dialogue.

Further undermining the grounds on which the 'sexual mores' films generally carry out their investigation is the tabloid-press style of exploitationist 'exposé' social observation, already mentioned. Translated into film terms, this licenses the films for their regulated measure of tits and bums, of justifiable rapes or other short, sharp acts of violence towards the women characters ('Nothing cooked up about this, just look in the newspaper any day'); of women positioned as recipients of lust and the odd bit of violence according to the tired stereotypes of bitch, whore, heart of gold, and doormat.

Not only are the female characters generally stereotyped marginalia to the rake's progress of the male protagonist(s); they are accorded none of that vitality of vernacular speech and gesture that energises the declared or latent celebration of male Australianness/Australian maleness that is the text or subtext of most of the films. They are not proposed as initiators of action, except for odd occasions of revenge, nor as people able to slip outside the eternal embrace of sexual combat and hostility. There is no guerilla-like rebellion against the victimization that such warfare finally forces on both sexes.

Underlying the slightly ocker exposé quality in most of these films is an edge of what Meaghan Morris has identified as an hysteria about the body. It surfaces in motifs of vomiting (the ocker-approved ritual of 'chundering'); in the persistence of sex and toilet jokes in the energetic play of male vernacular; in the punctuation of scenes by verbal or physical gags of bodily violence ('up yours', 'get stuffed', etcetera), and in the coyness of depictions of the male body, alongside the 'sexploitationist' depictions of female actresses.

It is impossible to detach these anxious, recurrent tics and habits of the films and account for them as signs, simply, of their truth to Australian life. They make the films, as a whole, bleak and blighted correlatives of the sexual blight and the ferocity of its workings, rather than any kind of a corrective to the communal picture of how sexual relations might work. They add to the impression that this group of films, which occupies such a rich terrain of possibilities, is nonetheless an old-fashioned, conservative, unchanging, unresponsive, aesthetically despressing body of work; an impression that can too frequently bleed across into generalisations about Australian film itself. This old-fashioned quality persists as depressingly late as *The City's Edge* (1983), *Fantasy Man* (1984), *The Naked Country* (1985).

The exceptions are few. Tom Cowan's *The Office Picnic*, and his later experimental feature, *Journey Among Women*, both propose strong women not completely subject to the will or meaning of the system. *Journey* takes that possibility into a realm of utopian feminist fantasy that is interesting, if flawed putting period imagery to a very different use from that of the AFC genre. Ironically, the film did well in its local release because its images of naked and lesbian women sold it — however incidentally — as sexploitation/titillation. *Puberty Blues* speaks from a teenaged female position that acquires some strength and authority and undergoes a shift by the end of the film. *Just Out of Reach*, *The Singer and the Dancer*, both short features, and *Maybe This Time* also have female protagonists, and involve some conscious probing of the false exits from the trap of male definitions of female sexuality. *The More Things Change* is also partly in this group. But *Maybe This Time* especially seems entrapped by mainstream male expectations of 'this kind of film', and it emerges as one in which nerve has failed on both sides. As a woman's-eye view of Australian maleness (in which there is no room for even an 'enlightened' or 'progressive' woman) it is too subject to the traditional 'Will she strip well?' and 'Is she a representative sample?' expectations which had become entrenched in this type of film by 1980. Finally, *Monkey Grip* and *The Devil's Playground* have only a couple of toes in this cycle: their mixture of aesthetic interests place them more strongly as eccentrics, considered in more detail in later chapters.

The Male Ensemble Film Variant
'Male Ensemble' Film
(* denotes scripted or from a work by David Williamson)

1971 *Stork**
1973 *Libido: The Family Man**
1974 *Petersen**
   (Stone)
1975 *(The Removalists)**
   Sunday Too Far Away
1976 *Don's Party**
1977 *Backroads*
   (F.J. Holden)
   (Summer City)
1978 *(Newsfront)*
1979 *The Last of the Knucklemen*
   (Mad Max)
   (The Money Movers)
   The Odd Angry Shot
   (Palm Beach)
1980 *Breaker Morant*
   The Club*
   (Stir!)
1981 *Gallipoli**
   (Mad Max 2)
   (The Man from Snowy River)
1982 *Attack Force Z*
   (Runnin' on Empty)
   (Midnite Spares)

1983 *Phar Lap**
 (The Highest Honour)
 Buddies
1984 *(Streethero)*
 (Razorback)
 (Strikebound)
Male Ensemble TV mini-series
 The Dismissal
 Waterfront
 Bodyline
 The Last Bastion*
 Cowra Breakout
 The Anzacs

The male ensemble film, in its first phase up to *Breaker Morant* (1980), is also strongly influenced by the posture of the ocker; blunt, loud, hedonistic and conservative in the populist manner. Its working-class or lower middle-class male figure is not an appeal for class solidarity, but a gesture towards the classless common man as last bastion of 'real' Australian virtues and vices. And, of course, the vices are cheered on as sardonically as the virtues; an Australian man is 'cut from a whole cloth', and the mix can't be argued or refuted. However satiric the mode of address, the bias is 'offensively Australian', an announcement that the era of self-apology is over. Ocker speech is naturally colloquial to the point where the exclusion of non-native speakers from a full understanding is the point. And it is rude, full of four letter words and crudely sexual imagery — the assertive use of vernacular is empowered by the feeling it is breaking with old taboos and the old, staid past; with a sense of freeing the irreverent larrikin spirit. The irony, by no means wholly unconscious, is that influential writers like David Williamson pitted this spirit against the conformities of male group behaviour, in which even male 'freedoms' were prescribed and ritualised.

As the films began to be conditioned more by a national self-consciousness of the imagined gaze of the world, vernacular speech became more muted, more segregated. For example, in *Gallipoli* larrikin energy is assigned to the minor group of mates, and not permitted very far into the more precious area belonging to the central male couple.

The populist male ensemble film, inspiring powerful identification. Bryan Brown, Graham Kennedy and John Hargreaves in *The Odd Angry Shot*.

Gregory Apps with Max Cullen as the contractor in *Sunday Too Far Away*. Cullen epitomises the male character actor who is acutely able to produce both spot-on characterisation and off-centre Australianness.

The other important point is the way that this current of energetic speech at once excludes women as interesting characters, and compromises their position as audience members. For example, Bryan Brown's line in *Breaker Morant*, 'A slice off a cut loaf is never missed', referring to his sexual liaisons with Boer women left alone on farms during the fighting, raises a loud laugh among men and women alike. To take some exception to the sexual politics involved is to be cold and unmoved by the spirited larrikin irreverence injected into staid, British court-martial evidence. That is, for women at such moments, a choice is forced between accepting the invitation to self-recognition and affirmation, and a share in the all-Australian familiar — or falling out.

The male ensemble film began with *Stork* and *Petersen*, perhaps *The Removalists* (all David Williamson screenplays), but the form crystallises with Ken Hannam's *Sunday Too Far Away*, written by John Dingwall from the shearing experiences of his brother-in-law. *Sunday* is a workplace milieu study which both celebrates and laments the isolated all-male ethos that governs a group of shearers. A comparison of *Sunday* with the Williamson films shows up Williamson's stronger inclination towards satiric deflation; *Sunday* has more painful ambivalences towards the male group. If Williamson discloses a fascination that is almost admiration for his male characters, Dingwall seems caught between love and dismay. Nevertheless, throughout the male ensemble films there is, increasingly, a tendency to celebrate male Australianness as essential, recognisable, likeable Australianness. And, as we trace below and in the following chapters, it is in these films, and in the corresponding television mini-series, that an iconic register of male Australianness begins to be felt. It forms the core of conscious articulation of national Australianness in the aesthetic field of the industry.

Initially, the male ensemble films probably reflected Williamson's stage training in fringe houses with economical casts, groups of perhaps half a dozen characters. Williamson's naturalistic satire organises these around sub-cultures or institutions — a football club, an election-night party, a group household, a university department and later on a group of soldiers. Group mores, hierarchies, norms, rituals and ritualised, prescribed freedoms, are the subjects. By *Breaker Morant*, and even more sharply, *Gallipoli*, the 'buddy' couple has defined itself against the group of mates. By the time of John Dingwall's *Buddies*, this theme has become explicit, although it is incipient as early as *Don's Party* in the mordant mutual sentimentality of the drunken Don (John Hargreaves) and Mal (Ray Barrett) observed by their wives with increasing scepticism.

This group of films corresponds almost like a talisman to the W.K. Hancock and Russel Ward tradition of Australian cultural history, in which the essential Australian is male, working-class, sardonic, laconic, loyal to his mates, unimpressed by rank, an improvisor, non-conformist, and so on. These virtues are defined and refined under the hard conditions of the bush, workplace, war or sport, in which women, and the feminine qualities, are considered to be beside the point. Since this cycle of films has spilt over and proliferated into television mini-series bustling with male actors, and given its central place in the iconography of the national self-image, it has had some marked effects on the pool of actors and actresses for films and the range of roles available. These effects, and their relation to the populist invocation of Australianness that has dominated the male-ensemble film, deserve some closer scrutiny.

Icons, Actors, Roles, Sexual Difference

Like the 'humanity ads' of the late seventies-early eighties (see Volume One, Chapter 1), the male ensemble film makes a *populist* appeal to an audience it projects as homogeneous (even if overlaid by an apparent diversity), conservative, nationalist, optimistic, ordinary, simple, attractive and sentimental. After *Breaker Morant*, the cycle of films becomes less apologetic, ambivalent and satirical in its invocation of its audience and Australia. It is increasingly disarming and calculated in its mythologising and commercial motives. The desirability and perceived authenticity of this invocation seems to have reached a peak around 1983 and subsequently fallen off. The confidence for this direct (rather than ambivalent) invocation of a populist Australianness became apparent in the style (and success) of *A Town Like Alice*, *Breaker Morant*, *Gallipoli*, *The Man from Snowy River*, *Phar Lap*, *The Dismissal*, perhaps *All the Rivers Run* and *Bodyline*. Five of these are clearly male-ensemble pieces.

There is a certain discontinuity between the qualities we like

The Aesthetic Force-Field   63

to think of as 'essentially Australian' — self-awareness, an oblique, self-effacing, non-exportable, vernacular form of irony and humour, the quality of 'being on to yourself' — and the peak of confident, extroverted nationalism in this cycle that occurred between *Breaker Morant* (1980) and *Bodyline* (1983). Earlier stages of the male-ensemble group of films were marked by double-edged icons of Australianness in the form of Jack Thompson's Foley, in *Sunday Too Far away*, or Bryan Brown's roles up to *A Town Like Alice*. *Breaker Morant* marks the change; from *Gallipoli* onwards, we find protagonists who are increasingly purified cyphers of mythic intention, to the point where Gary Sweet's Don Bradman, in *Bodyline*, and Tom Burlinson's Jim, in *The Man from Snowy River*, become unutterably good, models of approved behaviour. It seems that this shift is at least partly explicable as an increasing awareness in the industry of a calculated notion of what is export-quality and will gain approval overseas. The merging of the AFC genre and the male ensemble films, starting with *Breaker* and completed with *Gallipoli*, is indicated by this shift from a mode of irony to one of calculated innocence, from a more equivocal, indirect and definite assertion of Australianness, to an earnestness robbed of all lively contradiction.

From within the male-ensemble group of films, above all, particular lead roles, performances, and actors have acquired an ability to inspire a powerful consensual form of identification, an ability to signify 'Australia'. One can include the single-hero films, *Mad Max*, *Mad Max 2* and *The Man from Snowy River*, because the male ensembles of their supporting casts accord iconic force to their isolated, maverick heroes. The word 'icon' carries overtones not just of portrayal but of portrayal both widely recognized and invested with a sacramental force; the process of recognition involves some degree of audience ritual and bonding. An icon involves a symbolic construction recognised by a group, who thereby recognise their membership of the group. The successful, usually male ensemble, films containing iconically Australian roles, actors and performances have not found an audience; for a time they have instituted one.

It seems that the pool of male film actors in Australia has been both enlarged and subtly organised by the history of male ensemble acting and its intimate relationship with rousing and articulating a consensual Australianness. The few clear-cut 'stars'

— Mel Gibson, Bryan Brown, Jack Thompson, and perhaps Paul Hogan and Sam Neill — have each been moulded by roles and performances that are iconically 'Australian'. To some extent, the more iconic the performance, the more it is played down, reduced to a set of stances, gestures, brief and sardonic deliveries, gaze.

The new, lesser pantheon of recent stars, might include Tom Burlinson, Colin Friels, Vince Colossimo, Hugo Weaving, Gary Sweet and John Hargreaves. They have generally risen not through male ensemble feature parts, but from television and stage drama. Again, television has been as important as feature film in putting into circulation stereotypes with increasing iconic power. But outside the mini-series, the effect is less prestigious, endorsable, exportable. It is also more dispersed — they get more screen time overall, but in shorter segments of more diverse genres, like TV news, current affairs, advertising, documentaries, game shows and talk shows, as well as serial and series drama.

STARS	ACTORS	
	1) 'Australian' character actors	2) 'Actor' actors
Mel Gibson	Max Cullen	John Waters
Bryan Brown	Bill Hunter	Richard Moir
Jack Thompson	Bryan Brown	Norman Kaye
Paul Hogan	Graeme Blundell	Simon Burke
(Colin Friels	Bruce Spence	Sam Neill
Tom Burlinson	Dennis Miller	Gerard Kennedy
Vince Colossimo	Peter Cummins	Mike Preston
Hugo Weaving	John Hargreaves	Bill Kerr
Gary Sweet	John Meillon	Bud Tingwell
John Hargreaves	Harold Hopkins	Michael Pate
Sam Neill)	Chris Haywood	Alan Cassell
	David Argue	John Gregg
	Graham Kennedy	(David Gulpilil
	Reg Lye	Tommy Lewis)
	Garry Waddell	
	Ray Barrett	
	John Jarrett	
	Tony Barry	
	Steve Bisley	
	John Ewart	
	Tim Burns	

Then there is a large 'pool' from which films tend to draw either gifted character actors, usually used to support and give texture to the plebiscitary, populist male ensemble Australianness, or 'actor' actors, partly able to be used in the same way, but more often used to carry less culturally-specific meanings. The first group of actors, although individual and specialised in the particular quality they give to the articulation of Australianness, are cast as groups of concordant individuals who create a rich background orchestration for the threnody which is the loner hero icons. The list on the previous page is representative, not exhaustive.

And what of female roles, performances, and actresses? Clearly, the male-ensemble films have not created roles and performances and opportunities for actresses, especially after the marriage between male-ensemble and quality period film took place, and the birth of the all-male diorama approach to the re-staging of great sporting or military defeats from the hall of memory. Women, both as actors and roles, have generally been denied a part in the development of an iconic vocabulary of Australian faces, gestures, 'typical' responses, ways of speaking and looking, largely because of the central place occupied by the male-ensemble film and its dedication to the project of articulating male Australianness, or Australian maleness. The elision of 'male' into 'Australian' virtues has partly meant that female roles have acquired iconic force only when they approach certain 'male' virtues; for example, Judy Davis' Sybylla in *My Brilliant Career* borrows from the male tradition of the larrikin to achieve 'brilliant' non-conformity and hero qualities, and, by AFC-genre standards, spectacular success.

There is — perhaps as a consequence of this almost exclusively male interpretation of Australianness — only a small and uncertain list of female stars. In fact there is (or was) probably only Judy Davis, in the sense that she registers on an international consciousness. Sigrid Thornton is becoming known, but can still be assigned, after large popular successes like *The Man from Snowy River* and *All the Rivers Run*, claustrophobically passive and limited supporting roles such as in *Street Hero*. And yet this is consistent with the fact that her successes have been in traditional melodrama where female spiritedness is tameable, and softness and prettiness finally distinguish a woman in a timeless, placeless way. Her role in the anachronistic 1987 re-creation of the male ensemble film, *The Lighthorsemen*, supports this analysis. Angela Punch McGregor, Wendy Hughes, Helen Morse, Jo Kennedy, Judy Morris, Noni Hazlehurst and Greta Scacchi have all distinguished themselves as can be seen from the list of films with starring roles for women. But these have tended to be roles in the AFC genre soft option of representing tasteful Australianness, not the male ensemble hard option with its energy and power to confer iconic status. Noni Hazlehurst's role in *Monkey Grip* is a partial exception, perhaps because the inner-city sub-cultural milieu that she inhabits has incorporated feminism as a given in its history. Jo Kennedy is another. In *Starstruck*, her character walks, delightfully, the fine line between dilliness and supreme, unstoppable resilience.

The majority of Australian actresses — whether they have had lead or supporting film roles — fall into the 'actor' actor category. There is only a small list of actresses whose work in odd places (usually the eccentric list of films) has been permitted to contribute to the background richness of iconic Australianness; a list would include Kris McQuade, Pat Evison, Liddy Clark, Lorna Lesley, Jacki Weaver, Noni Hazlehurst, Carole Skinner, Jane Harders and Tracy Mann. Outside the AFC genre films, the second most likely group to accord women lead roles is the social realist film; as was noted in that section, women figure strongly in or as marginal, minority powerless or dispossessed groups or figures; often, they are the social issues.

Films with Starring or Strong Female Roles
(* indicates AFC genre; parentheses indicate a weak, questionable or minor example.)

1971 *(Stork)*
1972 *Shirley Thompson Versus the Aliens*
1975 *The Golden Cage*
    (Break of Day)*
    Caddie*
    (Picnic at Hanging Rock)*
1976 *(Eliza Fraser)**
    Oz
    A Promised Woman

1977 *(F.J. Holden)**
The Getting of Wisdom*
Journey Among Women
(The Mango Tree)*
The Singer and the Dancer
Love Letters from Teralba Road
1978 *Mouth to Mouth*
The Night the Prowler
(Patrick)
Third Person Plural
1979 *Cathy's Child*
Dawn!*
(In Search of Anna)
Just Out of Reach
(Kostas)
My Brilliant Career*
1980 *Manganinnie**
Maybe This Time
(Touch and Go)
Hard Knocks
1981 *The Killing of Angel Street**
Puberty Blues
Winter of Our Dreams
1982 *(The Best of Friends)*
(Far East)
Going Down
Heatwave
Kitty and the Bagman*
Lonely Hearts
Monkey Grip
(Norman Loves Rose)
Starstruck
We of the Never Never*
(The Year of Living Dangerously)
1983 *The Settlement*
(Buddies)
Careful, He Might Hear You
Undercover*
Winds of Jarrah*
1984 *Annie's Coming Out*

One Night Stand
(Run Chrissie Run)
Strikebound
(Warming Up)
Silver City*
On Guard
1985 *Emma's War*
Fran
On the Loose
1986 *For Love Alone*
The More Things Change
Two Friends
The Still Point
1987 *The Umbrella Woman*
The Place at the Coast
High Tide
Shadows of the Peacock
The Tale of Ruby Rose

The two remaining categories discernible within Australian film since 1970 have been far less active in organising the aesthetic field than those discussed so far. They are, in a sense, made in the interstices of the industry organised by those other, stronger trends. There is some danger, at this point, of endlessly assigning 'left-over' films to smaller and smaller, less and less defensible groupings — for example, that tiny group that could be labelled 'about intellectuals': *Between Wars*; *Newsfront*; *Third Person Plural*; *Winter of Our Dreams*; *Sweet Dreamers*; *Monkey Grip*; *Man of Flowers*; *Wrong World*. But the two still worth discussing — 'interior films' and 'eccentrics' - can indeed be situated as distinct moves or counter-moves within the aesthetic force-field organised by the major tendencies.

Interior Films

1968 *2000 Weeks*
1970 *Beyond Reason*
1971 *A City's Child*
1972 *(Shirley Thompson versus the Aliens)*
1973 *Libido: The Priest*
(Dalmas)

(The Office Picnic)
(Matchless)
27A
1974 *Between Wars*
1975 *The Firm Man*
     How Willingly You Sing
1976 *Illuminations*
     The Trespasser
     The Devil's Playground
     (Jog Trot)
1977 *Inside Looking Out*
     Journey Among Women
     (The Singer and the Dancer)
1978 *Third Person Plural*
     The Night the Prowler
     Solo
1979 *In Search of Anna*
     (Just Out of Reach)
     (Kostas)
1980 *(Maybe This Time)*
     Exits
1982 *Lonely Hearts*
     Plains of Heaven
     (Monkey Grip)
     Sweet Dreamers
1983 *Man of Flowers*
1984 *My First Wife*
1985 *Wrong World*
     (The Boy Who Had Everything)
1986 *Cactus*
1987 *(Belinda)*
     The Year My Voice Broke

This group is the closest that Australian cinema has really dared to come to the European 'art film' of subjectivity, inner states, private chambers of action, dreaming, argument or struggle. It includes much of the work of Paul Cox, who has recently begun to be that most rare thing within Australian film; the instituted *auteur* publicly exploring a personal domain. Peter Weir, probably the only other contender, has drifted away from this to other forms of privilege. It is a strikingly underpopulated grouping, yet it persists as a kind of answer to the sociologistic expose strain of the 'sexual mores' and male group-behaviour films, to the impermeable cold and plastic veneer of the 'purely commercial', 'genre in a vacuum' films that disown all cultural precision, and the soft, sentimental school of sensibility-dressed-as-period films of the AFC genre, which is the other near contender for art film status. In fact, the interior films have rarely achieved prominence, or the status that comes with showcasing for overseas display and consumption. Most have been made on relatively tiny budgets, for circulation in relatively obscure circumstances. Without a Channel-Four-like mechanism for funding occasional feature films about ideas and/or 'interior' subjects it is surprising that they have found any sheltering niche at all, especially given the range of aesthetic consensual wisdoms patrolling the bureaucracies and financial bodies of the Australian industry.

In fact, it might be proposed that this group answers the ideology of 'industry', 'business', and 'professional standards' (in terms of crew sizes and organisation, not accreditation) more clearly than any other. 'Everyone knows' that such films cannot make money, or find a large enough audience to make a profit. These films hold open a small place for other aesthetic possibilities, smaller audiences, criteria that may not be those either of profitability, or the industry showcase. Perhaps their presence allows the occasional 'eccentric' film to get through.

Yet, at the same time, they may more often succumb to the mere trappings of art-film 'art': bravura editing, camera work or processed imagery and sound for their own sakes; the signs of 'art' rather than of hard intellectual work. In turning their back on commerce and popular form, these films risk missing the flow of energy between film and the freely attuned moment of audience desire. The conscious art film also risks a certain academicism in its obedience to that particular canon — and just as the strictly commercial film invites a sterile cultural limbo, so this one risks a functional blindness towards the immediate living signs of the local and the regional. To their credit, most films in the group have avoided the excesses and pitfalls of their position; but there may well be more creative energy and expressive power available in the 'Australian Gothic' and 'eccentric' areas than here.

Speed and derangement. John Laurie and Gary Waddell in an all-night cult road movie, *Pure Shit*.

The Eccentrics

Eccentrics

1970 *Jack and Jill: a postscript*
1971 *Wake in Fright*
1972 *Shirley Thompson versus the Aliens*
     The Office Picnic
1974 *Between Wars*
     The Cars That Ate Paris
     Yakkety Yak
1975 *(Sunday Too Far Away)*
     Pure Shit
1976 *The Devil's Playground*
     Oz
     Surrender in Paradise

       Mad Dog Morgan
1977 *Journey Among Women*
       Queensland
       Backroads
       F.J. Holden
1978 *Mouth to Mouth*
       Newsfront
       The Night the Prowler
       Third Person Plural
1979 *Apostasy*
       Mad Max
       Palm Beach
       (The Money Movers)
1980 *Exits*
       Wronsky
       Hard Knocks
1981 *Against the Grain*
       Mad Max 2
       Winter of Our Dreams
       (Puberty Blues)
1982 *Going Down*
       Goodbye Paradise
       Lonely Hearts
       Monkey Grip
       Starstruck
       (Heatwave)
       Greetings From Wollongong
1983 *Buddies*
       The Clinic
       Man of Flowers
       The Settlement
       (Careful, He Might Hear You)
1984 *(Fast Talking)*
       My First Wife
       One Night Stand
       Strikebound
       BMX Bandits
       Future Schlock
1985 *(Bliss)*
       Bootleg

>   *The Coca-Cola Kid*
>   *Traps*
>   *Unfinished Business*
>   *Wrong World*
> 1986 *Wills and Burke*
>   *The Big Hurt*
>   *Dead-End Drive-In*
> 1987 *The Tale of Ruby Rose*
>   *The Year My Voice Broke*
>   *(Warm Nights on a Slow Moving Train)*

These are the films that resist simple incorporation into any of the major tendencies in the aesthetic field, making it difficult to generalise about them as a group. They may play with elements of several. For example, *Monkey Grip* moves between social realism and the 'interior' film, and establishes a resistant, non-exploitative eroticism against the grain of the sexual mores film; *Newsfront* resists the AFC genre enough to establish a genuine stake as a history film, incorporates some elements of the male ensemble film, but finally defines its main character as a loner, and establishes the virtue of refusing to accommodate a dishonourable group consensus. Or they may position themselves defiantly within one or more conventional established genres (of cinema at large — that is, largely U.S. cinema) and work against the generic grain to articulate not a generalisable Australianness, in the populist, nationalist male-ensemble sense, but a critical local or regional sense of place and culture. For example, *Palm Beach* mixes documentary, surf movie, detective film and experimental film to laconically explore a highly specific sub-cultural and regional domain: the surf and drug alternative living in Sydney's northern beaches peninsula.

One might expect, as the industry matures and analyses its strong successes, like the *Mad Max* films, to see an increasing confidence in the use of generic conventions from within, to tell specifically Australian stories, a growing trust in Australian audience sophistication in this regard and in the market-worthiness of such films outside their home territory. But the industry is slow to change its thinking or to put any trust in this 'eccentric' aesthetic ground, rather than the polarised groupings established in the seventies, explored at the start of this chapter. This seems to reveal on the part of the industry a lack of cinematic sophistication, a slow uptake, a certain lack of interest in the histories, shifts and differences of its own culture, let alone the wider world film culture. It seems that the eccentric films which tell so much about how the aesthetic field is centred, are made despite, not because of, the intrinsic character of this industry. (It is interesting to note how many 'got through' in the boom of 1982, along with a larger number of 'cold' films.)

The big money-makers like *Mad Max* spawn imitations; *Midnite Spares, Runnin' on Empty, Chain Reaction, Razorback*, and a host of projects that never got beyond the prospectus stage, consciously derived something from the style of *Mad Max*. But they do not seem to imitate the *Mad Max* films' mix of genre, cinematic literacy, invention and notions of myth and story archetypes. The smaller eccentrics, like *Goodbye Paradise, Starstruck, Newsfront, Going Down, Winter of Our Dreams*, are not honoured by imitation, even though many provoked wide interest and comment both here and overseas.

The aesthetic field of the present industry, as formed in the mid-seventies and perpetuated into the late-seventies, seems peculiarly immune to the eccentric presences that come and fade. It seems, incredibly, to be satisfied with its established quotas and delegations of a small set of adequate virtues: 'national identity' in the male-ensemble film and its later developments; quality and taste and a gentle 'sell' of Australia in the AFC genre; commercial pragmatism and 'nous' in the the coldly commercial films, with their dismally uninformed sense of genre; compensatory social conscience in the low-budget social realist, social issue film. Perhaps this nervousness and limited vision stems from the smallness, insecurity, and insularity of this industry, as well as its reliance on the goodwill of changing Australian governments for its existence. Certainly it militates against there being many aesthetic surprises or delights among its films, many intellectually and/or emotionally challenging films, or very much genuine and precise engagement with local and regional articulations of culture.

PART TWO

We now come to explore the specific ways in which Australianness has been articulated, inflected, promoted, and even marketed, in the course of the revived industry to late 1984. In this part we trace the outlines of a cultural nationalist project within the films themselves. We focus on the films that are interesting, if not exemplary, in the way that they mark out a stage or extreme or experiment in that loose project. The films are discussed in varying detail and are treated mainly in order of release.

We are not attempting an exhaustive list of all films that speak about or from an Australian point of view. Instead, this is an attempt to sift through and select, on a symptomatic basis, those films that show signs of the problems, tensions, contradictions and pleasures of trying to articulate that which is Australian. Of particular interest in each case is the 'voice' of the film; its mode of addressing an Australian audience; its stance towards, or within, Australian history; its treatment of place, of landscape; the distinctions and tensions it maintains around the questions of sexuality, class, and race or ethnic identity; what assumptions it makes about genre, what formal decisions it makes.

3

The First Phase (1970-75): The Prototypes Emerge

In retrospect it can be seen that in the first phase of the industry most of the prototypes that were later to circumscribe the aesthetic range of the cinema emerged. However, the start was made in a virtual vacuum. There was no immediate body of work to provide a context, no patterns of successes and failures to allow a glimpse of an audience. There was, in fact, a great danger of finding oneself 'midway between Texas and Manchester', as Tim Burstall put it.[1]

The local theatre revival offered some direction — a vigorous use of lovingly observed Australian vernacular and behaviour, a defiant localism, a concern with Australian group rituals and social life — and its failings — from a point of view that flirted openly with 'ockerism'. The posture of the ocker was blunt, loud, hedonistic. It asserted that Australia was all right and Australians good blokes, and that if you had to combat philistinism then barbarism had a lot to recommend it. The ocker's appeal was populist and conservative. Its blue-singleted working-class male icon was not a signal for class solidarity, but a gesture towards the classless common man and last bastion of the 'real' Australian virtues — which included a sardonic, humorous appreciation of uncontrite coarseness, grossness, even stupor. The ocker displaced the 'knocker', announcing in the least subtle way available that the era of self-dissatisfaction was over. John Singleton traded most successfully on the image and its moment of populist appeal in the mid seventies, and demonstrated that it could serve a kind of 'private ennerprise', strongly anti-union, tory radicalism. Paul Hogan — and in a sense Prime Minister Bob Hawke too — still trade on it in the mid-eighties, winning public approval for a genial, unapologetic roughness of manner that intimates working-class egalitarianism without really implicating it in any way.

Ocker speech was colloquial speech pushed to the point where the exclusion of the non-native speaker *was* the point. It was also rude. The four-letter word, after such protracted banishment from polite society, gave power to the new assertive use of vernacular. It helped to give the early plays of the local theatre renaissance an air of being unconventional, making a new start, repudiating a staid, inauthentic past and freeing the irreverent larrikin Australian spirit.

The title of Alexander Buzo's play, *Rooted*, in 1968, nicely exemplifies this playful release of unofficial language into the public arena. 'Rooted' is a vigorous, sexually crude way of expressing exhaustion. Yet in its adverbial function it has a tongue-in-cheek innocence; perhaps even homage to a respectably titled play like Arnold Wesker's *Roots*. A skilful use of double-entendre with a bias as 'offensively Australian' as you could want.

Changing censorship laws gave another kind of guidance in the early seventies with the introduction of the 'R' (Restricted) certificate and the consequent loosening of exhibition restrictions. So it is not surprising that early film production looked to the libidinous possibilities and novelty value of Australian R-rated material. In fact, eminences as *grise* and respected as H.C. (Nugget) Coombs were quoted as recommending that the fledgling industry should create an initial financial stake by producing frankly pornographic material. Stopping short of hard-core porn, the R-certificate tolerated full-frontal female nudity, but did not permit glimpses of erectile male tissue. Thus the sex-romps and soft-core porn of the 'Emmanuelle' novelette variety or the pseudo-documentary of night life or sexual problems that were suddenly permissible and briefly popular in the early seventies for their novelty, wherever they came from, focussed on the special, compromised titillation of naked women and less revealed, less disrobed men.

Then there were the influences of existing sixteen milimetre independent and underground film and television drama previously

The First Phase (1970-75): The Prototypes Emerge

discussed. The constantly changing relationship between mainstream and independent cinema has been described in Volume One, but here we shall see frequent evidence of a relationship that is sometimes contributary but more often mutually exclusive, as though one were the negative impress of the other, or as if each side of the relationship delegated odious responsibilities to the other, and could then hold both the responsibilities and the 'other' in some contempt.

Nevertheless, there was a vacuum of feeling for what might constitute an Australian feature film audience or where to find it. But the first moves to summon and address an audience, in that near vacuum of knowledge and history, were not quite stabs in the dark. Some points of contact and response were known from theatre, television and film audience patterns in the early stages of the new censorship codes, and from the low-budget area of filmmaking. But when films made contact and drew box-office responses, it did not necessarily follow that they had touched on profound universal needs seeking expression and gratification. Critics in the early period rarely approved of those films, mainly ocker or sexploitation comedies, that succeeded at the box office. An almost exactly inverse ratio existed between critical acclaim and box-office success, to the point where Tim Burstall could characterise the situation as a 'death-bed scene regularly attended only by most of our critics, the film buffs, the festival people, the trendies, the underground'.[2] John Hinde was moved in 1979, at the lowest ebb of the second phase, to question whether the *Alvins* and the *Bazzas* were not, in fact, true starts to an indigenous film industry, ruled 'false' by critical reaction and governmental desire for approval in 'the sacred groves'. He suggested that the strong audience approval for these films indicates that they were after all in touch with some half-conscious self-recognition in an audience wandering in the impoverished sexual limbo of our culture; that they offered, in effect, crude sketchy maps which might have enabled later films to make a more detailed, exploration of this terrain.[3] In this view, the critics were, however unconsciously, conforming to an ancient streak of wowserism and prurience in the Australian psyche, and further explorations were aborted, replaced by the tasteful, copy-book period drama. It is an interestingly provocative line, but one that overlooks the pragmatic, exploitationist motives guiding these early probes for pay dirt. Perhaps it also overlooks the way the interesting, eccentric films have virtually depended on the passive repressiveness of the 'official' industry. Their less guarded, more idiosyncratic, even accidental routes to production remind us of what has been repressed in a haphazard, frustrated, half-coherent fashion. But incoherence can be more suggestive, more persuasive, and even more articulate than the polished surfaces, discreet charm and self-conscious innocence that our institutions have tended to endorse.

It is interesting that the first film of the seventies to work as a confident essay on an aspect of Australianness — the effects of isolation, booze, relentless masculine company, in a hot, flat interior landscape — was achieved by a hybrid American-Australian production company which imported a Canadian director and three British lead actors. *Wake in Fright* (1971), directed by Ted Kotcheff, seems to be more intimately connected to a 'tradition' of dramatising Australia for itself than many a film with technically pure Australian credentials.

It is an outsider's essay, a kind of Australian heart of darkness, but at moments a deeply perceptive and unadorned one, without either false politeness or undue reversion to gross stereotype. It is an early example of the male ensemble film, and the presences of Jack Thompson, John Meillon, Chips Rafferty and Peter Whittle balance the imported Gary Bond, Donald Pleasence and Sylvia Kay. The adaptation of Kenneth Cook's novel helps to anchor this co-production in this culture; it is also worth speculating that Ted Kotcheff's Canadianness presented less of a problem of cultural difference than would have been the case if an American or British director had been used. Dominion provincialism, a geography of extremes and great isolation, and a similar sense of a cultural coming of age in the seventies: Canada and Australia had a lot of common ground.

Gary Bond plays a teacher stranded at a a remote inland school, a genuine outsider desperate to escape back to the coast, at least for his holidays. He loses his savings — escape money — in a drunken two-up game as he waits at the nearest railhead town for the connecting train. Landlocked, defeated, he sinks into an alcoholic haze and abandons himself to a night in which he descends into hell at the hands of the menacingly friendly townspeople.

As the alcoholic tide rises, the film drifts from realism —

dramatising the strangeness of human society in extreme isolation — into grotesque exaggeration, poised painfully on the threshold of the comic. At the heart of this disorientating process is the drunken kangaroo slaughter with four-wheel-drive and spotlight, in which repression, violence and masculine ritual are suddenly on display in the most destabilising moment of the film.

Wake is curious and interesting because it manages to portray a horror at the heart of Australia that is about the conditions of sexuality, as Meaghan Morris says, by being about repression, violence and male self-segregation.[4] Yet it manages also to withhold the heavy hand of judgement above and outside. It was one of very few films of that early period to look at contemporary Australia and not shy away from its commonplaces, as though they were unbearably emptied by sheer familiarity. To understand this point, it is necessary only to look at other co-productions of the time — *Nickel Queen* and *Side Car Racers*, for example. The frozen address of these films, the stillborn narratives, the threadbare cinematic resources: John Laws as the hippy gigolo of *Nickel Queen* is much more a foreigner in this, his own country, than is Donald Pleasence, in *Wake in Fright*.

Walkabout (1971) makes an interesting comparison, as a co-production of this early period. *Wake in Fright* turned a deliberately blind or jaundiced eye towards the beauty of the interior landscape; it was about the impoverished terrain of white, civilised humanity in that overwhelming emptiness. *Walkabout* is its Siamese twin, facing the opposite direction but from the same point. Urban Australia, coastal city and small inland town, is seen as a perverse denial of the essential innocent truth of Australia. In this film, the interior is still brim full of a spiritual infinitude which answers the needs of Eurocentric mankind escaping from a shrinking Europe. It is seen as the the great, dry heart of a last reserve of natural power, of a wilderness knowable in its spiritual, Aboriginal truth. The land-forms, plants, animals and Aboriginals still able to transmit the Dreaming are seen as the sole positive human forces in the landscape. If they are rejected at this level, the film proposes they are fragile and may lose their power and die.

Lost in the desert, two children who have survived their father's attempted family suicide, acquire an Aboriginal guide played by David Gulpilil in his first feature role. His presence begins to translate their battle for survival into a form of ritual walkabout, a spiritual reacquaintance with the land, a reawakening of Eden. The older child, a teenage girl, is already too aware of a fallen world; she cannot penetrate the experience to its fragile heart of innocence. Only the small boy can completely understand, relax with the landscape and be at home. The girl (Jenny Agutter, a British actress) rejects the courtship rituals of their guide without a full understanding, even with ridicule; and so the two worlds fail to achieve symbolic union. Rejected, the fragile ancient world, the Aboriginal, slips away to die. The failure also condemns the invader to a kind of death-in-life. The girl is seen, grown older, bound to a conventional married life in the city and dreaming of what she once glimpsed; she sees her own world as artificial and moribund.

The allegorical form, heightened by close-ups and landscapes of the natural world almost surreal in their intensity, makes the equation 'nature equals paradise lost'. As we will see, later films such as *Journey Among Women* and *Long Weekend* also explore equations between nature, guilt and sexuality. Many Australians share with a moral vengeance the guilt *Walkabout* deals with, and perceive the white history of Australia as invasive, destructive and life-threatening, like a cancer. The guilt is felt as deepening sexual repression, economic rapacity and phobia-ridden relations with the land. But while it is a product of this perception, *Walkabout* also has a certain platitudinous, Rousseau-like simplicity partly arising from its allegorical form, partly linked to the fact that it is the vision of a European outsider who perhaps needed a dark continent for mythological investment, and therefore needed to apportion blame for the wronging of this continent.

An utterly different kind of 'first start', wholly Australian-made (in fact, virtually wholly Jim Sharman-made), is *Shirley Thompson Versus the Aliens* (1972), a striking, early example made with great confidence. 'Being ignorant meant we had no fear', said Jim Sharman of this film. Joseph von Sternberg at the 1967 Sydney Film Festival, when asked why he thought there was no film industry in Australia, replied, 'I don't know, you have cameras, don't you?'[5] In this spirit, Sharman provided the whole $17,000 budget himself to make the film he had talked up with Helmut Bakaitis.

The First Phase (1970-75): The Prototypes Emerge

The film draws lovingly, with unhesitating energy, on a Gothic vision of Australia in the 1950s, mediated through the madness of the institutionalised heroine, Shirley (Jane Harders), in the sixties. Fifties' subculture — bodgies, widgies, bikes, milkbars, Luna Park (that timeless place of Sydney's memories), the Harbour Bridge and the sci-fi teen horror flick itself — is used as a means of talking about Australia without the spectre of drabness and over-familiarity even being considered.

Shirley Thompson was the first feature-length venture on to the terrain of Australian Gothic. The suburban Australian household is where horror lurks, in this instance. Drummoyne is beautifully chosen as its site — front yards with their lone, spindly shrubs, 'Emoh Ruo' over front doors, kitsch interiors, in which Mixmaster arm descending to its task in the bowl can be savoured by the camera as an epic moment, just as the subsequent hurling of the Mixmaster through the kitchen window can have a force that is both comic and frightening. Between these two moments, two shots, the wide-angled stare of the patrolling camera discovers a variety of absurd objects in the over-regulated zone of the house, and we are permitted the full range of pertinent emotions. We see bed dolls, shells, wrought-iron bookcases, tap shoes, koala cushions and rose-emblazoned tea towels.

Here Shirley is pressured to conform to her parents' wishes and marry the nice boy Harold, who takes her for milkshakes on the Bondi esplanade. But she has a secret life as Shirley, queen of her motorbike gang — an obvious and necessary answer to her home life. 'Home' is dissonant with Shirley's hopes for life, but consonant with her 'madness' — she receives warnings from alien beings lodged in the river caves at Luna Park, and struggles to transmit their warning to the world. Later, in the sixties, we see a drugged, restrained zombie-like Shirley in another kind of home altogether. When Shirley relays, pirate-fashion, the aliens' message of warning for the world over the radio, followed by an 'Aeroplane Jelly' commercial, no one cares. 'So it's true, so what?', says her father. The aliens, transmitting their warning from the papier-mache river caves, are more familiar and finally less alarming than the people back home; the family is the truly alien and alarming presence.

The film reverberates with controlled hysteria, beautifully centred on Jane Harders' performance, but also flowing from all of her surroundings. Sharman's successful generic mix of sci-fi, rock musical, art film, and semi-comic, but horrifying, fifties' style case-study is a perfect abandoned kind of vehicle for hysteria that brings the repressive qualities of Australianness into sharp focus. The female hero has a confident Australian voice that denotes a strong character. Admittedly she's mad, or heading there, but mad in the tradition of failed heroes, as much as suffering heroines.

The film has worn extremely well, and this isn't just because of the return to favour of fifties' and early-sixties bric-a-brac in the eighties. It is more to do with the complete lack of coyness or hesitation about 'speaking Australia' in the same breath as speaking genre, repression, and even apocalypse, alongside a genuine fascination or affection for the Australian past.

Libido was a project put together by the Producers' and Directors' Guild of Australia in 1972, a *portmanteau* film to provide a kind of portfolio of available film industry talent — especially directors. John Murray, Tim Burstall, Fred Schepisi and David Baker each directed a thirty-minute story with some loose connection to questions of sexual behaviour and mores. The title gave the film a touch of class by the use of a high-culture word as its title, and simultaneously an R-rated promise of saltiness.

What is most interesting about the film from the present vantage is how much its four short films anticipate large tendencies in the work of the decade that followed. Remember that this was a film made to demonstrate quality and commercial sense; it shows a tentative movement towards several avenues which would be well-trodden in pursuit of critical and/or commercial success.

The Husband, part one, written by Craig McGregor and directed by John Murray, is a kind of comedy of middle-class manners, centred on an elegant Paddington household in which the too-trusting breadwinner is being gently cuckolded by his pretty, idle wife and the friend who was his best man several years, and two small children, ago. The film borrows touches from sixties British films like *Morgan: a Suitable Case for Treatment*; for example, the zoo mimickry, the 'swinging London' feel given to the Paddington social scene and the gentle dissolves between 'pretty' scenes for ironic effect. It also borrows from European art film imagery: the final scene has the wife lying naked on the matrimonial bed to flirt with her lover by telephone. She is given lines like, 'Don't worry darling, I'm not a whore. I'm your wife.' Its archness finally suggests television soap rather than a direction for feature film.

Tim Burstall's section, *The Child*, scripted by Hal Porter, has a period upper-class setting, and follows a child's growing awareness of the sexual undercurrents of the world within the boundaries of his own high-walled garden and palatial house. Finally, in a state of almost sexual jealousy, he causes the death by drowning of his governess' lover; a death which recalls his father's ungrieved demise on a business trip on the *Titanic*. In its assumption that wealthy settings befit and evoke period spectacle, in the kind of natural association formed over several decades of British television drama, and in its lyrical, celebratory camera style, *The Child* clearly anticipates much of the AFC genre — and much that Burstall would repudiate in his later work.

The Priest, Fred Schepisi's piece from a script by Tom Keneally, is the most 'intellectual', in the sense that it takes the form of an argument about the issue of sexual passion and purity of motive in the face of Catholic celibacy. Arthur Dignam plays a priest suffering a breakdown over his desire to repudiate Church authority and marry a nun (Robyn Nevin). Their encounter occurs in a single closed room, and acquires a kind of chamber-theatre intensity as the camera circles and enacts their entrapment by their religious vows. Again, this part has the virtue of 'quality' television drama — but this is because of the emotional intensity achieved in a confrontation that is chiefly waged at a level of passionate but frequently abstract debate. At the end, Dignam's face is ravaged by the trauma of exorcising 'faith' - it is like a map of the battleground Schepisi explored later in *The Devil's Playground* and even *The Chant of Jimmie Blacksmith*, also scripted by Keneally.

The Family Man was David Williamson's contribution, directed by David Baker. This story concerns two men out on the town after the wife of one of them (Jack Thompson) has given birth to a third daughter. ('Girls give me the shits!') It is confident Williamson territory: male rituals, group mores, sexuality as the Achilles heel of the Australian male ethos, 'natural' misogyny and a satiric naturalism in the service of a sort of *National Times*-style exposé of middle-class reality. This film, more-so than *The Child*, assays the ground that Burstall would cover, generating a small but persistent cycle of films. None of the *Libido* films offer much hope for relations between the sexes and none are from a female point of view.

The Family Man comes closest to a Pyrrhic female victory. It cuts deeply into male sexism and exposes its white-anted interior. But the women in the film — two faintly 'liberated' women and a long-suffering wife — are not allowed any real force or credibility. They are given lines like, 'She's a very committed person. She won't be exploited', while the men have lines like, 'Ken'll go through you like a packet of salts . . . He'd go through a knot hole in a fence'.

If the women strike back, they also anticipate recurrent defeat, almost as ritual victims. The male universe is presented as the interesting one, with its verbal vigour, and even an element of tragedy. This pattern is repeated in *Petersen*, in many aspects of *Sunday Too Far Away*, and in the male ensemble films such as *Don's Party*, *The Odd Angry Shot* and *The Club*. It is even mirrored, in a way, in the one counter-example within this cycle of films: *Maybe This Time*. 'Femaleness' is manifest in characters who are ciphers to aspects of the male or to 'maleness'; Australian women suffer a characterless 'non-male' existence of one kind or another, with brief moments of reprieve if the plot permits them to enact a small revenge.

Stork (1971) is interesting to consider beside the two other foundation comedies of the period, *The Adventures of Barry McKenzie* (1972) and *Alvin Purple* (1973). These three comedies in a sense introduced the possibility of box-office success for Australian mainstream features. *Stork* is the first David Williamson play adapted to film, and the first Burstall-Williamson collaboration. It was linked very clearly to the Melbourne-based Australian theatre revival. In its early promotion the fact that it was an Australian film was deliberately omitted. Nevertheless, *Stork* participated energetically in the release on to the screen of suppressed Australian idiom which had become so much a part of the local theatre revival.

The Coming of Stork is a male ensemble play: the film *Stork* singles out the main character with an especially ironic scalpel. Bruce Spence plays the gangling, shy, anti-intellectual, crass, hypochondriac, insecure central male, whose very height suggests the playwright himself. He fleshes out his character's nicely complex mess of stereotypes with painfully awkward attempts to grab centre stage such as the old oyster-up-the-nose party trick. Stork is in fact a little like Tal Ordell's Dave in Raymond Longford's *On Our Selection* — not the central character but the most sublime in a comic ensemble piece.

The film seems, in fact, to test the wind for ribald comedy with strong ocker touches, in a sixteen milimetre, low-budget trial run. *Stork* was a success, with its generally light, playful rhythm, sexual picaresque and deliberately unrounded story.[6] As one might expect of a theatre-renaissance piece, it has plenty of specific local cultural referents stitched into it: Bolte-isms, anti-Vietnam demonstrations, production-line jobs at GMH, Carlton terraces.[7] The ribaldry comes out in the open, where it should be. Tag lines like, 'You can't keep the old Stork down', put 'stork' into a class that would include 'pecker' and 'cock'. (Is this another authorial trace of David Williamson? In *Gallipoli*, another bird metaphor is used to describe the author as he plays football on screen. He writes in his own epithet as 'that tall streak of pelican shit'.)

Stork is, relatively speaking, typical of the strain of naturalism and serious but ironic social comment that runs through most of Williamson's work before *Gallipoli*. *The Adventures of Barry McKenzie* is, by contrast, literally the stuff of comic strips, thanks to Barry Humphries' pushed-to-the-brink comic invective. The revue tradition meets *Private Eye* magazine: grotesque and exaggerated comic self-criticism becomes celebration, and no one is forced to own the criticism. It is a highly transitive form of satire. *Bazza* delighted Australians with its anti-Britishness, and the British with its anti-Australianness. Nobody ever admits to receiving the wound that Humphries' satire inflicts; nobody recognises themselves in his grotesquerie; everyone shares his cruelty at the delicious expense of someone else, some *other*.

Indeed, it is a tussle between Barrys — Barry McKenzie (Barry Crocker) and his Aunt Edna (Barry Humphries) — to establish with whose voice the film finally speaks. Barry Crocker brings a boyish geniality from his family television singing specials to the part in the form of a genial idiocy which is used to cover large measures of vulgarity and scandalous behaviour. His spade-like chin is an almost perfect replica of the cartoon drawing.

But Barry Humphries' Edna (Edna Everage, now Dame Edna, megastar of media events) is felt as the force that sketched young Barry into being, determined the narrow poles of his psychic world, and governs it as its chief influence and presiding genius. With that presiding genius in drag, it is hardly surprising that all the characters inhabit a kind of half-world, and are distorted by strong pulls towards their sexual opposites or contraries.

The Australian Film Development Corporation fully funded the film as its first major investment. Tom Stacey, then Manager, is reputed to have called to Bruce Beresford as he left for London to shoot *Barry*, 'For God's sake, don't put all those terrible colloquialisms in the film!' The 'terrible colloquialisms' are, of course, the motor of the comedy and its appeal to Australian audiences. They provide a comic invitation to warm yourself at the fireside of the familiar — and the daring. But to be aligned with the language is to be aligned with the protagonist, which takes you into some strange places. Vomit is not particularly funny, but 'chunder' and the threat of chundering are, especially when it is at the expense of the less expansive, fastidious, recoiling culture of the 'mother country".

Barry McKenzie was the first contact with that rich pay dirt of Australian film that continues right to the present: anti-Britishness, or at least a repudiation of the old desire to win the mother country's approval, to meet her standards. Barry's 'full-colour chunderama' is a manifestation of the errant child's refusal to believe in family tradition. He comes 'home' and disgraces himself through uncontrolled or indecorous bodily functions and even, in one terrible misinterpretation of television studio signalling, through full-frontal exposure of himself on prime-time BBC television. Meanwhile, in parody of the long-standing Australian desire to please Britain, Barry acts always with only the best of filial intentions; and in parody of the British view of Australians as naives abroad, he allows himself to be taken by cab from Heathrow to London in a round-trip via Stonehenge, wearing his ever-ready beer mug on a dog chain around his neck. It is a two-way current of hostility. As the poet Les Murray once said, 'Much of the hostility to Australia, and it amounts to that, shown by English people above a certain class line can be traced to the fact that we are, to a large extent, the poor who got away'.

Edna Everage carries a little of this current of hostility; she often flatters herself that she resembles the Queen, and before her advancing presence many treasured British shibboleths are bulldozed into view at all kinds of strange angles. But she carries a stronger hostility of another kind; with the drag-queen there come not only a range of female stereotypes from the sharp to the vicious, but all the archaic fear-and-loathing-of-women jokes that women have laughed at through the ages out of uneasy fear of contamination. If everybody is seen to laugh at them, they must be harmless, mustn't they? And at least halfway true? Edna has proved to be Humphries' most famous and enduring persona. At the start of the 1984 Los Angeles Olympics, she presided over Olivia Newton-John's boutique party for Australian athletes and film stars; the new patriotism had reached the point at last where it could not only tolerate but craved her overblown, drastically puncturing presence. In 1972, Australia needed her strong comic deflection to focus the future.

Edna has been gradually embellished over two decades with ever more outrageous characteristics. She has been menopausal for a very long time indeed; a menopausal suburban witch from the Moonee Ponds from which Patrick White's suburbia grew and never escaped. Her husband Norm was a long time dying, eventually fulltime on a kidney machine. The image suggests a shrivelled victim bound securely and sucked dry in a spider's larder, the kind of blood-sucking vampirism implied by many portrayals of women who in any way exceed their male partners. One of Edna's favourite words is 'little', and she attaches it to her most outrageous characterisations in order at once to inflate and discount, decorously, their extravagance. At the same time, this very genteel, 'feminine' word becomes a symptom of the littleness of female vision, tunnelled through a terrifying respectability which reduces the world to petty moves in an inconsequential flow of gossip. In nightmarish contrast to the absurd niceties that cloak her speech, Edna is endlessly full of 'juices' and vigour sapped from the male victim, of course. Often this takes the form of double entendres. She has a fearful devouring sexual vitality which, at especially ambiguous moments, is almost admirable. She is a monster of blindness and egotism growing more bloated every year, her grotesque appetites feeding on ever-larger pastures of respectability. It is salutary to reflect that Edna, even as a deeply misogynist creation, was one of the strongest, most distinctive female roles for many years outside of a few in period films and the inestimable Shirley Thompson.

The other early comic success, a huge one, was Burstall's *Alvin Purple* (1973). The running joke in *Alvin* is the wimp, a waterbed salesman, who makes good with scores of women who can't resist him; in fact he makes better than good, better than his desires, energies and staying-power will allow. Finally, he is on the run from jealous husbands, but the convent that gives him asylum promises little relief from his problem. The comic dissonance between the hero (Graeme Blundell) and his apparent attraction for women is a slim joke, constantly reiterated. It is fleshed out a little in brief send-ups of certain agents of social authority: the psychiatrist, the police, the press. But these are passing, and never permitted to interfere with the simple repetition of slapstick social attack and evasion.

Even though Blundell did a good job just in remaining a sympathetic character, the popularity of the film appears to have rested on the titillating circumstances of the playful humour, with the male both hero and comic butt. To state this does no more than describe the main constituents of a sex romp. In the first heady days of the R certificate, when full frontal nudity was novelty enough to keep films like *Swedish Fly Girls* and *Bedroom Mazurka* doing long-running business downtown, *Alvin Purple's* slight edge was enough to reach a large audience, who ignored the offended critics. The film offered *Australian* female nudity, whole crowds of it in fact, and a protagonist who could be both liked and offered as victim at the same moment. And Blundell was a recognisably Australian wimp, even if the idiom and local referents were less carefully worked in Alan Hopgood's *Alvin* than in Williamson's *Stork*. Where *Stork* had one willing girl, Anna (Jacki Weaver), and a cluster of men, *Alvin* had countless willing women and one only minimally elaborated male.

The comic dilemma provides the titillation of lots of flesh, but stays almost wholesome through Alvin's inadequacy for the task. If the audience had any remaining dubiety about permissive sexuality, then this is the capping joke that let them off the hook. If you objected at some level to the simple sexploitation of the film, you had the perverse satisfaction of seeing the tables turned on the traditional myth of the male's boundless sexual appetite. That's if you didn't object even more strongly to the unspoken

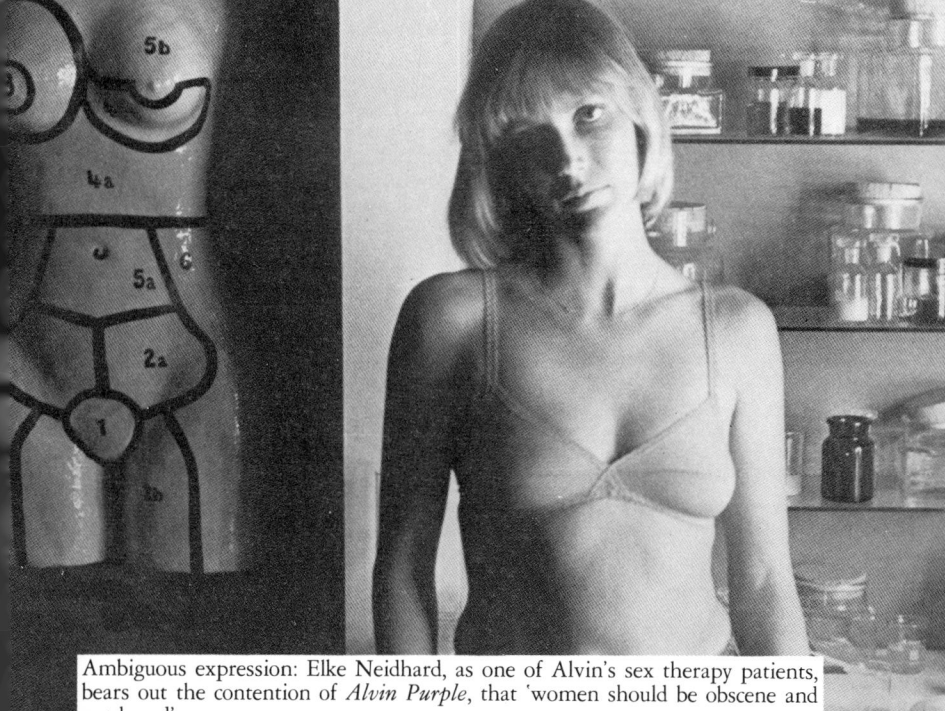

A tussle between the Barrys: Barry Humphries and Barry Crocker in *The Adventures of Barry McKenzie*.

Ambiguous expression: Elke Neidhard, as one of Alvin's sex therapy patients, bears out the contention of *Alvin Purple*, that 'women should be obscene and not heard'.

accusation of *vagina dentata* levelled against women in this reversal, which begins to establish a point of kinship between *Alvin* and its ocker stablemate, *Barry McKenzie*.

At least it can be said that *Alvin* concentrates sufficiently on its comic-porn genre to be utterly relaxed, even unconscious, of its address to an Australian audience. Australianness in *Alvin* is not loud and rude in order to be definitely present, as in *Barry McKenzie*. It is not worth commenting on. It is just there, if you like, in the voices, the Melbourne street scenes, and the neutral suburbscapes. If Australianness inflects the main 'concerns' of the film at all, it would be in the very modest inversion of male sexual prowess in the character of Alvin. And, perhaps, in the confidence this film could have in its local audience response at the breaking of such a long, restraining drought.

Both *Alvin* and *Barry McKenzie* had sequels, which quickly played out the small remaining reserves of interest in their audiences, and comedy in their devices. While a third *Alvin*, *Melvin, Son of Alvin*, was made in 1984, and a third Barry Humphries film, *Les Patterson Saves the World* was released in 1987, both quickly dropped from sight, and, generally speaking, the gross or ribald comic mode did not survive the first phase. It began to wither after the slow response to the bedroom-farce style chosen for *Eliza Fraser*, Burstall's project of 1975-6. *Eliza Fraser* was a period film that did not adopt the moral viewpoint of its AFC-genre neighbours. In fact it adopted a variety of viewpoints, opting out of the consequences of all of them except a *Tom Jones* kind of feyness.)

Between Wars (1974), the first period feature, was also on a different moral footing from the AFC-genre films to follow. It was left-footed, even left-wing, and oblique in its style; a little different from the gentle but earnest AFC genre that was to come. *Between Wars* shows an interest in history as distinct from mere 'period'. Written by Frank Moorhouse and directed by Mike Thornhill, the film traces the period in Australia between the two world wars, from the post-war shock and stumbling economy to deep uncertainty and Depression. It covers a period that was culturally provincial, conservative and repressive.

It uses the device of an unheroic protagonist, a small-town doctor, a bit part on the stage of history, an on-looker from a marginal but not unprivileged vantage. Trenbow, played by the English actor Corin Redgrave, is a recessive, trans-cultural figure, signifying a whole generation of privately-educated middle-class British-Australians who were restrained and modest in the exercise of their privileges. Relieving his general greyness is Trenbow's interest in the new, not yet reputable, science of psychiatry, kindled during his experiences as a medical officer treating shell-shocked soldiers. This, along with his mild flirtation with radical social experiments, like the local fishermen's cooperative, carries him into waters troubled by some of the larger issues of the times. We gauge them from the way they touch his life; from a distance. Our investment is mitigated by his veneer which makes him seem slightly vague and aloof.

A later film, *Newsfront*, plays off against the processed history of the newsreel through another post-war period: the late forties to late fifties. *Between Wars*, by contrast, has only the already oblique Trenbow as a device through which to read how world history was experienced from a distance by Australia. The episodic scenes are constructed as long sequence-shots which allow the trivial to surface in order to reveal the subtle undercurrents of the scene and the historic moment. Where *Newsfront* generates energy and intensely affectionate moments of recognition through its old newsreel footage, *Between Wars* has an existential distaste for much of what was Australia in those respectability-ridden decades. If people in their sixties at its time of release were meant to revisit their past in the film, as the publicity suggested, it must have been a bleak homecoming.

Between Wars in fact has as much to do with the art film of the fifties and sixties as it has to do with Australian history. Trenbow is a mildly disaffected, disengaged, drifting sensibility. Whole scenes are given over to philosophical conversation between men at loose ends. The point is that they do not connect, do not act, and only sometimes suffer the world acting on them; but that is a difficult point to dramatise, especially when the same view also governs *mise en scene*. The action is static or short-lived, the camera is disengaged and slightly distant, the art direction is carefully neutral except for the killer splash of red when the town's nymphomaniac makes her entrance. *Between Wars* is world-weary rather than lyrical, sceptical rather than affirmative, analytical rather than spectacular; but in other respects it initiates many of the AFC-genre characteristics with its undriven narrative based in character rather than plot, its art-film overtones and occasional drawing-room, period feeling. However, it is not in the business of selling innocence or likeable Australiana. Landscape is simply not an interest of the film; it would probably be incompatible with the film's case-history-like interest in the psychic terrain of a class, and to some extent a nation, over a specific period.

The Cars That Ate Paris (1974) is another film of the time lacking box-office success, but with a strong connection to its culture and bearing seeds of the future. *Between Wars* has its roots in Australian intellectual history of the late fifties and sixties, particularly the first definite signs of cinephilia that led to the rise of film societies, and the left-wing caste of Sydney libertarianism under the influence of Andersonian realism.[8] *Cars* could be said to have much of its origins in the Sydney underground film tradition, and a tap root into the unconscious of Australian car culture as well.

It is, in fact, the first car crash movie, a genre that became recognisably Australian and intensely popular in the wake of the first *Mad Max*. However, this early example is very differently paced from *Mad Max* or any of its imitators; it is, again, a kind of art film out from the underground, translating the subversive fantasy of the one domain into Australian Gothic in the other. It does not attempt to be a tearaway genre success. The conscious authorial impress of Peter Weir is more firmly felt here than any instinctive sense of genre or other sub-stratum of storytelling. The seeds it carries of later car-culture fantasies are probably inadvertent.

Weir had already experimented with subversive fantasy in the underground film, *Homesdale* set in an isolated guesthouse, with strange guests, compulsory games, and grisly surprises. Australian Gothic permits undiluted Australianness to be presented obliquely. It is just as involved in the Australian ethos as the ocker comedies that shouted above the din of their own anxiety. As with *Shirley Thompson*, the distorting, wide-angled stare of Australian Gothic pushes normality a stop or two, until it begins to flare with strange, grotesque possibilities. The 'normal' twists stubbornly away, towards the perverse and malevolent. The protagonist must escape from the murderous confines of the normal, either physically or into madness.

The First Phase (1970-75): The Prototypes Emerge 95

The Cars That Ate Paris turns its gaze not on to the home but the car. In the small, imaginary country town of Paris, the rule of the car is almost complete. Arthur Waldo (Terry Camilleri) is driving with his brother, combing the countryside for work, when detour signs divert them towards Paris, and into an unavoidable car crash engineered by the inhabitants. Paris, like the Yabba in *Wake in Fright*, is not the preserve of innocence and virtue we have come to expect from the long-running split between city and bush in our culture. It is a coffin that closes on the unwary.

Arthur regains consciousness in the Paris hospital to learn that his brother is dead and that he, as the unexpected survivor, must be incorporated into the strange community as parking officer. Gradually he discovers that the entire economy of Paris is dependent upon the car — or more precisely, the carnage of the car. The wrecks are scavenged, the survivors recruited if they are still able-bodied. If they are not, they join the ranks of vegies and zombies under the vigilance of an experimentally-minded doctor.

But a human pestilence is breeding in Paris from the unacknowledged violence of the car's regime. A horde of youths is building killer cars, monsters reconstructed from the bloody wreckage, with spikes like the spines of dinosaurs. A dance is held. Though it is populated mainly by hospital zombies on furlough, they are barely distinguishable from the other townsfolk. That night the cars turn on the town: Arthur must overcome his paralysing phobia about cars if he is to escape; but if he escapes by car, will he have escaped at all?

While it reverts to the oblique and grotesque in its approach to the question of how to be an Australian film, *Cars* doesn't strain for its answer. It is, of course, commenting on something deeply embedded in the Australian ethos: that we would die without our cars, and to prove the point we daily risk dying in them. The spike-encrusted cars coming out of the darkness to prey on civilisation form the crowning image; but *Cars* produces equally suggestive menace of a quieter kind, like the way the Mayor's car with its long fins slides like a shark among the long grass and dappled shade of an otherwise lyric landscape. It works as a suggestive, dark, comic fantasy, uneven in its success, but rich in some of the perversity it unearths from the underside of the

Australian psyche. It endows its sense of cultural identity with considerable malevolent force, and a wry face.

It's not quite the opposite of the broad, overtly ocker celebration of *Barry McKenzie* because both stem from a sense of uncertainty about the acceptability of Australianness, and in both, in very different ways, the male ethos is clearly felt as the burden of the films. But where *Barry McKenzie* takes a stance only through exaggeration and satire, *Cars* takes one only through oblique, suggestive distortion.

4

Transition 1 (1975): Touchstone Successes

Sunday Too Far Away and *Picnic at Hanging Rock* were made and released on the cusp between the first and second phases in 1975. Each prefigured important tendencies. *Sunday* is a workplace *milieu* and ethos study — Australian shearers in 1955 — and it intersects social realism with labour history in a finely made narrative structure. Its comic, episodic story set a pattern in 'male ensemble' films. *Picnic* is 'period' rather than 'history', in the way that *The Gift* (the second part of *Libido*) is, but here it serves with even more dedication the creation of an evocative lost world, lost innocence. *Picnic* is a contradictory film — a delicate fantasy horror film, in which the horror consists of the suggestion of inescapable, fatal links between Nature, female sexuality, and sacrifice.

Sunday Too Far Away created in film a truly confident, likeable icon of male Australianness. It points out the difference between history and period, though it finally wavers in its choice. It mobilises wit, strong language and a highly literate, but never high-brow, sense of story within a tradition of realism that owes much to the government documentary tradition of the Commonwealth Film Unit and later Film Australia.

For *Picnic at Hanging Rock*, 'period' with an opulent feel and the sensibility of the European art film was chosen, a daring decision in its day. Although traces of Australian Gothic are just discernible, they are transmuted by the bias of this project towards a look of quality and good taste never really undermined by content. Its wholly unexpected commercial success established a trend in films — the AFC genre — in many ways remote from the intentions of this film.

Both films, in totally different ways, began the process that occupies the second phase: establishing areas of safe ground, and then wondering if they might also be commercially fertile.

It is interesting, and far from incidental, that it was a role in *Sunday Too Far Away*, a film set in the fifties, that suddenly made Jack Thompson into the first icon of essential Australianness. The potency of the icon had a lot to do with short-back-and-sides, hump-back Holdens, old-fashioned country pubs with an old-fashioned radio on, short sleeved sports shirts, blue singlets and shearer's traditional aprons, Globite suitcases, sheep . . . and living but distant memory, both ours, and Jack Thompson's. By contrast with his role in *Petersen*, Thompson is completely at home. He described John Dingwall's script as 'The most extraordinarily accurate, almost diary portrayal of the Australian proleteriat, with all its pride and sort of craft mystery . . . It looked like day after day of my life in the 1950s, when the film was set, when I worked in the bush. I recognised Foley . . .'[1]

The character of Foley is an endearing collection of all the most general Australian-male attributes. Equally, he is riven by its contradictions and failings. He has the stature of its heroism in full measure, and the full tragedy of its failure as a way of being in the world. The film maintains a sometimes painful ambivalence over its burden of male ethos, with both love and dismay for its subject. This is different from David Willliamson's naturalistic representation of a particular social register or enclave of Australianness accompanied by satiric deflation, so that the ground is never certain beneath your feet. But some of the same techniques and interests propel *Sunday*: male ensemble characterisation around an emblematic centre; narrative punctuation and dynamic provided by verbal or sometimes visual jokes that are vigorous and earthy; the invitation to enjoy familiarity, the pleasure of recognition. That pleasure had powerful novelty value in 1976, even though it is tempered by a sceptical wit exercised as much by characters as by narrative. The difference is perhaps that Dingwall tells a more traditional story; he has

Foley (Jack Thompson), a shade past top shearer, on the downward slope in *Sunday Too Far Away*.

an instinct for archetypes, while Williamson's work is angled to send splintered reflections of contemporary milieux to his audience, in the interests of what he calls tribal self-awareness.

Sunday portrays a six-week shearing contract just prior to the last great shearer's strike with national economic consequences, in 1955. This provides an oblique approach to a deeper concern: the rise and decline of the prowess of a gun shearer. The story is an analysis, or at least a chronicle, of the working conditions and economic predicates of a shearer's existence as a skilled, competitive labourer. Underlying all of this is the essay into rural working-class maleness, situated just far enough in the past to be seen in emblematic purity, just before the present begins to cloud the picture. The strike itself is left at the margins, not really negotiated as a destiny of the narrative.

Foley's emblematic stature is clear. He is a past champion (gun) shearer at the height of his power. This six-week shed marks a moment when he is poised at the beginning of his descent into mediocrity, booze, and gradual physical deterioration. Michael Simpson (Gregory Apps), the first-time 'roustabout', and Old Garth (Reg Lye), the nearly broken, frail drunk, are his past and his future. On the long car trip out to the sheep station, the camera finds Foley half asleep, Old Garth dead to the world and Michael Simpson awake and waiting anxiously for a cue. One by one the camera pans across the faces in the back seat of the car. The shed will bring Foley to his defeat, Old Garth to final exhaustion, and young Michael to his first competence on the lowest rung of the shearer's ladder. Foley's other mates — Ugly (John Ewart), Basher (Jerry Thomas), Tom West (Robert Bruning) and Tim King (Max Cullen) — are not representative stereotypes, not foils to Foley, but further reiterations of Australianness, his mates. (It is worth making this point for the contrast it offers with *Petersen* or *The Family Man* section of *Libido*, where the Jack Thompson character is elaborated by reactions to female stereotypes, and relation to individual, male, 'mates'.)

However, the Max Cullen character is not simply a mate any more. As a first-time contractor, he has stepped across the divide between his shearing mates and the isolation of a private businessman and boss. There are two other male characters of consequence. Dawson (Philip Ross) is the 'cocky' or owner of the vast sheep station, Timberoo, and Arthur Black (Peter

Cummins) is an unknown shearer from New South Wales whose taciturn silence and aloofness earns him the name Black Arthur. Black Arthur emerges as Foley's nemesis, the force from elsewhere who will inexorably topple him from top dog, gun-shearer status, and start his decline towards the destiny that engulfed Old Garth. Black Arthur is a black knight figure, the one who cannot be beaten. His arrival effects a painful self-evaluation for the protagonist, and signifies, in a sense, Foley's inevitable death. His character, and the tripartite configuration Garth-Foley-Simpson, are signs of the narrative archetype and symbolic register present in the work.

There is other evidence in the many symmetries worked into the 'naturalism' of the story. The exit of the defeated, lemon-essence-addicted cook on the back of the mail truck is poignantly echoed by the removal of Old Garth's body. The undertaker attempts to put the corpse in the back of his utility, but Foley sits Old Garth's body upright in the front seat instead. When the rhyme is revealed, the first gag takes on a blacker, more tragic shade.

Another set of symmetries is revealed through the way the rhythm of the story is invaded by semi-documentary shearing sequences. This punctuation of life by repetitive work mimics the rhythm of the six-week shed, with leisure times experienced as time displaced from purpose, intolerably vacant, miles from anywhere. Work rigidly dictates both the timetable and the quality of time. But the five main extended shearing sequences are stitched into a story by the drama of the sub-verbal rivalry between Foley and Black Arthur. A duel gradually mounts. These sequences themselves have an internal symmetry hingeing on the middle one, in which the cocky's daughter gets her way in sitting through a run of shearing as spectator.

This sequence is shot from a female point of view. A wide-angled, slightly see-sawing lens tracks constantly during a discordant, nauseous version of the theme music. We see the electric combs cut into the flesh of the sheep, the subjugation of sheep and men to the process, the efficient extraction of wealth from an animal resource. The first shearing sequence details the regime of time-clock, piece- work rates and mutual competition that pits the men against each other and keeps to a minimum the life of the shed. The arrival of the men at their quarters is cross-cut with that of the first flocks to the yards. Now, however, the shearing is seen from a viewpoint almost perfectly excluded from the shearer's self-conception and life: the female. It makes plain the lack — the exclusion — of the female in the ethos of the shearers.

Sheila and Ivy, the barmaid in town and the only other female character, represent Everywoman. As Sheila approaches the shed, the rousie's cry goes up: 'Ducks on the pond!' The bestial imagery signals instinctive fear, fear of women, and warns of an unnatural intrusion into the secrets of a skilled and competitive male workplace, where men are possessors of the necessary, painful, secret knowledge.

Sheila wins the right to look on by means of a veiled threat. In order to defeat their cook — 'the poisoner' — Foley made a midnight raid on his stores of essence of lemon. Sheila hints that she might tell her father, and the men are forced to let her stay. At first the men overcome their tension at her presence by clowning around. Finally they simply do not permit themselves to look at her, nor hear her say thank you as she leaves. From this point onwards the film descends towards Old Garth's death, Foley's attempts to maintain his increasingly beleaguered position on top, and his eventual defeat.

Three scenes answer to this single 'female' sequence. There is the sullen, comic rivalry of Ugly and Foley at the wash-tubs when they spat with each other, bitching 'like women' over stains left on clothes despite a vigorous, competitive scrubbing that makes their buttocks jiggle, 'like women'. Then the day Old Garth is found dead in his bed, Foley breaks down and cries like a girl in front of Sheila — not over Old Garth directly, but over a sense that his life struggle for superiority in the terms of male esteem must inevitably finish in defeat. The repressed and banished feminine, carried like a recessive gene in male Australianness, comes comically or painfully to the surface in these scenes. To some extent, even the production history of the film conspired to suppress the feminine. In the re-editing, Sheila's role was reduced, and so was the relatively girlish and receptive role of Michael Simpson.[2] Jack Thompson's grief for the self he has made within the dictates of maleness comes, as edited, as an unconscious eruption, welling up and spilling over, as though in defiance of the film's sense and its other, more conscious, decisions.

The good Catholic marriage scrapes on the rock of fifties politics. Bill Hunter, Jone Winchester, Angela Punch-McGregor, Kay Eklund and John Flaus in *Newsfront*.

The third scene is a passing moment when the young married shearer, Berry, chooses to write to his wife rather than go with the men 'to look at tomorrow's sheep'. He is accused of being 'queer'. Foley yells at him, 'What the bloody hell's wrong with you!'. It follows closely on the scenes showing the arrival of the new cook, Wentworth, who is plump, softly spoken, positively feminine in his devotion to cleaning up the store and kitchen in the wake of the abominable Quinn. Wentworth's little feminine touches are humoured and indulged: they are so appropriate in the kitchen, and they produce such satisfying food. Quinn was filthy, lazy, a mean bastard and a 'poisoner'; he was too big for Foley to fight and dispose of in the normal way. In short, he was wrongly gendered in every way except his weakness for lemon-essence, and therefore did not belong in the kitchen. The complete consensus of all the men 'proves' the aptness of his replacement by the fastidious, feminised Wentworth. The whole routine comically confirms the affinity of feminine virtues and women's work.

Running as a thread in the background is the occasional radio discussion of the possibility that the shearers' prosperity bonus will be withdrawn in response to the graziers' case that the clip is down this year. The men are 'union'; in the first shearing sequence they elect Foley as rep for the shed. ('All those in favour?' Silence. 'Against?' Silence.) Meetings are called on the spot to modulate ill feeling towards the 'cocky' and to resolve ways to express a collective contempt for him and his hovering presence and constant interference during the shearing of the expensive stud rams, where the differently valued masculinities of sheep and men rub sourly against each other. But union business itself is often simply the accepted form of ritual insult for bosses, including Tim (Max Cullen).

When the prosperity bonus is withdrawn on the last day of the contract, the long 1955-6 strike begins, adding insult to the already poor seasonal wages that are in the shearers' lot. The last movement of the film, after Foley's defeat by Black Arthur, is organised around the shearers' return to town where they plan to gamble and drink the spoils of six weeks' hard labour. The strike-breakers quickly appear, under guard, and agitation against them begins. The final scene is a pub brawl that echoes the first challenge to Foley's reputation as top shearer by Franky Davidson (Ken Shorter). That first encounter had been settled by a poker-like battle of bets and wits; later on, in a fist-fight with the giant Quinn (handicapped by six dozen bottles of lemon essence), Foley has had one glorious, flushed, cathartic physical victory. But in this final fight, the punch he aims at Frank Davidson's face step-prints and slows to a freeze-frame before it can arrive, with Foley's face blurring and distorting with the effort to unload his burden of defeat. Instead of catharsis, we see a montage of idle sheds, the melancholic music of the middle shearing sequence, and two successive graphics, that between them extract the story of the strike from the action of the narrative:

> The strike lasted nine months. The shearers won.
> It wasn't so much the money. It was the bloody insult.

And so the narrative shifts into an elegaic mode, to be 'capped', in the way of many sequences, by a comic punchline.

But what is the effect of this punchline? It invites sympathy with an ironic, amused view of strikes as a matter of perverse principle, a kind of stubborn, ritual class antagonism expressed in established, tolerable form. The subject of strikes and unions that figures so strongly in Australian history and in traditions of working-class identity, is not just *contained* within this comically brief description, it is also, in a sense, *missing* from the narrative by being enclosed within these two titles. The subject stayed missing from the field of Australian film narrative until *Waterfront* (1983) and *Strikebound* (1984), a decade later.

Meanwhile, *Picnic at Hanging Rock* took what for the industry would be decisive steps in a very different direction, with its effusion of lyricism, bush picturesque, Edwardiana, and horror (or is it celebration?) on the theme 'Women who vanish into the embrace of Nature'.[3] The blonde Miranda is, as Meaghan Morris puts it (capturing the absurdity of the proposition with deadpan accuracy), '... the chosen one of the Rock, reserved for a meeting with a strange and phallic force of nature which takes her beyond the impure physicality of this world.'[4] In *Sunday Too Far Away*, the outback landscape is there, taken for granted. It is the element of male Australianness, as we are invited to see it, enforcing isolation, self-sufficiency and strong mateship upon its inhabitants. But in *Picnic*, the landscape is loaded with beauty, power, and even gender. Fatally so. The foreign beauty of the young girls, perversely exotic in their period whites, is offered by the film as sacrifice to the aroused male force of the land. Is this an act of appeasement, for the 'guilt' of intrusion, or a 'natural' mystery in which young girls willingly offer themselves like ripe fruit for the picking, in a violent and seductive surrender?

Certainly, *Picnic* has an air of perverse Britishness — or Europeanness — seeking the *frisson* of contact with the necessarily mysterious, alien bush, and the disturbing Rock that protrudes from it. It unfolds with the pacing of a full-blown art-movie, lingering over the effects of sunlight, flesh-tones and lace, infused with classical music, in the fashion of *Elvira Madigan*, which had earlier been a considerable box-office success in Australia.

Picnic was adapted from a modestly-successful novel by Joan Lindsay. The pattern it set went beyond the visual novelty of period costume, especially female clothing, in the newly photogenic

Australian bush, modelled in strong yellow light against intense skies. There are echoes of British television drama. The authority is drawn from literary adaptation; there is a sense of strong class differences as the hero or heroine ventures across class borders, though the emphasis, for its sheer visual spectacle, falls upon the upper classes. Also, there is an emphasis on character and sensibility, rather than strong story lines. We too have a history and sensibility, says the film. The first, retrospectively, proved our solid identity; the second demonstrated our worth, albeit in curiously out-dated terms, fairly remote from what was normally demanded of mainstream commercial cinema. It was hard to see in those days that such films, with their devotional cinematography, in rapture before the richly textured Australian landscapes and detailed period art direction, were 'uncinematic' — a kind of cinematic taxidermy, as Pauline Kael later put it.

Woven through all of these elements in *Picnic* is a web of metaphysical voice-overs, mainly spoken by Miranda. 'What we see and what we seem are but a dream. A dream within a dream.' 'Everything begins and ends at exactly the right time and place.' Hot-house erotic undertones can be felt in the confines of an exclusive, all-girl boarding school, presided over by the repressive Mrs Appleyard (Rachel Roberts). The soundtrack spins a suggestive web, too: silence is prolonged into eeriness, broken by insect sounds or leaf rustles; a silence of shimmering heat, languor and portent. At the Rock, pan pipes replace the slow second movement of Beethoven's Fifth Piano Concerto. Three girls, blonde Miranda, dark Irma, fat, complaining Edith (Anne Lambert, Jane Vallis, Christine Schuler) are roused from their languor by a compulsion to climb the Rock. Miranda leads the way, rarely pausing, never hesitant. Edith brings up the rear, resisting and finally running away in abandoned fear when the two girls slip from sight into the cleft between the tors. Fleeting, unexplained images feel as though they are the successive points of view of unseen presences. Two points of view are attributed — to the blond, upper-class Michael (Dominic Guard) and the dark, lower-class Albert (John Jarrett). Michael watches Miranda; Albert watches Michael, trying to fathom his response. Later, Michael is drawn back compulsively to search for the girls. The loyal, uncomprehending Albert finds him walking dazed on the Rock, clutching a fragment of the lost reality, a piece of material torn from Miranda's dress. Michael is lightly wounded by his other-world experience: above his right eye is the same small incision that is found on Irma's forehead, when she is, inexplicably, ejected from the transcendental embrace of the mountain, days later. Perhaps her hair is the wrong colour.

Miranda, Irma, and the mathematics teacher who goes to search for them, transcend the limits of space, time and recountable story. The supernatural, of course, must be beyond explication. Perhaps the rapture on the mountain is only horrifying, like the promised 'raptures' of Jerry Falwell's Armageddon scenario, to those who prefer to be excluded. In any case, the story has been accused of wandering afterwards without narrative purpose for another forty-five minutes into a maze of inexplicability of its own making, coming to rest when finally defeated. Even Peter Weir admits to no clear sense of what was working through him or the story after the disappearance. It is true that most of the film's lyrical energy is expended building up to the ineffable moment upon the Rock. But the events after and including those on the Rock have a discoverable logic worth looking at, even if the ineffable loses something in the process.

Ian Hunter has pointed to the Victoriana of *Picnic*, 'honorary pre-Raphaelite, despite the gum trees'.[5] His comments touch on the economy of class and sexuality that generates the story, pointing with his title, 'Corsetway to Heaven' to the deformity in the culture that can equate sexuality with necrophilia, purity and transcendence with self-repression, innocence with corruption, art and beauty with suffering. As he says, 'the ladies have their corsets, the director his punishing but rewarding art'. And the lower classes have their instinctual life, the upper classes their masochistically refined sensibilities.

The gardener comments to the handyman, 'Some questions got answers and others haven't.' While the film attempts to account for itself through this kind of instinctive, stubborn knowledge of the lower classes, as well as through the more metaphysical utterances of the acolyte, Miranda, it is not sufficient for the narrative. Other, less mystifying accounts are unconsciously on offer, with less remote implications.

The underlying class narrative is as follows: the upper-class inmates of the exclusive girls' boarding school live under a sexual regime that perversely and erotically denies sexuality, linking the denial to class duty. The lower classes — servants all — are by contrast blessed with a happy, uncomplicated animality in their sex lives, and the narrative links this to a stoic acceptance of the burden of service and duty to others. They are more responsive to the demands of nature — but at a less sensitive, less meditated level. The self-repression of the upper classes earns them both the retribution and the transcendence of the Rock. It is as if their perversity sets up a powerful antagonistic force — or tunes into one — in the land itself, which fulfills a violent and 'inexplicable' set of destinies as it discharges itself. To the upper classes, this is harrowing. The force plays itself out in unnatural disruption and death. To the lower classes, it is merely another of the questions without answers that are to be darkly accepted, like the one of eternal service and subordination itself. These class oppositions relentlessly dictate every articulation of plot and character, however frequently they are pronounced inexplicable.

The character of Sarah (Margaret Nelson) shows the pattern most strongly by way of aberration. Sarah is marked out for a troubled destiny by being parentless, a charity-case, *and* dark-haired. Blond hair is the absolute sign of purity; Miranda's fairness 'explains' why she should be so perfectly attuned to her transcendent destiny, while Irma's darkness accounts for her eventual rejection and re-entry to the world forever changed, forever silent about her experience. When she goes — dressed in the red of sexual experience — into the physical culture class to farewell her old classmates, general hysteria breaks out. By contrast, Michael pictures Miranda as a white swan, an image which evokes not only grace and beauty, but purity, sacrifice and coupling between animal, human and god, as in the myth of Leda and the swan.

When the picnic party sets out on St Valentine's Day, Sarah is excluded. She has already declared her feeling for Miranda in the exchange of love tokens; now Miranda calmly intimates that she may never return from this outing. It is Sarah who rushes to the late-returning coach in darkness, to see to her horror that Miranda has indeed failed to return. When she falls ill with grief, Mrs Appleyard turns on her as scapegoat; as pupils are withdrawn she determines that Sarah must be sent back to her institutional origins to 'pay for' the school's rapidly declining fortunes. Sarah is found dead in the greenhouse among shattered flowers, having crashed from a school window through the glass roof. In turn, Mrs Appleyard's own mysterious demise is exacted by the unknown. Are we to understand the headmistress, source of repression, as the wrong doer of the narrative, whose attempt to scapegoat Sarah must be punished? If so, then only at the most superficial level. It is Sarah's function in the film's economy of sexuality and class — her desire, her lack of means, her percipience, her impurity — that dictates her inexorable movement to the debit side of the ledger. If she had not jumped, someone — or *something* — would have had to send her through that window to die. Her fall symbolically cracks open the fragile lid that sealed the hot-house world of the school and its delicate blossoms, raised to be plucked and die. In this scheme of things, Mrs Appleyard's death is a bonus, to satisfy only our crudest sense, at the surface of the plot, that Sarah was unfairly treated. And the narrative, far from losing itself after the high point on the Rock, can be seen merely to run its well-determined course.

5

The Second Phase: 1976-80: Seemly Respectability

There was almost unseemly haste in these years to bring the new industry to a stage of seemly respectability. Film by film, one investment decision at a time, the consolidation of the aesthetic field around its dominant groupings was accomplished.

Following the success of *Picnic at Hanging Rock*, Fred Schepisi's *The Devil's Playground* (1976) was now able to work on quite different art-film territory with none of the AFC-genre characteristics. It is a true 'eccentric' of its time. Its fictional 'period' - the mid-fifties — doesn't qualify for costume-drama lyricism, and it is semi-autobiographical rather than literary in origin. It is European in flavour only because it deals with Catholicism. Australian Catholicism has a flavour of its own which was strongly Irish in the fifties. Nevertheless, the subject has strong lines of European descent. Furthermore the intensity and austerity of the film are reminiscent of the *kammerspiel*, the chamber film tradition. The seminary is closed in behind high walls and closed doors. Even the swimming pool visited downtown is an indoor pool. The echoes in its tiled enclosure are a lovely metaphor for unnatural repression. Like the *kammerspiel*, the film is an introspective look at the passions that arise and are forced by enclosure and systematic repression to find indirect expression. But the imagery is drawn more from the documentary than from expressionism. This plain, unforced imagery communicates well the texture of provincial urban Australian life in the period, and

The Second Phase (1976-80): Seemly Respectability 111

the quality of a Melbourne Catholic adolescence poised painfully between surrender to Church strictures and a sexually impassioned break for freedom, however traumatic.

In many ways, the film extends the territory of *The Priest* segment of *Libido*. Arthur Dignam is used again, this time as the obsessive Brother Francine, who humiliates the protagonist (Simon Burke) about bedwetting, and nude showers in breach of the rule that underpants must be worn. The details of the film have the idiosyncratic force of personal memory and also the necessary measure of painful universality to strike chords for those with non-Catholic memories of adolescence. The next film to achieve such a balance of horror, poignancy and dark comedy is *Puberty Blues*, in 1982, developed from memoirs of a very different adolescence, but with similar feelings of bleakness, and the tyranny of conformity and acceptability. *The Devil's Playground* is about a small world made up of intimate contact between adults and children, with sexuality as the structuring absence rather than the openly ruling tyranny. The film moves constantly between the world of the boys — straining to please as acolytes in the system — and that of the brothers with their varying vocations, none unequivocal. The Australian inflection is unstrained but present, as in the contrast between the large, benign indifference of the Antipodean sky, and the narrowness of the retreat priest's fire-and-brimstone evocation of Hell.

Caddie (1976), even more than *Picnic*, elaborated the AFC genre, even though it is not all a gentle period piece. It is based on the oral-history-like memoirs of a Sydney barmaid during the thirties' Depression, battling to keep and raise her children after her marriage breaks up. *Caddie* explores aspects of sexual double standards, sexual harassment, and breadline survival. But it is a fundamentally aesthetic poverty, with genteel suffering and a psychologically cushioned descent into working-class hell. The setting is inner-city picturesque, using Balmain in a way that visually echoes the Woolloomooloo working-class cityscape of *Sunshine Sally* (1922). But where *Sunshine Sally*, or what remains of it, yields a strong, angry iconography of women down but not beaten, *Caddie*'s central role (played by Helen Morse) is always restrained, groomed, considerate, un-gritty. In one scene with her romantic interest, a Greek businessman (Takis Emmanuel) she lashes out briefly at the double standard he unconsciously adopts by caring about her exploitation while vigorously exploiting his own female employees. But apart from this eruption, the film flows far too smoothly; her strongest character traits are dignity and a well-groomed presentability: not the stuff of powerful female Australian iconography.

A desire to please a middlebrow audience asserts itself over the material. A workplace *milieu* study like *Sunday Too Far Away* gives comic larrikin energy to its shearers even if they do, in the end, reveal themselves as bound and strung up between the mores and rituals of the male group, the job, and the union. *Caddie*, however, doesn't want its concern jeopardised by comedy, or its pleasantness marred by strong language or excessive energy. However unconsciously, the film projects the spectre of feminine respectability; a kind of substitute strength used to maintain women in a position of weakness that is unthinkingly accepted.

When *Caddie* became a quiet but definite box-office success, a pattern was set. Certainly it is confidently written and made, with strong period production values that belie the film's relatively modest budget. The appetite for a respectable film industry was translated into general appreciation for a respectable film, especially one with a respectful, proto-feminist attitude towards its attractive central character, and charming period detail, authenticating our sense that we have a history of our own. The pattern for 'worthy' films was set.

> There's a certain ambivalence in my attitude toward Australian behaviour... There's some endorsement of the vitality and energy of the social ethos, at the same time as there's a condemnation of the excessive chauvinism, materialism and cynicism of the milieu. But it's an inextricable blend: I can't loathe this country because I don't. A satirist like Humphries, who uses much larger, more blatant stereotypes, is really into an area of loathing; my level is a lot more ambivalent.
>
> David Williamson. *Meanjin* interview, 1979.

Don's Party (1976) has a kinship with both *Sunday Too Far Away* and *The Adventures of Barry McKenzie*. One has a male ensemble with a supporting gallery of female sexual types, idiomatic humour and a degree of naturalism; the other is an outright satiric lampoon that allows both affection and revulsion for its object of study. In other words, *Don's Party* is an ocker comedy with subtler, more ironic, sardonic inflection and group of males as the central device for exploring the Australian ethos. Bruce Beresford is an understandable choice for director, three years after *Barry McKenzie*.

The male ritual under Williamson's scrutiny is the election-night party. Of course, there are women involved, too: Don (John Hargreaves), the failed novelist-turned-schoolteacher, has his wife Kath (Jeannie Drynan); his older mentor from university days, Mal (Ray Barrett) brings his wife Jenny (Pat Bishop); Simon, the Liberal-voting wimp (Graeme Blundell) brings his flirtatious, apolitical wife Jody (Veronica Lang); then there is Mack (Graham Kennedy), whose wife has just left him, Kerry (Candy Raymond), the sculptor and man-eater, who brings her anal-obsessive dentist husband Evan (Kit Taylor) as a kind of afterthought, and the mythical Cooley (Harold Hopkins), eulogised for his wont to 'go through women' like a crate of oranges, who drops in for a time with his current girlfriend Susan (Clare Binney), who likes anything in pants, and strips like a shot. Kath and Jenny are offered as two varieties of women who weigh their men down with domestic regimes, children and complaints — one younger, one older and therefore less desirable. None of the women, except Kerry, are characterised by anything but their relationship to their men; and Kerry's art is treated as little more than a further fabrication in the web she spins for men.

The concentration is on the men, especially Don and Mal, who form a couple more enduring than any other we see. For one brief moment, cut short by the return of the men, Kath and Jenny commiserate and flirt with the possibility of closer contact, but otherwise every scene is focussed on male action and male response. The women are props for male self-awareness. They are shuffled between the men, shared in rituals of bonding or exclusion. Dramatically, they exist as ciphers of male desire, male expectation, male ideology. The actresses concerned — especially Pat Bishop and Veronica Lang — manage to make their characters memorable, but they work in the interstices of the drama, not its conscious or uppermost intentions. They are rarely allowed the satiric lines; they are destined, as in most traditional comedy, to be the butts rather than the makers of jokes.

This is not, of course, to deny the stereotyping among the male characters, nor the fact that male egos are punctured throughout the film with the regularity of balloons at a children's party. The difference is that the men have full human status and the central male characters are permitted to exceed their stereotypes. They have the vigour, inventiveness and self-aware comic energy of strong language and well-written, articulate idiomatic Australian speech. In this regard, the women are left virtually speechless. The men speak with ocker assurance and crudity, thus inviting a warm general identification with the ethos that speaks itself. The film is a critique of the suburban desert in the midst of plenty (the original Melbourne setting was Upper Plenty), of middle-class self-indulgence and self-obsession, of an enfeebled, ritualistic political tradition, and even of male piggery and female bitchiness. But the display is always enjoyable, and the revulsion is an affectionate one.

The historical position is worth noting. Williamson's original stage play was written and produced in 1971, and depicts the 1969 election in which government was narrowly retained by the Liberal party. By 1976, the setting was too recent to feel historical, but still did not easily fit into the present because subsequent political events had moved too decisively. Each election after 1969 had a character very different from Labor's edge of the political wilderness. In 1976, the close conjunction of real time and screen time seemed odd — and there seemed to be too little precise historical content in the film for the 1969 setting to matter. In 1982, however, after the success of *Breaker Morant* in the U.S., this much earlier Beresford film was released there with considerable success and a certain degree of period curiosity.

Don and Mal's emotional investment in a gradually evaporating Labor victory is used more as a sign of the 'intellectual"s automatic genuflection towards the radical. Mal, however, has given up his tutorship in psychology for a private consultancy, and Don has slid from his literary ambitions into that last resort of the failed intellectual: school teaching. Barracking for Labor is not connected to material success or mortgaged survival; it is a choice as natural to their self-images as their preference for beer. Wimps vote Liberal and wear jackets with little leather patches at the elbows; men vote Labor and share the pathos of what was then a perennially honourable, perennially lost cause.

Oz (1976) is an early example of the way Australianness could be handled artlessly and directly under cover of a genre. It is an energetic, low-budget rock-musical that converts *The Wizard of Oz* to the story of a groupie pursuing her dream to see the popstar, the Wizard.[1] Dorothy (Joy Dunstan) is a small-town rock fiend who gets involved in a road accident with the local band. On her journey through unconsciousness, the sexually-ripe Dorothy draws the pursuit of a malevolent truckie, bent on rape, and three 'helpers', or rather, dependants: the gentle surfie Scarecrow (Bruce Spence); the lustful, acned mechanic, Tin Man (Michael Carman); and a chicken-hearted motorcyle yob, Lion (Gary Waddell), all dream variants of actual band members.

Maleness is both the threat and the lure in the story, which is always an undisguised projection of Dorothy's fantasy. It is an interesting fantasy in which the tables are turned on desire and fear allowing the girl to move on, a fraction stronger and better armed, after each incident. The film tunes in to that highly creative moment in a young girl's sexuality in which magical events that might rapidly transform her and carry her to a high plane of union with a star are always about to happen. Then the perspective shifts an inch, and suddenly the whole idea is as distant as childhood. As if mirroring the urgency of desire, the rural landscape is all beauty, clear light, and great promise. The city, too, is heightened. Every written sign is a portent. It is also the place where she falls back into 'reality', or realisation; in this sense, a traditional division between city and country is restored. Dorothy 'comes back to herself' in her place, the country, after her imaginary journey into city experience.

Backroads (1977), Phil Noyce's low-budget short feature, also accurately articulates its time and place in a relaxed way by thinking through genre. It is an existential road movie, directionless on outback roads, leading nowhere. The landscape is relentless and monotonous from the viewpoint of a car in transit. An ocker white (Bill Hunter) has a knife-edge mateship with an Aboriginal (Gary Foley)[2]. They journey towards the coast in a stolen Pontiac Parisienne, collecting people and also a kind of residual racial violence that must finally discharge. Places like the black shanty town and roadside cafe are given documentary realism, and John Emery's script is finely attuned to naturalistic speech and the lazy violence that can lie beneath its laconicism. But the world inside the car is emblematic, not documentary. Black and white, male and female, enclosed within a detached alienation, speeding nowhere. Bill Hunter adds to the repertoire of Australian male iconography that already includes Jack Thompson's Foley in *Sunday Too Far Away* and John Hargreaves' Don in *Don's Party*. If Foley is the top dog in a group of mates bound by work, and Don is one of the boys, an amiable self-flatterer with what the Americans call 'a shit-eating grin', Bill Hunter's Jack King is the solitary Australian, moving with other men but beholden to nobody, and with the capacity to turn rogue bull.

It is interesting to compare two other films made later: *The Chant of Jimmie Blacksmith* (1978) and *Wrong Side of the Road* (1981). *Wrong Side* is a low-budget road movie about the Aboriginal reggae rock band, No Fixed Address, on the road from point to point in South Australia. It's a kind of re-enacted musical documentary, scripted by the band from their own experience: racial illegitimacy and harassment from outside both test and sustain the 'inside' sense of black community, undiminished by physical distance.

Jimmie Blacksmith was a very different kettle of fish. In some ways it was a film bred purposely to be a champion of the film industry, of Australian culture, and of raised consciousness about race. Based on Thomas Keneally's novel, it traces the reasons for and aftermath of the legendary violence against whites (including undefended women and children) by the real-life Aborigine, Jimmie Governor, at the turn of the century. Its budget exceeded one million dollars — only the second film to go so high. (The first, *Eliza Fraser*, was still struggling to get back its costs in that year, 1978). There was much pre-publicity suggesting that *Jimmie Blacksmith* was the great white hope (irony intended) of the industry. Its acceptance as the first Australian feature into competition at the Cannes festival crowned this expectation.[3] Publicity over-ran itself and the film's failure to win the competition came to overshadow its success in achieving such acceptance.

Jimmie Blacksmith is an essay in contradiction, but one which is itself founded in a partial contradiction. It addresses the tensions of race and gender between the black male and a white regime, and the appalling violence that is the logical result. But it is still an art film, directed towards an international, liberal middle-class white audience, which, it seems, in Australia, was finally overwhelmed by the violence, or its logic. The scenes of violence

Cars, capitalism, the Western suburbs, scarred roads: the recurrent beauties of the city-bound Australian road movie.

The algebra of race and gender: black male in a white regime. Ray Barrett and Tommy Lewis in *The Chant of Jimmie Blacksmith*.

exceeded the expectation or capacity of an audience that expected something different from an Australian period film with a heavy 'cultural' reputation preceding it. The spectacular way *Jimmie Blacksmith* was shot — from landscape-consuming pans to extreme close-ups of tiny insects or reptiles — confirmed audience expectations so well that when the violence struck, the audience emerged angry, with the feeling they had been misled, were 'lambs to the slaughter'. The period film — even the art movie — in Australia in 1978, could not carry the burden of the film's painful proposition.

The underlying proposition is something like this: Jimmie's quest is for adulthood in a white society, where adulthood, in the sense of psychological, sexual and social autonomy, is never completely granted to blacks. When Jimmie and his brother run amok with an axe among undefended white women and children, they are striking out for that denied freedom in a way that is not paradoxical, but relentlessly logical. Jimmie (Tommy Lewis) is a good boy, an assimilated Aboriginal. He is even a cop, though confined to the most menial rung of power. But he makes mistakes. In marrying a white girl, Gilda (Angela Punch), whose child he may have fathered, he slips too far out of the Oedipal yoke of white colonisation, which makes the sexually mature but non-white male an eternal boy. The white women of the station arrange to take Gilda and the child away from Jimmie's hut, an act they see as generous. The terrible punishment exacted is more the result of meanings enacted through them than by them.

Arguably, the contradictions facing a black male in white culture centre on white women. Since women in general are sexual subordinates in almost every culture, the greater social power of white women presents black males with a deep contradiction. So, in a sense, white women can be read as more powerful signs of black oppression than the white males who oppress both. This is the complex of deferred meanings expressed by Jimmie's action when he finally snaps from social paralysis.

Finally, there is a slight contradiction in the way that landscape is presented simultaneously for our delectation, and to prick our consciences as dispossessors of Aboriginal Australia. By searching out spectacular and lyrical imagery in the land, the film invites an ahistorical, transcendental contemplation. In one scene, Jimmie and Mort (Freddy Reynolds) take refuge among huge boulders,

The Second Phase (1976-80): Seemly Respectability 119

an Aboriginal sacred site shown to have been desecrated by white graffiti. It is a reminder of the extraordinary meaning of the land for its traditional inhabitants. Yet this reminder sits uncomfortably with the film's invitation to a kind of beatific bush tourism, enjoyable though it is. There is something a little too close to a patronising fetishism in our late desire to admire and aesthetically claim the landscape. The basis of Aboriginal meaning — in political terms, land rights — is offered today only as a possibility so flimsy that it can blow away at the slightest shift of the economic winds. And when the film was made, land rights barely merited a mention by Australian governments.

The F.J. Holden (1977) is a suburban road-movie in which the protagonists, Kevin (Paul Couzens), Anne (Eva Dickinson) and Bob (Carl Stevens) get nowhere, trapped in the maze of Sydney's western suburbs: Bankstown, Panania, Chullora. This is another essential Australian landscape, not one that asks through the camera to be claimed by the senses, but one which claims — or at least accommodates — the Australian heart. Australians disparage their suburbia in aesthetic and cultural terms (or occasionally make undue counter-claims for it). They criticise it for its stupor and praise it as the last bastion of hedonism in the western world. They deplore its monotony, repetition, sprawl, but concede that it leaves open a small space for freedom. Each separate household block can support genuine idiosyncrasy, be a place where Australians can exercise the remnants of old domestic skills with chicken runs, tool sheds and choko patches. It isolates households, placing particular stress on women, and celebrates the privacy of the family unit in a way that can strain it unbearably. It is the largest and smallest boundary of community. It has been held to account for the sluggishness of Australian political life. Home building rates provide a barometer of the economy and home ownership remains a sacred cow for all political parties. Suburbia is the open space in which the cow ranges and dominates.

Jimmie Blacksmith — and many of the AFC-genre films — provide spectacular and picturesque landscape as both compensation and denial of the suburban quotidian. *F.J. Holden* is remarkable for the degree to which it embraces suburban life as a powerful and underrated reality. Nevertheless, it is by no means free of contradictory attitudes towards its subject. The film is *for* suburbia, insofar as the covert anarchism and overt hedonism

of the kids during the brief space between sexual maturity and
enlistment into marriage-and-mortgage is celebrated as a kind
of primitive libertarianism. On the strength of this, the film moves
very close to its material in some scenes, offering such sympathetic
intimacy with the defining moments of a character that you can
see the glint of pain in the movement of an eyeball. It is delicate
in its handling of the non-story, particularly the way Kevin and
Anne's romance fizzles out under the pressure of beer and the
stronger demands of mateship, that other suburban holy cow.
The film also shows great care for the character of Anne, her
proscribed life as substitute mother to her two much younger
brothers, and as sales assistant in Bankstown Square. Her few
moments of freedom are snatched in between, in the form of
a drink at the pub and the opportunity to meet a few boys. She
impassively pays for her imitation-romance on the first night
by letting first Bob, then Ken (whom she really likes) 'go through
her' in the back seat of Ken's F.J. Holden. Anne is a truly memorable
character despite the drabness beneath which she lives her life
and maintains her dignity. Her strength is accessible because of
the film's strong empathy for her, even in banal scenes like the
one in which she chops carrots for her little brothers' tea while
they fight in the bath.

We are given unfettered access to the houses and their small
domestic comedies, as if we belong to a privileged team making
a voyeuristic television documentary in the *Checkerboard* or
Willesee style. When the film is sympathetic, we feel the privilege
rather than the voyeurism; but when it mocks, we are suddenly
embarrassed intruders. There are moments when the film is not
from or with Bankstown, but from way across the city, somewhere
in the better-educated eastern suburbs, and Bankstown's objects
and rituals are suddenly picked off for our amusement.

On balance, the film does look for long stretches with acceptance,
seeing, in the manner of Eastern European social realism, with
an eye to comedy. It takes in Bankstown's narrow range of
vocations, brief summers of freedom condoned for boys if not
for girls, followed by single, double or triple-fronted conformity.
It is equally aware of the pleasures, securities and limitations of
the world it assays, veering between comic improvisation, an
intense, almost lyrical social realism, and an odd obedience in
some scenes to the teenpic genre. There isn't the nostalgia of

The Second Phase (1976-80): Seemly Respectability 121

American Graffiti, although the comparison is interesting. The F.J. Holden car that is progressively restored through the film is a model strongly invested with fifties' nostalgia for the generations of Australians who grew up with it. Terry Larsen's original story is a short, sharp, when-I-was-a-kid story about Bankstown. Sexuality is treated with a special poignancy. The film is almost nostalgic, or wistful, about what it sees as a plentiful suburban sexuality, but the division of gender is seen as so deep that communication is a very delicate and tenuous affair, a minimal story constantly threatening to be a non-story, exactly like the film's narrative.

> I wanted to explore philosophical, political or psychological subjects generally with an ethical basis to them plus an interest in the exploration of characters. Those have been abiding and continuing interests.
>
> John Duigan, in *35mm Dreams.*

Mouth to Mouth (1978) is a much more classical social realist film, very low-budget, which established a pattern with its success: issue or problem-centred films, usually focussed on marginal or *declasse* segments of society, unemployed youth, derelicts, delinquents, drug addicts, single mothers. *Mouth to Mouth* completely avoids the case-study, concern-from-above feeling that afflicts, for example, *Fighting Back.* Where *F.J. Holden* is wryly comic, *Mouth to Mouth* has more taste for tragedy and melodrama. The narrative is generated from the interactions of its four characters, the two girls from reform school, Carrie (Kim Krajus) and Jeanie (Sonia Peat), and two boys from the country, Serge (Serge Frazetto) and Tim (Ian Gilmour). They wind up living together in an abandoned building, tenanted downstairs by a metho-drinking derelict, Fred. Their urge is not simply sexual, it is communal — a community of outcasts, keeping a friendly eye on Fred (Walter Pym). Melodrama is at work under the surface, though, and the tragic fate of Carrie as a prostitute is offset by small victories: loyalty, love, the integrity of Jeanie despite her return at the end to the reformatory.

John Duigan, who wrote and directed the film, used the same four-character device in *One Night Stand* in 1984. It allows the formation of the couples to give an underlying structure while leaving the narrative free to digress and sample. In both films four friends are deeply thwarted on a common, unarticulated quest — for security as social refugees in *Mouth to Mouth*, and for security and shelter as nuclear hostages in *One Night Stand*. But the earlier film is far more successful at making its characters 'engaging and accessible to as large a public as possible . . . no matter how different their world might be from the audience's world'.[4] It is striking for the way it made the language and culture of youth ring true for a wide audience, and for its ethical sense. It is also notable for its vision of Melbourne, financial capital of the country, as a landscape harbouring poverty and dereliction, indifferent to both.

An earlier film to assay the down-and-out in Melbourne, with bleak poetic realism, is John Ruane's short feature, *Queensland* (1976). This is a winter film, set somewhere like inner-city Richmond. Doug (John Flaus) is a single factory worker entering middle age with an invalid pensioner sidekick, Aub (Bob Karl). The film follows their efforts to break the cycle of work, drink, boarding houses and desolation just enough to get out of Melbourne to an imaginary fresh start in Queensland, 'the Sunshine State'. Queensland is the other place, not easily reached from Melbourne, mid-winter, when you get your car back from being in hock over gambling debts and find it will barely make it to the corner, let alone out of the suburb. Aub realises he's not going after all, and Marge (Alison Bird), Doug's resurrected romantic interest, has waited too long in the drizzle at the appointed corner and goes before he gets there. The final, epic crane shot up from street level watches Doug's broken-down Holden start, stop, and crawl uncertainly through the maze of streets, a thousand miles still to go. Doug's quest is deeply futile, locked in the city. *F.J. Holden* uses a few similar epic crane shots; the final one pulls up and back from Kevin's entrapment at last by parents, police, and a stunted future. It is interesting to compare this, for its wry comedy, with the corresponding shot in *Queensland*. The latter's tone is never comic, but its images have their own claims to beauty. Trains, signs, industrial clutter, bare working-class pubs are all part of the old, inner-city working-class landscape.

Another low-budget short feature of the period, *Love Letters From Teralba Road* (1977) made an impact with a similar austerity and obliqueness. Its writer and director, Stephen Wallace, generates a story from a small bundle of real letters he found in an old

Dreams of another place, not easily reached from working-class Melbourne. Bob Karl and John Flaus in *Queensland*.

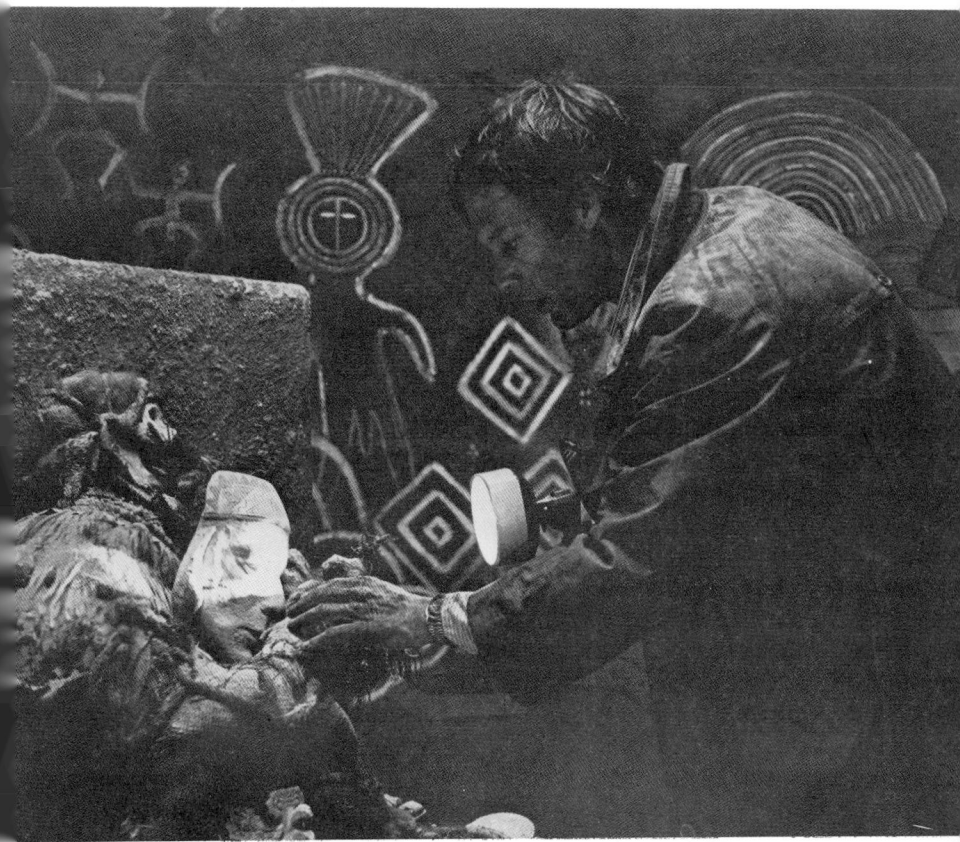

Appropriation. Richard Chamberlain in Peter Weir's sometimes brilliant post-Daniken film, *The Last Wave*.

house. It is the story of two people assessing the damage of their failed marriage, harbouring hopes by letter that can't stand up to a meeting in the flesh. The letters are used in voice-over, and they have the power of strong emotion that has no adequate means of expression. As in the best moments of *F.J. Holden*, it observes its subjects acutely with a sympathy that never sentimentalises. *Love Letters*' black-and-white cinematography by Tom Cowan works to portray the grim urban landscapes of industrial Newcastle and working-class Sydney. Again, sexuality is explored as a gulf between two species who need, but may not survive, each other. The narrative is in fragments in the way that letters are, with their tangential sentences that declare the difficulty of speech. Bryan Brown's role as Len — his first lead role — is a powerful addition to the iconic repertoire. Len is a working-class male with traditional expectations, crippled by his inarticulateness, a person for whom tenderness is almost impossible. But Kris McQuade's Barbara is at least equally powerful. She is strongly portrayed as a tough character who may once have been vulnerable, as though she were Anne, of *F.J. Holden*, a few years further on. Hers is not an heroic, virtuous icon, but she has an attractive, if uncertain, strength that contributes to the small film gallery of Australian females.

The Long Weekend (1978) and *The Last Wave* (1977) form a pair, of sorts, in their attitude to nature. They are linked to *Walkabout* and *Picnic at Hanging Rock* and their theme of unnatural crime preceding natural retribution. *Last Wave* explores what the French call *la fantastique Australienne* in a dreamlike first-person; *Long Weekend* has a hard-edged, half-surreal approach. In *Long Weekend*, crimes against Nature lead to the torment and death of a holidaying couple at the hands of Nature. In *Last Wave*, the prescience of impending catastrophe seems linked to white guilt, the guilt of the despoilers, recent arrivals, unable to recognise the gods of the country. *Picnic* attempted to tie Nature, sexuality and suffering in a Gordian knot in the Victorian tradition. Peter Weir's natural apocalypse in *The Last Wave* is isolated from almost all the traditional 'causes' of retribution in the horror-film canon. It is not linked to unnatural sexuality, condemned or celebrated; there is little sense of social disease that could draw such massive punitive response. The repression of Aboriginal Australia, the bland, heedless lotus eating of white Australians, and an apocalyptic cycle in the mythic history of the continent are all involved. But the atmospheric is much stronger than the discursive. Deluge, obliteration, doom, perhaps purgation, are simply in the air. To look too closely at this sometimes brilliant fabrication of a looming watery apocalypse in the driest of continents brings us up against the von Daniken-style persuasions underlying it.

Long Weekend, by contrast, is right inside the horror genre, with its Old Testament view of adulterous sexuality (and subsequent abortion) as the key transgression against Nature. The marriage has apparently deteriorated since Marcia's (Briony Behets') bored, extra-marital adventure. When Peter (John Hargreaves) insists that they spend the long weekend camping 'wild' (with all their expensive camping paraphernalia) at a beach with difficult access, Nature begins to exact an eye for an eye and a tooth for a tooth. Their crime is more than personal. This is a couple heavy with post-industrial guilt, embodying conscious and unconscious crimes against the environment with their litter, insect-sprays, processed foods and senseless actions against wildlife and trees. Their last covenant with Nature is Peter's ageing black Labrador, Cricket (ironically namesake of Pinocchio's moral conscience, Jiminy Cricket). His last-minute inclusion in the trip provides the final bit of luck Peter has. The dog is attuned at some level to the natural realm. His loyalty sees Peter through as far as his last crazed flight into the forest when he leaves the dog barking in the locked car. He is released from the clutches of the bush only to be struck down on the road by a truck, just as he struck down a dazzled kangaroo on the way to the campsite.

John Hargreaves' character carries the film's sense of Australianness. It is another *Don's Party* role: boyish, half-attractive, half-repulsive. They are not an attractive couple, but at least he has a little vigour and rudeness on his side. The implacable Old Testament logic of the film confines Marcia in her archaic role as the sullen original sinner; and the remote peninsula is a lonely Eden, made ominous by the directions '. . . just past the abbatoirs', the circular maze of tracks in its precincts and the eerie calls of the dugong. The beast is taken as a threat and shot like the harmless albatross of another story. Though dead, it continues to creep up the beach, a silent accuser, until the couple is pushed over the brink of insanity. *The Long Weekend* accords with the self-loathing of liberal Australians for their material and spiritual sins against the continent. *The Last Wave* supports this judgement, but concocts a South American visitation myth, purportedly part of Aboriginal knowledge, in which second-sighted emissaries from that other continent always come to Australia with warnings when the destructive phase of the eternal cycle is beginning. Richard Chamberlain, as the foreign corporate lawyer with South American ancestors is that person.

It can be noted here that Dominic Guard, in *Picnic*, Richard Chamberlain in *Last Wave*, and Mark Lee in *Gallipoli* can all be read as stand-ins, of a sort, for Peter Weir in his films. Weir is the Australian director most invested with the myth of the *auteur*; publicly he has neither propagated nor dismissed that investment which has helped to market his work. The three actors all bear some physical resemblance to Weir, and have in common a receptive quality atypical of the Australian male ethos. They visualise, witness and are finally impotent, though not 'infertile'. The last of them, in *Gallipoli*, is pre-ordained for self-sacrifice in the way that is the customary destiny for heroines in melodrama.

In 1977, a highly successful children's film based on a popular novel by Colin Thiele took up the theme. *Storm Boy* is the story of the tug of war between right and wrong attitudes to the wilderness. The wild Coorong is a presence in the narrative as strong as any of the three main human characters: the child Storm Boy (Greg Rowe), his taciturn, reclusive father Tom (Peter Cummins), and his guide to the world of the Coorong, the Aboriginal Fingerbone Bill (David Gulpilil). This is achieved partly through bravura cinematographic passages on the landscape itself: the dunes, beach lagoons, dense bird-life and wild weather. More importantly, however, the Coorong constructs the characters. Fingerbone is its intelligence, Tom its recluse, Storm Boy its initiate, and Mr Percival, the pelican, is its token of blessing and acceptance bestowed on the boy. The Aboriginal is close to nature and the wisdom of the land, a go-between. Gulpilil's role here is strongly reminiscent of that in *Walkabout*. With the guidance of this emissary, the white inhabitants of the Coorong survive the moral and physical trial of Nature, and good wins as it must for this audience. And never a woman in sight.

Hatted Australians, the last honourable generation of males. Len (Bill Hunter) and Chris (Chris Haywood) hope for a 'close shave' in the 1955 Redex car reliability trials in *Newsfront*.

Jim Sharman's *The Night the Prowler* (1978) is a hybrid, blending Patrick White's literary metaphysics of suburbia and Jim Sharman's Australian Gothic. Like *Shirley Thompson versus the Aliens*, the film takes respectable suburban Australianness as an all-too-solid and stable construction, and puts it to the test of tragi-comedy. The film sets explosives in its darker, deeper basements. It views the edifice as a storehouse of repression.

The film is set in Patrick White's own Sydney suburb, Centennial Park, a middle-class enclave islanded by parklands in one direction, and less salubrious suburbs in the other. White is not known as a lover of women, nor indeed of mankind; but this film concedes some interesting strengths to its female protagonist. Felicity Bannister, ungainly and wilful, is apparently raped by a prowler in her parents' house, suffers a mental disturbance and turns herself into a prowler of sorts. She proves a close cousin of that earlier suburban heroine, Shirley; just a little more heavyweight, a little more objective towards herself, frighteningly impassive. As the story progresses, we learn that she took advantage, in every sense, of the prowler she trapped in her bedroom, and seized on his presence as a weapon with which to make a radical break from her family and childhood. She acts instinctively, following step by step the logic of her move, until she is dressed at last in black leather, prowling the night, threatening, breaking and entering, taking revenge on households that mirror her own. Finally, she comes across a man reduced to the state of a poor, bare, forked animal, alone in a derelict house. She is moved at last, and so she comes to the end of her psychosis. She had needed it to escape beyond the smothered madness of her earlier life.

The weight of property and proprietorial duty comically burden and distort the mother (Ruth Cracknell), father (John Frawley) and overweight daughter (brilliantly played by Kerry Walker). When the mother is not on the phone in the hall — an easily-invaded confessional, where the best face is presented tirelessly along with the worst news — she is obsessively smoothing over the surfaces of her house and life. The father makes himself as scarce as possible, or otherwise resorts to a complete and perfect blandness. The Gothic is more subtle; because it is not openly declared it gains a sly power. The qualities in Australian, or perhaps any, suburban life that give so much scope to the Gothic response are the trained smallness of mind, the careful blindness of eye, the litany of trivial responses, the deathly quest for security. They are all small signs of death. One asks oneself, 'Did I see that? Or is it only I who see it that way?' The small signs slip from sight, but their ceaseless repetition inures and makes them natural. That is the quality that Sharman captures here. To capture the enemy, he rarely needs to go over the top.

The film changes gear towards the end, however, dropping parents and flashbacks from sight and following Felicity's nights on the loose a little too literally. She is first seen as a tensely-guarded island of impassive resistance in the smoothed-over madness of her parents' household. Later, she becomes a comic spectacle, making it difficult to maintain the identification we have cautiously invested in her. If she is psychotic, did we misread the earlier parts and laugh at the wrong things? Apart from this hesitation, the film is bold and direct in its address: it is as though the first part belonged to Sharman, the second to White. Between them, the film is neither simply comedy, nor art film; and the two tend to exclude each other. It is unselfconscious about genre, untroubled by the question of how to be Australian.

Felicity Bannister, like Shirley Thompson, is that rare, strong, memorable female Australian film character, even a hero. But is she offered as a positive, imitable icon of Australianness, to give us warmth and security as Australians? In 1978 even male film protagonists were not so whole-hearted. The moment had not yet come when the positive Australian icon would be thought a good risk. Bryan Brown was not yet a call to born-again Australianness. Yet, as we have seen, even the more equivocal heroes in the mould of Foley were offered as an invitation to the pleasure of recognition. The fact that this pleasure was almost exclusively invested in the post-ocker male is striking. Exceptions like Kerry Walker's Felicity prove the rule.

Newsfront (1978) was a landmark film; it established a partisan Australianness in a form genuinely analytic towards the history of its setting, not merely period in its decor. *Newsfront* starts in 1948 with the beginning of intensive post-war European immigration under Chifley's Labor Government, through the 1949 defeat of Labor as an early casualty in the Cold War; the establishment of the Menzies Government that would last a generation; the clear start of consumerism, the suburbanisation

A woman at large (at last?) Kerry Walker in *The Night, the Prowler*.

Felicity Bannister (Kerry Walker) takes advantage of her prowler (Terry Camilleri) to break out of the pattern of her life in *The Night the Prowler*.

and Americanisation of Australian life, to 1956, TV and the Melbourne Olympic Games. It traces the fortunes of a 'Cinetone' newsreel cameraman and his off-siders through the last years of the newsreel.

This provides the richest device of the film as history. The found Cinesound and Movietone newsreel footage provides a complex mixture of iconography, folklore and history, as well as a way of speaking about the representation of history in general and the history of the Australian film industry itself. Bob Ellis, credited with 'original screenplay', is passionately at home with this project and the opportunity it affords for a radically nationalist, sentimental, intellectual elaboration of his theme, 'Be true to your culture'. The post-war period for Australia, as for much of Western Europe, was a time when we were extremely vulnerable to the flood of American foreign investment and export culture. Rock-and-roll was a symptom of the process — and a sudden, sharp sign of which generation one belonged to. The consequences of television were a more serious one. It formed an inroad, a royal road, to the national unconscious for Americanising influences. For Ellis, the test of individual honour and integrity is the ability to be instinctively Australian, 'on to yourself', sceptical towards the blandishments of the new culture, aware of the Faustian price-tag attached to its most seductive invitations.

Hence comes the character of Len Maguire (Bill Hunter), one of the last of the 'hatted Australians'. He is a cameraman, Labor man, loner with a nationalism that both guards his honour and threatens to make him reactionary. Hunter's role is a beautifully understated advertisement for another possible position: that Australia is habitable as a culture, inoculated against the American disease by a maverick larrikinism that cannot be bought or sold. Of course, this view is intensely nostalgic, reinforced by the iconic power of the newsreel footage to summon a quainter, simpler and purer past. Len Maguire is of the generation which parented the post-war 'baby boom' and is invested with the power of 'the time from which our time has come'. He is portrayed as part of that bulwark which stood firm for us; and he is posed as a question to our consciences on the matter of cultural integrity.

Diverting the flow of nostalgia, and keeping it under some control, is Ellis' acerbic wit which, nevertheless, is usually deployed in deeply sentimental causes. Len Maguire himself keeps any kind of excess under control. Australians are defined as more modest, less pompous, more attuned to austerity and dry humour than Americans. Len's brother Frank (Gerard Kennedy) provides the contrast as the one who literally goes over to the Americans, misses the point of integrity, and sells his birthright for a mess of pottage (or should that be a 'potted message'?). But Len's restraint is part of the deeply sentimental construction of his character. While filming a water polo match between the USSR and Hungary at the 1956 Melbourne Olympic Games, Len captures the bloodthirsty fight that erupts from Hungarian hatred of Soviet occupying forces in their country. It is the most commercially valuable footage that will ever pass through his camera. Frank attempts to buy some of the film from Len on behalf of his American employer. Len stands true to his company, country and self, and refuses. Amy (Wendy Hughes) explains this to the uncomprehending Frank by simply saying, 'He's just a bit old-fashioned'. In director Phillip Noyce's version of the script, this is the capping line as Len walks towards us, shouldering his camera as a sign of his lonely burden of integrity and small-time heroism. Not only does Len resist selling company footage for profit to his turncoat brother; he also resists selling ammunition for the Cold War in which he, as a loyal Labor man, has already sustained small, private wounds to which he would not admit.

Len and Frank Maguire are working-class Catholic characters, not just for local colour, but because of the historic role played by this part of the Australian electorate in splitting off, in the majority, from traditional Labor to form the right-wing, anti-communist Democratic Labor Party. This divided the working-class vote so successfully that Menzies secured an unparalleled sixteen-year run in office by raising the spectre of 'the Red menace' in the Labour movement at each election.

In the political polarisation of the Catholic community, Len holds to his own counsel, and questions his priest's right to hand out 'Vote Yes' leaflets on the eve of Menzies' national referendum to ban the Australian Communist Party. But he bows to his Catholic wife's strict rejection of birth control, and watches his marriage crack under the strain.

Around Len and his brother there is a small gallery of male workmates and one female, Amy, secretary to the boss. Again, the male group elaborates the theme of Australianness. Even Chris

The Second Phase (1976-80): Seemly Respectability 133

(Chris Haywood), Len's assistant, a new-chum Cockney, is quick to learn and fits in easily. Bryan Brown plays Geoff, the 'ageing radical' film editor on the team who eventually leaves for England as the place where his talents, and political leanings, might be better tolerated. His supporting role lets him develop the combination of laconic casualness and spirit that he perfected later in the supporting role of Handcock in *Breaker Morant*; a role which was recognized as the very incarnation of Australianness.

And the female roles? They are in every sense 'supporting'. As Meaghan Morris points out, Len's wife Fay (Angela Punch-McGregor) 'is portrayed as the unfortunate bearer of the false morality which denies life but treasures social conventions, while the husband's space is not only endowed with warmth, sensuality and independence of mind, but political integrity'.[5] It should be added that Angela Punch-McGregor makes something quite memorable and not altogether negative out of this role; she portrays a conventional person damaged by her own strict rules and adherences, shifting over time to a position shaded a little more by pragmatism and experience. She strikes a genuinely historical note with the early fifties, embodying it the more fully, perhaps, for her muted presence and limited screen time. Her position is reversed in *We of the Never Never* a later film in which Lewis Fitz-Gerald almost mutely, and from the periphery, incarnates the period in which that film is set in a way that Punch-McGregor, in the lead role, cannot rival.

Amy is the career girl whom Frank discards, after many years of never really intending to get married. Len discovers her in a first really sexual moment of realisation, before his own marriage has truly dissolved, on the night of young Chris' wedding. She is a frustratingly unrealised and neglected character, whom the script makes strong in odd moments. She is the independent, attractive woman, but one who functions too much as a pawn in the male-centred plot. She is apparently prepared to wait decades for one or either brother even though they age, turn into Americans, or else shy away from her, masking their fear with indifference. The insecurity of the narrative around Amy is expressed in Len's reluctance to face a sexually strong female; it is a symptom of the narrative's failure to face this challenge to the construct of Len and the male Australian traits and virtues invested in him. Thus Len forces Amy to recognise what sudden, strong meaning her sexuality has for him in the scene at the dance, initiates an affair with her, but then rapidly sinks into the quandaries of middle age, often hardly dares to meet her eyes, and walks away from her and Frank in the final frames of the film.

Formally the film is a richly textured play of black and white and colour, newsreel compilation and period recreation of shooting those newsreels. Len's loyalty to the disintegrating remnants of the last surviving Australian film company, his doomed marriage, his ageing and looming displacement or redundancy in the age of television: all function as motifs of the passing of an era; of the older, truer, more honourable Australia. The newsreel segments have a syncopated relationship to this melancholy theme; they speak the voice of history accomplished, history to be cheerfuly borne, lighter moments to be laughed at, thrills to entertain — but nothing that can ever be beyond the clear, knowing, fatherly gaze of the narrator. Folkloric events like singing dogs, round-Australia car rallies, or the curious spectacle of cars being driven in balletic leaps into Sydney Harbour are alternated with the key moments in political history and with natural disasters like floods and bushfires.

One lovely device incorporates the very process by which filmed images acquire nostalgia with time. Chris takes home-movie footage of the day when all the blokes from work form a working bee to build on a new room for Len's rapidly growing family. Some years later he drowns in the Maitland floods, soon after his forced, but not wholly unwilling marriage to the country girl he met for a night when covering the Redex trial of 1955. In 1956, the film is taken out for the children to view during one of Len's routine visits. On the screen, Chris sets up the camera in order to stage a visual gag in which a man walks into a post at the height of his groin. He is seen peering into the lens as the film runs out and fades to white, an image now full of the sense of his death.

Thus *Newsfront* incorporates and acknowledges the sentimental potency of all such moving images of the past. As the film finishes, instead of leaving us in the fifties — or rather, leaving itself in the fifties and us here, unconnected with the lost and seductive past — a final newsreel montage under the end credits takes us rapidly forward through the bowing-out of Menzies, the

The Second Phase (1976-80): Seemly Respectability 135

Vietnam war days, the succession of post-Menzies Liberal prime-ministers, and the advent of the Whitlam Government. On one level, this connects the lonely figure of Len in the tunnel under the stadium, in the depths of the Menzies era's entrenched conservatism, with Whitlam's brief light at the end of the tunnel: one hero of Australian nationalism linked to another. But on another level the public moments of history are the connective tissues between 1948 and the contemporary era (in 1978) of 1972. In 1978, to show the scene of Whitlam's victory was still a defiant act, proclaiming someone a saviour who had been a scapegoat in raw and shameful recent political history.

My Brilliant Career (1979) was Gillian Armstrong's debut feature, as *Newsfront* was Phillip Noyce's. *Newsfront* works a period adjacent to the present, and conducts a commentary about the major influences shaping Australian destiny and identity over a stretch of years sharply formative of the present. *Career*, set in the 1890s, came at the point when even critical support for the AFC genre was exhausted, and yet it managed to win a large audience and become the jewel in the crown of the worthy period-film cycle.

It both exemplifies and exceeds the characteristics of the genre. Its origins in a literary classic are exceeded by the proto-feminist stance of Miles Franklin's novel, and its status as period costume drama by a moderately feminist rejection of the central romance. It is certainly a romantic rejection, posed as a decision in favour of art and independence, and experienced as indefinitely extending the delay of gratification, the staple of romantic fiction. The slow, sensuous pans over the landscape and beautifully-dressed sets, the camera's lyrical exploitation of beautifully-lit women in richly-textured costume, are all there, but they too are exceeded by a sharp eye for witty or efficient *mise en scene* and the nice contradiction of a spirited, eccentric heroine whose characterisation approaches the larrikin — and therefore the heroic?

Miles Franklin's precocious self-irony is overlooked, but her boldness and cheek are not: the confident title and semi-autobiographical heroine lend a scandalous, endearing sort of egotism to the entire project. Here was a woman who doesn't play herself down, who doesn't sublimate her passionate contradictory desires, who doesn't choose the destiny set up by this narrative and by almost every other. No, here are a number of such women whose identity flows on from Miles' Sybylla. Gillian Armstrong, directing her first commercial feature, Judy Davis, with her first feature lead role, Margaret Fink, producer, Eleanor Witcombe, writer, and Luciana Arrighi, production design, were also part of the mildly feminist publicity-narrative surrounding the time of principal photography and post-production.

Others have noted some of the niceties of the film's *mise en scene* as a constant indication of Sybylla's character, sensibility, and growth to maturity.[6] Certainly, the film is cohesive, and relatively economical in the way it uses the relation between camera, actor and physical space to centre on Sybylla as she moves through each of the three main stages of her development. Possum Gully, her parents' home in the bush, is flat, dusty, threadbare, a place of drudgery and hard labour. Her grandmother's house, Caddagat, is watered, green, an oasis of nature and culture — and wealth and elevated society. The McSwat's farm is almost Dickensian in its impression of the rude, teeming, dirty animalistic lives of the rural working class. They are Catholic and child-ridden, kindly but ignorant. Through each of these tests of pleasure and travail, Sybylla moves with a first-person intensity that the camera relays through *mise en scene* verging always on the subjective, but never relinquishing the objective gaze which focusses on her character. The aim is always to make this character, in her vigour and eccentricity, exceed and upstage the feast of merely visual pleasure.

A good example is the scene apparently devoted to the elaboration of the picturesque — red parasol, pretty girl composed with book at the foot of a tree, sunlight and green reflections as the camera advances with ample slowness towards the object of its desire, along with Frank (Robert Grubb), Sybylla's unwanted upper-class English suitor, and the bunch of flowers he will present to fix her in her place as grace note in the composition. Frank goes, his mission completed. Then the rain begins and Sybylla dances in it with a dry-country appreciation of rain as an occasion for excitement and celebration. She refuses to be an element in picturesque composure — she dances, gets wet, disarranges her hair, clothes and prettiness. The bouquet lands in the water with the raindrops. And so the film rejects its awards for mere good taste, taking the side of its 'difficult' character who refuses to surrender to the erotic pull of the story towards Harry (Sam

The Second Phase (1976-80): Seemly Respectability 137

Neill), marriage, the wealth of Five Bob Downs and a writing career on the side, the way of most women writers. The film has its cake and eats it; it has the lyrical passages and its resistant narrative; the erotic and romantic currents run strongly, but there is still the 'feminist' rejection of sexual passion, dependence, and child-bearing, in favour of a literary career and independence. The traditional pattern of deferred gratification is taken one step further, as a feminist variation on women's fiction.

Yet here it misjudges both the force of that traditional pattern of audience desire and the weakness of its attempt to vary it. We never actually see Sybylla as a person fanatically invested with the desire to do her own work. Her pronouncements on life and art are at least as adolescent and 'tried on' as her pronouncements on marriage, love and woman's lot. There is a perversity in the way the film devotes itself to scenes like the pillow fight between Sybylla and Harry at Five Bob Downs — a scene charged with sexual tension — only to switch course and topple audience expectation. It is the film itself that has it each way, having its cake and eating it, watched by an audience denied the cake that they have been offered. The novel — produced from thin air and sent off into the sunrise to a British press at the end of the story — seems very like an afterthought.

Mad Max (1979) is in the opposite corner of the aesthetic ring. Its pattern of funding, address, genre preoccupations and rhythm all mark it out as possibly intentionally frustrating the AFC genre and its dedicated construction of a middle-of-the-road safety zone. *Mad Max* is that rare phenomenon of its time: a film entirely privately funded. It was also George Miller's and Byron Kennedy's first film, and it was the first Australian film to reinvent a genre and achieve strong commercial success at home and abroad.

It is difficult to discuss the first *Mad Max* in isolation from *Mad Max 2* (1981). The contrast shows the relative poverty of myth in the first, and its much greater reliance on exploitative gimmicks. The most important of these is the way women and children are set up as victims. *Mad Max* pushes the car crash/bikie film towards a slightly more mythic level. The forces of evil are the Nightrider's gang, mechanised horsemen of the apocalypse, breeding in the advanced rot that has set into Australian society some time in the near future; a society broken apart by

The expendability of women, children and the domestic sphere: anxiety and joy enmeshed in *Mad Max*.

Sybylla (Judy Davis) refuses to be an element of the pretty picture in *My Brilliant Career*.

a catastrophic oil drought. The film uses the outskirts and hinterland of Melbourne as a deliberately unpicturesque setting, elaborating the victory of urban-industrial sterility over the landscape. The empty roads are a labyrinth in which a gladiatorial struggle takes place between the last zealots of law and order, and the growing forces of darkness. Max (Mel Gibson) steps from one kind of moral ambiguity, working for the police, to another, acting out of sheer unshakeable revenge, to become the hero who can meet these dark forces. He successively loses Jim Goose (Steve Bisley), his offsider, then his wife Jessie (Joanne Samuel) and their child before he becomes 'Mad' in a holocaust of revenge.

In the opening sequence of chase, crash and close escape, a shot of a woman wheeling her child in a stroller is intercut with the approaching catastrophe of speeding cars, slow-moving caravans, and freaked-out drivers. This proves to be a beat-up of audience expectation. We are let off the hook. The woman and child are miraculously safe, although the fragile 'home' of the caravan flies in exploded fragments all over the road. But in being let off, we are also set up: Jessie and Sprog, the most strongly characterised woman-and-child dyad of the film, are increasingly placed under threat by the Nightriders, who seek revenge against Max for the death and capture of their members. Max quits the corrupt, ineffectual Halls of Justice, which are given a Gothic treatment surpassed only by the extreme anti-naturalism of the Nightriders. They are led by the Toecutter, played extravagantly by Hugh Keays-Byrne. Max wants only a quiet life with his family.

Naturally, the family must be targeted. Jessie and Sprog can't escape. In a sequence with the feel of that nightmare in which you try to outrun fate with legs that barely move, Jessie flees down the road with the child in her arms only to be run down by the Nightriders. The child is dead; Jessie may as well be (and in fact does not survive her catalogue of grisly injuries, to reappear in the sequel). In a narrative closer to horror comics than the *Boys' Own Annual*, the woman and child are not just naturally at risk, but are created as sacrificial victims, to fuel the moral economy of the narrative. For female viewers there is the paralysing fascination of enacted fears: rape, mutilation, harm to children. For male viewers, all this and more, with the extra possibility of vicarious pleasure from identification with the perpetrator and avenger, and never simply with the victim of the narrative.

The film falters stylistically. It is at home with the Gothic treatment of the Halls of Justice, and the hyberbole of the action sequences with their hundreds of fragmented, wide-angled close shots cut at a speed which emphasises the pace, creates tension and increases the power of suggestion between the shots. A comparison of either *Mad Max*, but especially the first, with Eisenstein's *Strike* would be revealing in terms of imagery as well as montage technique. The family-idyll part of the film, however, is shot with obvious insecurity about dialogue, sentiment, and how to make it interesting in the absence of action.

Is the film especially Australian? In some ways the more mythically timeless *Mad Max 2* is better able to incorporate sly Australian jokes and to make Max (Gibson again) and his new off-sider, the gyro-captain (Bruce Spence) more interesting elaborations of nationality than anything in the first film. This is despite the fact that the first film contains so many emblems of a contemporary Australian 'social imaginary': an ambiguity towards the forces of law and order, an acceptance of an aggressive car culture, and its ironic vision of a future where petrol scarcity and the old tyranny of distance combine to create a purgatory in the post industrial wasteland. We will come back to *Mad Max 2* in the following chapter.

James Ricketson's *Third Person Plural* (1978) and Albie Thoms' *Palm Beach* (1979) form another pair; both are low-budget, sixteen millimetre features, and both are semi-improvised unconventional drama features created on the editing bench. The similarities go further. Both use the Sydney northern beaches peninsula as their setting, both cast Bryan Brown in similar lead roles; and both experiment with a non-synchronous sound track and narrative cross-cutting in a kind of cubist approach to narrative which creates a sense of simultaneity and the interpenetration of narrative moments.

But the styles of story are quite different. *Third Person Plural* is audacious, in Australian terms, in generating characters from philosophical and ideological positions. The story is minimal: the different philosophies of two men and two women are set in play over a two-day boating weekend. Couples form, and, in the following weeks, are strained or fall apart. Bryan Brown plays

The Second Phase (1976-80): Seemly Respectability 141

Mark, an entomologist specialising in ants. He is a sceptic in search of the miraculous, tortured by a sense of idealism and its futility. He is attracted to Danny (Linden Wilkinson), who makes 'political' documentaries and works at a community settlement for underprivileged kids. She believes that life is about finding the working thesis that fits your feelings most comfortably. She wants to believe that it is possible to change the world, make it 'better'. Mark likes her clarity but cannot leave it unchallenged, nor trust her do-gooding impulse. He senses the pragmatic emotional reserve behind it, and wounds himself on it.

Beth (Margaret Cameron) is a gentle, sheltered soul who should have caught the bus to Nimbin. She has a husband, a child and an open marriage that begins foundering when she convinces herself that she is in love with Terry (George Shevtsov), who owns the *Volita*. He is a dispassionate, playful sceptic; a hedonist who plays devil's advocate with dinner-party wit, and doesn't stay around for the consequences. He has only a mild, pleasurable interest in Beth and returns her child-like behaviour in kind.

The film concentrates on the first couple. It cuts back and forth throughout over their hesitant relationship, which possibly gets somewhere through a war of words, arguments, stalemates over questions of the world's amenability to change, and the nature of the desire for it. Some scenes are seen more than once, some pieces of dialogue continue over more than one scene, usually full of immobilising, existential questions. The concern with character, subjectivity and existential position, plus the discontinuous treatment of time, place this film in art film territory. But the shooting style is flat, as in *cinema verite*. It follows the scene and anticipates little.

Palm Beach is much more conscious of story. Superficially, the visual style is similar, but on closer examination the long takes reveal themselves as highly planned sequence shots. The film plays with several genres — detective, documentary, social-realist narrative, even surf-movie — in its essay on a specific urban place: Sydney's northern beaches peninsula, its surf subculture and surf-related economy. It approaches this specifically urban Australianness with historical irony and considerable self-awareness. Several peninsula stories are told over the two days of the narrative: the private detective from Bondi, Larry Kent (John Flaus) is hired by a distraught woman to find her missing daughter Leilani (Amanda Berry), who may be getting in with the drug scene down on the beaches. A surfer (Ken Brown) from Maroubra, a less salubrious south-side beach, heads north to Palm Beach to see his old friend, Ned (Nat Young), and get hold of some acid; in fact, he has been busted for marijuana, and must try to uncover a source of LSD to satisfy the police, who in return will lift the charges. His search is fruitless. For a day, he travels with Ned from point to point through the sub-culture, from the Manly Silver Screen picture-show in the south to surf-shops, surf-board factories, health-food shops, going north. Paul (Bryan Brown), is unemployed, bored, living with his girlfriend Kate (Julie McGregor), who does a wonderfully repulsive dance act at the RSL club for a living. With the exception of Larry Kent, who never looks in the right place at the right time, all the characters come together at the party on the first night. The only connection made is between Ken and Leilani, who spend the night together. Leilani has several refuges; one on a trimaran down at the marina with an American friend who is just waiting long enough to sell some acid and be off further around the world.

Leilani offers to connect Ken with her source. While this is arranged, Larry Kent, tie flapping in the wind, fruitlessly walks Palm Beach in search of Leilani, never quite in frame, or looking in the right direction at the right moment, and attracting contempt with his clothes and binoculars.

Meanwhile, at the party Paul connects with nobody and becomes still more isolated. In a chest of drawers belonging to his host (who is known only to some of the party-goers) he discovers a gun and lifts it, along with one or two other valuables. Next day he walks to a Coles New World shopping-centre and sticks up a super-market cashier for a few dollars from the till. His farce goes badly awry: a policeman challenges him in the street. Paul shoots him and runs on till he reaches home; then he retches violently into the sink. He decides to hide out on Barrenjoey headland. Kate's Mini-Moke is open-roofed, so he disguises himself for the journey in the absurd wig used in her act. In the early morning light Larry Kent returns to his lonely flat in Bondi, removes his toupe with a sigh, and a helicopter shot travels over the spit and circles Barrenjoey at the extreme northerly tip of Palm Beach peninsula. Its objective eye picks out uniformed police

The Second Phase (1976-80): Seemly Respectability 143

descending on Paul's inadequate hide-out; then it circles and returns towards Sydney, looking down on some of the city's most expensive real estate. The aggressive words of the theme song, 'You've got the best, why not take the rest?' sound ironically over Paul's fate in the midst of affluence.

As Noel Purden observes,

> The last shot of *Palm Beach* could be straight out of *Cop Shop*. But what is rigorously avoided is the inner structure of television narrative; the structure that, whatever the storyline, is provided by fast cutting, obedient reverse angles, trick shooting, up-classed set dressing, and a visual concentration on sexual and violent energy which is lied about by being at the same time glamorized and de-sanitised.[7]

Precisely with its looseness, the way it plays with genre, and its astute, ironic regionalism, *Palm Beach* both contains and far exceeds the limits of television drama.

It partakes in another discourse, too: experimental film. The hand-held *verite*-like camera work consists of extended sequence shots, with sometimes quite complex *mise en scene*. Movement in and out of a moving frame, presence and absence in the frame and composition-in-depth bring the disconnected stories into tangential relationship with one another. The sound-track is a rich mix. Dialogue overflows, bridging to or from scenes not present on the image, and choric radio and other location sounds are almost continuous. For example, a nice minor touch is the way Larry Kent is frequently accompanied by barking dogs or yowling cats. Like Richard III, whose shadow dogs barked at, Kent is the eternal outsider, the mismatched one, who wears his separateness like a hump, or, indeed, a toupe. The radio — or sometimes television — soundtrack brings both consequential and inconsequential information into the mix; it is habitual, trivialising, moralising, inappropriate, beneath contempt, and often subliminal. The disjunction between sound and image creates some superb moments. Bryan Brown steals a garden statue of a naked female figure and hurries down the road with it tucked under his arm while in voice-over from the preceding scene a woman lectures on media representations of women. Another example is a reading from D.H. Lawrence's *Kangaroo*, heard as Ken and Ned's car drives around some loops of bushland at dusk. The passage describes Somers in his garden house as he ruminates about the melancholy, ancient and unwelcoming Australian bush, in a rhetorical tradition that goes back to Marcus Clarke. So the film's consciousness of place is declared, and lifted from the finely particular to the ironically general.

Palm Beach itself is not just combed and documented for its particular sub-cultures and the surfing mythology on which it depends. Its particular inflection of surfing culture is compared with that of the poorer surfing regions to the south. in the person of Ken. Its economic infrastructure and sexual politics are turned out to the light with a deft and indirect set of narrative gestures. Ned's wife is sweet and servile; the nomadic surfing life is both an aesthetic quest for waves and a misogynist search for women; Leilani gives over, helps out, shuts up; the girls lie on the beach ('little spunk-buckets', as Ken says) while the boys surf. The narrative, which looks like an idle, open-ended picaresque, is in fact constructed to mimic documentary openness, while trapping in its coils a highly ironic, lightly didactic discourse on Australian culture — a world in a grain of sand. It has one of the cleverest and most underrated narrative structures of any Australian film. The kind of recognition which it sets up is sharply productive, not merely supportive and pleasurable.

In Search of Anna (1979) was another low-to-middle-budget feature to experiment with a complicated treatment of time. *Anna* is a curious marriage of the disaffected road-movie and the subjective art film with overtones of social realist 'issue' films like *Mouth to Mouth*, or Esben Storm's earlier *27A*. The film journeys progressively north, from Melbourne to Sydney, Sydney to the NSW north coast, growing always greener and closer to Eden. The disjointed flashback structure is a kind of metaphor for the fractured, post-prison consciousness of the central figure, Tony (Richard Moir). His journey in search of Anna, who's image was his life raft through prison, introduces him to Sam (Judy Morris), a dissociated personality of another kind. By the time he reaches Anna's threshold, he realises that the journey has really taken him to Sam, who came with him. It has stitched him back into time, enabled him to digest the past, including his betrayal by his friend and the death of his mother, and brought him to accept the hopelessness of trying to get back into his old life.

Richard Moir's character is an interesting inflection of male Australianness: sensitive, low-key, tough, with even a hint of a

The Second Phase (1976-80): Seemly Respectability 145

laconic intellectuality. Judy Morris' character is more stylised. Toughness teeters on the edge of breakdown, and less brittle qualities emerge when she leaves the fast lane of city life. The other character in the film is the old American Buick that carries them together, and finally lets them be together. This is somehow natural, for although it is Australian, it is nevertheless a road movie, in which fetishised Americana slides through a more un-American than Australian landscape. The art movie element comes to a slightly embarassing art movie climax in the montage of empty rooms, passages, paths, Sam framed in windows or doorways of the darkened abandoned house, while Tony, in the film's parlance, 'gets his head together'.

Maybe This Time (1980) is worth mentioning as a late companion-piece to *Petersen* (1974). It is opposite to it in almost every detail; in an odd way, it demonstrates the traits that link the sexual mores group usually authored by David Williamson and/or Tim Burstall. This film is the interesting exception. It takes 'a woman's view', tracing the crisis of a woman turning thirty as she tries to decide her life's direction in a kind of cold post-feminist dawn that doesn't offer many possibilities. It is a curiosity in Australian film, because it is a 'women's picture' that intersects with the male-based sex-and-relationships sub-genre. There are other 'women's pictures': *Caddie, My Brilliant Career*, perhaps *The Getting of Wisdom, Tim, We of the Never Never, Careful, He Might Hear You*; but these are mainly from the list of the most critically acclaimed AFC-genre films. The others in the AFC genre are less successful, probably because of their decision to centre on a recessive male instead of a woman who refuses to be completely recessive.

Maybe This Time is also interesting for its complete commercial failure, even in so far as failing to gain the confidence of a commercial distributor despite the excellence of its script credentials (Anne Brooksbank, primarily, with Bob Ellis), and its actors (Judy Morris, Bill Hunter and Chris Haywood). A lapse of some years between original script and production meant that by the time it was released in 1980 it was already dated. Events and sensibility in the film in fact suggest 1975 and the fall of the Whitlam Government. The shoot was uncomfortable, fraught with differences of opinion and a broken period of principal photography. Roadshow pulled out and the film fell between promises, intentions and inaction until it drifted into the AFI's small distribution and exhibition circuit.

The fate of *Maybe This Time* is in many ways symptomatic of the low point in Australian cinema towards the end of the middle phase. It was characterised by a lack of confidence and commerciality, and further hampered by unsympathetic, ill-timed release dates. It would have been a more interesting film in 1976; by 1980 it was strange to see how dated it felt, despite the bleak 'feminist' rendering of the choices facing a single woman of thirty. Judy Morris' character, Fran, reviews her long-running affair with a married political press secretary, Stephen (Bill Hunter). Stephen is a womaniser who doesn't care much for any of his women, including his wife, who has begun to retaliate against his infidelities. Fran retreats from this impasse, re-visits her home town for Christmas and contemplates marriage to her former sweetheart, Alan (Ken Shorter). She observes her married sister's unhappiness burdened by small children, however, and her suitor's ludicrous aspects, despite his money and security, are not lost on her. She revisits her old mentor, a private school teacher who deplores the absence of any 'real men', nowadays; then nearly makes the wrong move with a travelling salesman in her motel. Back in Sydney, she strikes up a desperate affair with the lecturer for whom she tutors (Mike Prescott), who offers sexual solace without emotional responsibility. In other words, there *are* no men nowadays — or none who answer the needs of a woman caught in a contradictory position. She has half unpicked her traditional expectations, but has no idea how she might now proceed.

Some of the distributors' reactions to the film seem to have been fear and distaste for that proposition. A woman who sleeps with three different men in fairly quick succession and finds all of them severely wanting is fundamentally unacceptable, even threatening. Yet Roadshow did set up the Hexagon production company in order to make *Petersen* (1974), which traces a male odyssey on a similar course through a series of sexual and emotional possibilities, all of which are eventually rejected. *Petersen*, written by Williamson, and directed by Burstall, was also part ocker comedy. In the end, Jack Thompson's Petersen falls out of his university experiment back into the rougher, 'truer' world of the unassuming tradesman, being his own boss, working hard with his hands, eyed on the sly by some of his stereotypically available women customers. By contrast, Fran in *Maybe This Time* goes abroad to join a female friend, only to learn on the plane that she has died in a car accident in Greece.

In both films, the issue of sexuality promotes them from telemovie to feature film. Their fairly flat visual styles are also comparable. In *Maybe*, the social-realist 'adequate' camera style is gentle, a touch lyrical in places; in *Petersen*, the style is more aggressive, in keeping with the surface drama of punch-ups, public fucking, nude romps on beaches, and a rape. *Maybe* is tentative, visually uncertain. *Petersen* tries to present repressed anger and attempts to be visually explicit. *Maybe* was rejected as unattractive and uncommercial, *Petersen* was promoted as wholly appropriate. Was this a matter of times having changed too much, or merely of the old double standard not changing enough?

Stir (1980) can be compared with *The Odd Angry Shot* (1979), another elaboration of the male ensemble film which prefigures the patriotic turn this form took with *Breaker Morant* (1980) and *Gallipoli* (1981). *Stir* and *Odd Angry Shot* are negative versions of the form; and *Stir* had only half a foot in this territory. While both are studies of men in groups, cut off from the world by prison or war, *Stir* has the force of a profoundly angry dramatised documentary which mounts to its grim climax with no place for humour, while the other film uses humour and episodic construction in the style of *Sunday Too Far Away* and other Williamsonian social comedies.

Stir uses Bryan Brown's China as icon of the prisoner alienated and pushed to breaking-point by the harsh, inhumane Australian penal system. The story follows very closely the well-known events of the Bathurst prison riot. The NSW Film Corporation, despite the fact that it is answerable to the state premier who at that time also oversaw the state prison system, strongly backed the film, which was developed by the Prisoners' Action Group, a body aimed at prison reform. The script is strewn with four letter words. Of course, prisoners' speech would have sounded crippled and tinny without them; but while strong language pleased audiences when deployed as part of male comic energy, it was disturbing when placed in the service of relentless anger and hatred.

This question of context is a matter of fine judgement. *Maybe This Time* shrinks from including the word 'fuck' in the script;

A curious marriage of the disaffected road movie and the introspective art film. Judy Morris and Richard Moir in *In Search of Anna*.

Phil Motherwell, Bryan Brown and John Maxwell in *Stir*: a strong sense of the Australian loner, more anomic than alienated.

when Judy Morris has to say to Mike Prescott, her university boss turned lover, 'Don't just fuck me, make love to me,' the word was changed to 'screw'. Though more 'acceptable', in a woman's speech it clangs. *Odd Angry Shot* included eschatological imagery of a vigorous and often misogynist kind, but never hesitated to judge this appropriate.

Stir captures extremely well the quality of repressive male cruelty to male. As breaking-point approaches, loners like China are pushed into initiating action without ever quite becoming leaders. When breaking-point is reached there is release and then the bleakness of the aftermath, with no ground gained. The film also achieves the sense of a placeless place, Australian in speech and attitude but without strongly flavoured landscape to invest it with with cultural exactitude. The dramatic pitch is somewhat monotone, relentless, unbroken by the many moments of black humour that might have found a natural place in its narrative purpose.

The character of China takes Bryan Brown's aura of alienation in *Palm Beach* and *Third Person Plural* to an extreme. Common to all of Brown's roles, with the exception of Peter Lalor in the mini-series *Eureka*, is a strong sense of the Australian loner, more anomic than alienated, but always slightly apart, even with mates: 'each man an island'. Also common to each role is a scepticism that makes the character honest, resigned, ironic, and yet fierce when pushed, capable of heroism. He is not strongly assertive, but a shade introverted, not egotistical, 'on to himself', and yet unconscious of how attractive this quality can be. It doesn't take much to push this characterisation over the line to become a potent, partisan hero like Handcock in *Breaker Morant*. Keeping the role just off centre-stage makes him acceptable.

Where *Breaker Morant* and *Gallipoli* are, for the first time, directly in the business of intoning Australian myth, *The Odd Angry Shot* belongs to the previous historical moment which indirectly and slightly apologetically celebrated an Australianness, deflected through representative, less-than-heroic men. Furthermore, of course, the Vietnam War did not inspire a national sense of heroism; shame, guilt and failure were plainly associated with it, long before it was declared to be over. It cannot be taken as just any war and used to illustrate the effects of war on the men. The film both knows this and denies it. Written and directed by Tom Jeffrey, it is on one level a 'Williamsonesque' entry in the tradition of that dark humour which treats war as absurd situation comedy and includes *The Good Soldier Schweik, Catch 22, Sergeant Bilko* and *M.A.S.H.*. In such films, verbal and physical jokes are interrupted by real deaths and mutilations. On another level it admits that this was a specific war in which expeditionary forces were to have an ambiguous relationship with their own societies. So the film gives several set-piece apologias to the older, more experienced, fatherly figure in the platoon, Harry (Graham Kennedy). He has to step out of character to warn the boys that people back home won't want to know, and then lurch back from the sermon into his ribald comic mode, with an excruciatingly sexist line about hair round the hole in a beer can.

The male ensemble includes John Hargreaves, John Jarrett, Bryan Brown, Richard Moir, Ian Gilmour and Graeme Blundell. The narrative attack is very similar to *Sunday Too Far Away*, in which episodic construction is punctuated by verbal and physical gags. In *The Odd Angry Shot*, however, these are sometimes strained and over-anxious, as they work to compensate for the slightness of the film in the face of the richness of its subject. The film attempts to bond the audience by encouraging the recognition of a mythology that is typically and fundamentally male. Participation in the recognition ritual is also participation in sexism; women members of the audience laugh at jokes which are made at their expense, using the one self-defence that seems to be available. So the invitation to cultural identification cannot be fully accepted by all, or by any given audience equally. There are moments of deep implausibility for those marginalised by the film's male address, and this is true of all the male-ensemble films, whether on the sceptical, satiric side or the fully partisan, *Gallipoli* side of the continuum.

6

Transition 2 (1980-81): A Tentative Maturity

On the brink of a major shift within the industry from direct to indirect government support, there came a series of successful films: *Breaker Morant, Gallipoli, Winter of Our Dreams, Puberty Blues, Mad Max 2* and the television mini-series, *A Town Like Alice*. These were all of the second phase but their success spilled over into the third. In character they were all more Industry-1 than Industry-2, and their release just as the operation of Industry-2 was being transformed was undoubtedly important in keeping open a space for the values of Industry-1. As striking box-office successes, *Breaker, Gallipoli, Alice,* and *Mad Max 2* (released as *The Road Warrior* in the U.S.) each exerted a strong influence over the way 'Australia' would be screened in the third phase of the industry.

> Next time I go to a cricket match, I'm not going to throw empty beer cans at the Poms.
>
> > Comment to Bruce Beresford by an audience-member after a screening of *Breaker Morant*.

Bruce Beresford's *Breaker Morant* (1980) was a breakthrough which won audiences in Australia and overseas. It projects patriotism strongly, though mainly obliquely, as anti-Britishness. It proposes that three Australians executed by a British firing squad during the Boer War, in 1901 (the year of Australian

151

A knowing look from the sidelines. A shared female point of view subtly undermines the male preserve of surfing subculture. Nell Schofield and Jad Capelja in *Puberty Blues*.

Four different but concordant icons of Australian maleness. Jack Thompson, Edward Woodward, Bryan Brown and Lewis Fitz-Gerald in *Breaker Morant*.

Federation) were martyred by British pragmatism and the need to save face. Its definition of true-blue Australianness is channelled through the supporting role of Bryan Brown's Handcock, so that his lines cut in from the margins, from nowhere, through posture and protocol, to deliver the truth.

It is difficult to separate discussion of *Breaker Morant* from that of *Gallipoli* (1981). It is almost as if *Breaker* comes as a prophet of the shift to a 'simply' pro-Australian stance, combining a hard sell of patriotism, even narcissism, with a strong confidence that the audience's recognition would lead to commercial success. *Breaker* was slightly more equivocal, indirect, defiant, controversial. *Gallipoli*, after *Breaker*'s sucess, found a new use for the innocence of the AFC genre. In the service of a sharp Australian bias it was finally proven to be fully commercial. In doing so it persuaded commercial interests to lay claim at last to the traditional 'worthy' film.

Breaker Morant resurrects a half-forgotten, Ned-Kelly-like hero of the Australian expeditionary involvement in the Boer War. He is not a military hero, but a nationalist martyr of a slightly shameful war. Yet it is usually seen as the dress rehearsal for the Anzac legend of the bushman turned warrior, skilled at survival and success in a hostile environment; a special breed of man, physically magnificent, an individualist with initiative, contemptuous towards the caste system of the army — especially the British officers who took command; yet loyal to his mates to the death. The presence of a British command and British troops alongside the Australians is essential in both films.

In *Breaker*, the execution of two Australians for acting within inadmissible orders received from British command encapsulates the essence of the Anzac legend: an Australianness defined and revalued under British duress and contempt. And both cases — the execution of two Australians in one war, the massive and pointless sacrifice of thousands in another — offer Australian audiences an opportunity for pleasantly mournful contemplation of defeat in the most faultlessly honourable circumstances. If the actions of Morant and Handcock were ever less than honourable, the mounting injustices leading to their execution by British firing squad tend to bury that consideration. At the same time, both these films inspire an anger that unites the audience in a way that is quite seductive. The fate that cuts down the best is not blind, in this case, but cold, deliberate and *British*.

The Ned Kelly element in *Breaker* couples the spiritedness of the wild colonial boys with the inevitability of retribution from the old-world forces. The boys in *Gallipoli* play up, mock the pompous British officers in Cairo and refuse to take their war games seriously. They adopt an endearing casualness towards conditions in the trenches, though the rebellious larrikin side is played down in favour of a certain purity, and mateship is played down for friendship of a more individual and romantic kind. But the sense that the British value too lightly the lives of the volunteer Australians, especially in the diversionary manoeuvres of the Nek, is there again, in exactly the measure needed to sting Australian nationalism to life.

The oblique nationalism of *Breaker* is anticipated in the more ironic and historically specific *Newsfront*. There the animus of difference was the threat of post-war Americanisation, a more relevant stimulus than memory of turn-of-the-century British attitudes towards Australia. It's there too in a shrunken, equivocal form in *The Odd Angry Shot*, pretty well limited to the Scorpion versus Spider fight (in which the Australian spider loses to the American scorpion). It is as if the immense contention raised by American involvement in Vietnam, and the related tremors of doubt, shame and anti-American sentiment that our own even more odious involvement caused, did not exist.

But the nationalism of *Breaker* was founded on a far more exclusively male basis than *Newsfront*; so much so that it was described as 'the biggest line-up of male talent since *Sunday Too Far Away*.' The necessary association between Australianness and masculinity ('male talent') depends on a 'natural' absence of women from the picture. Gender difference scarcely figures at all, and the film is equally absent-minded when it comes to other factors that modify and undermine its simple, powerful constructions of race, class, and even history. This war which coincided with the first year of Australian independence from Britain was one of armed Boer rebellion against British colonial policy. The film draws no parallel between the manipulation of Australian and South African economies by the interests of British international capital; not even at the level of a throw-away comment which might have scored easy points. Breaker has a blind spot concerning any complications which might dissipate its focus on an heroic masculine Australian ethos.

Of course, the relative absence of women on such a field of battle is unremarkable. But their presence in flashbacks as pretexts or adornments to male action and virtue is so muting and marginalising that it heightens the sense of how profoundly they are overlooked by the film, and/or repressed by the military frame of mind. In *Sunday Too Far Away*, the exclusion of the feminine has the force of a structuring absence that distorts the male ethos. Not so in *Breaker Morant*.

The scene that stumbles most obviously because of this 'absent-mindedness' is the one in which Handcock (Bryan Brown) slips away to an assignation with the wife of a Boer farmer who is absent fighting. Later, the assignation becomes an alibi that he cannot really use because 'honour' forbids him from revealing the lady's name. But honour doesn't figure much on the woman's side. Clearly his masculinity completely overwhelms her scruples and commitments to such an extent that she sleeps with the enemy. Questioned about his morality, Handcock replies with a line calculated to bring the house down: 'They say a slice off a cut loaf is never missed.' The line invites slightly outraged amusement, and depends on Brown's likeable larrikinism to ensure that his misogyny is forgiven in advance. The line immobilises women as sexual prey, objects for male consumption, in a way that cannot be returned in kind because the implied reference to feminine virginity is gender-specific. Yet not to laugh is to be cold and humourless, unmoved by the spirited, plain-speaking Australianness of Handcock. Not to laugh is to be as much a victim of the line as if one had laughed and been caught out by its perfect timing.

The complications and contradictions of history are edited out as part of the film's dedication to a sentiment as simple as Morant's last written words, 'Australia forever, Amen!'. The drama of Australian manhood was played out on South Australian terrain, chosen to represent a South African veldt. We see a landscape that is Australian, but not presented as such. The South Australian location used to represent Gallipoli is not to be feasted on, while the South Australian location for Western Australia in that film *is*. Yet in *Breaker*, the similarity of the diegetic locale to Australian terrain is part of the film's meaning. The Australian Bushveldt Carbineers are more at home in the dry, un-European terrain than the British. They acclimatise quickly to the commando warfare, while the British line up their tents in tight, neat little rows, and shout in perfect unison, 'God save the king!' from inside, exactly at lights-out. Ironically, through the use of a disguised, renamed Australian landscape, the film concedes on one level the comparison and contrast that can be drawn between two subject nations. This is a little less fraudulent than the notion of a Boer woman waiting, mute and receptive, for her handsome enemy Australian, as if to demonstrate the instinctive affinity of Boer and Australian in 1901.

Each of the four main male characters in *Breaker Morant* articulates a different but concordant version of Australian maleness. There is a sense in which maleness may be the priority of the film, and Australianness its most natural domain. Harry 'Breaker' Morant (Edward Woodward) is Australian by election; a man of culture, a rhymer if not a poet; and a man of action, old-world Anglo-Irish and new-world Australian. Australia is represented most iconically by Handcock, the native son who speaks with a simple, blunt voice, on nationalism and the dawning anti-British feeling. Lewis Fitz-Gerald plays Whitton, the third convicted man, who is excused from the death penalty. His character is less central; he exists to show male Australianness at a younger, more innocent, less larrikin moment. And Jack Thompson plays Major Thomas, the Australian defence lawyer dragged from the obscurity of the back blocks into his first criminal case involving a capital offence. His early ineptitude belies skill that is not a part of the British plan. This courtmartial was intended as an exercise to appease Germany. Out of the ensemble, a couple is winnowed and formed: Handcock and Morant go to their firing-squad chairs on the hillside. Morant takes Handcock's hand in a gesture that is both moving and, retrospectively, complicit with the undertones of a romantic bond, perhaps a homo-erotic one.

The film is constructed as a court case, but does not resolve the questions about guilt. It proposes that prisoners were shot rather than taken to the overtaxed British concentration camps, and that a non-combatant German national probably was shot by those accused. But it proposes further that Morant's orders in each case were motivated by the wild justice of revenge for Boer atrocities committed against his dearest friend, Captain Hunt, and his men. Also, they were within the terms of British standing orders at the time — or genuinely believed to be. Even though the British desire to make an example of their conduct is hypocritical, coldly pragmatic, does this make them guilty? The film doesn't answer. It closely 'juxtaposes brutality and sentiment, a kind of lover's grief and savagery, machismo and homo-eroticism', technical guilt, and emotional injustice.[1] All ethical questions are clouded with strong feeling and nationalistic indignation.

Morant's character is invented as much as discovered. Historian Russel Ward depicts the historical Harry Morant as 'a confidence man, a cheat, a bare-faced liar, possibly the greatest male chauvinist pig of all time, a sponger, a racist, and a sadist . . .'[2] His earliest mythologiser, Sir Frank Fox, under the pen name 'Frank Renar', eulogised him thus: 'His supreme daring, his wonderful horsemanship, his buoyant good humour, his hardy drunkenness, all tended to make Morant a very king in the Australian bush . . . (who) could break words to his will as well as horses . . .'[3] Edward Woodward's Morant has just the faintest traces of the first account in the hardened gleam of his smile, the slightest measure of pre-meditation and study in his charm, the sense that he is a man's man to a fault; a small, forgivable one. Almost completely covering these traces is something like the second account, beautifully attuned to the perennial needs of male vanity and the more seasonal tide of nationalism. *Australian Playboy* wrote 'What a luminous and irresistible character he was! A personification of the idealism and national pride that marked the early Australian nationhood . . . If Harry Breaker Morant had not existed, it would have been necessary for the Australian Film Commission to invent him!'[4]

The characters in *Gallipoli* are not based, even loosely, on real people; they are functions of a mythologising urge more obviously than in any previous Australian film. The male couple, Archy and Frank, do not gradually emerge from the male ensemble: they are its organising principle. The group of mates, Billy, Barney and Snowy, are the shading which highlights the contrast of the friendship between the two romantic leads.

But theirs is a peculiar mythic speech which mutates history into something strange, unsustainable and utterly unreliable. It is an attempt at a visionary recall of the 'original' moment of the entry into myth. It is in fact more revisionist than visionary.

The obsessive concern over exact buttons on uniforms and configurations of trenches disguises the fact that this film is not historical. Rather, it is a period film which deals with a landmark legend. Attached to it are exact dates and names of a military campaign that every Australian school child learns. But the lines of history are smoothed and retouched as if with an airbrush in the name of artistic licence.

So in some ways, *Gallipoli* is the crucial example of the tendency for the AFC genre to produce a calculated innocence within the ambience of history, a delightful freedom from the burdens of experience and doubt, in the playground of the pretty and impressionistic past. The process started innocently enough, perhaps, with the gentle naivete of the early period films, oblivious to world history and film history alike. But this film tunes in to the same Australian yearning to love itself and its history that *Breaker Morant* recognised. The legend must be projected positively. *Gallipoli* identifies a responsibility to re-mythologise, as if the moment can be emptied of all but the contemporary myth and meaning. It rejects the stale glory of the myth that these young men went knowingly to self-extinction on behalf of country, King and Empire. It also rejects the long backlash of cynicism. It is oblivious to all the intervening generations of myth and counter-myth, view and reaction, right- and left-wing appropriations of the legend, as though the sentiments at the time the legend was wrought were right, simple and pure, unsullied by contradiction and conflicting political purpose. With *Gallipoli*, 'innocence' shifts something to be displayed as a winning aspect of Australia's slightly lagging culture, to a different, calculated innocence towards history and the process of reading it.

> Dear Australian Boys,
> Every Australian woman's heart this week is thrilling with pride, with exultation, and while her eyes fill with tears she springs up as I did when I read the story in Saturday's *Argus* and says, 'Thank God I am an Australian.'
> Jeannie Dobson, Ballarat Schoolteacher,
Letter to *The Argus*, April, 1915.

> There was not one of those glorious young men who I saw that day who might not himself have been Ajax, Hector or Achilles. Their almost complete nudity, their tallness and majestic simplicity of line, their rose-brown flesh burnt by the sun and purged of

all grossness by the ordeal through which they were passing, all these united to create something as near to absolute beauty as I shall ever hope to see in the world.'
Compton McKenzie, *Gallipoli Memories.*

I went back to the source of the myth and came away with a number of simple statements — and admiration for the type of man . . . a fascination specifically in their acceptance of death under certain circumstances.
Peter Weir, interviewed in *POL*, August 1981.

The 'source of the myth' was not the remaining trenches on the Gallipoli peninsula Weir visited; not even the relics of bone and metal, the empty bottle of Eno Salts he found as if handed from the grave, 'touched by history'. It was the immediately mythologising accounts of the British (Ashmead-Bartlett) and Australian (C.E.W. Bean) war correspondents who provided a powerfully romantic discourse at the very moment of national shock at the appalling casualty figures.

Weir stated that he 'wanted to show the men entering the myth', but we never glimpse them outside it. Bean's mythologising narrative depicted Australian youth as noble white savages, bred by the land for their destiny as warriors, upon whom the whole world looked in amazement. The film seeks to resurrect, as an act of 'originality', this earliest authorised version. It moves sacramentally from point to point through the chosen scenes of the legend like Stations of the Cross.

The first of three deserts is the site of boyhood where the Anzacs were formed, the Australian outback. It is the place where bodies are toughened and perfected, practical skills of survival and initiative are learnt, and a peculiarly Australian innocence is bred, strong on the right feeling, weak on the right facts. Here, Archy (Mark Lee) and Frank (Mel Gibson) meet as competitors in a running race. This was echoed as the very epitome of manhood in the 'British *Gallipoli*', *Chariots of Fire* (1981). Archy and Frank are an odd couple, fair and dark, candid and devious, bush and city, Anglo- and Celtic-Australian, winner and second-best, noble sacrifice and survivor, heroine and hero. They find themselves together, and travel the long way round to Perth, crossing a purifying desert on the way. They join up, Archy for pure, unexaminable reasons, Frank for less ineffable ones: better to be in it, and see the world, than not.

Gallipoli: the epiphany on the mountain: the male couple, Mark Lee and Mel Gibson.

The second desert is Egypt, the site of military training under British command, place of an ancient and devious civilisation in decay. Frank and Archy are reunited and climb a pyramid together, at dusk. The boys play pranks and sport before the big game begins. The final desert is the Turkish peninsula called Gallipoli, on the eastern-most shores of Europe, the old continent. Here, the fateful assignation is kept: Australian purity is tested and proved in fire and the noble white savages undergo their decimation at such a rate that even their survival in history is placed in question. Archy dies — or at least, freeze-frames; Frank lives because of Archy's self-sacrifice, to be the more enduring larrikin variant who survives the traumatic birth of the twentieth-century. As in *Picnic at Hanging Rock*, the blond are destined for sacrifice, the dark for ordinary survival.

What remains within the ritual of the narrative? Anti-British sentiment is keenly felt, but vague patriotism is substituted for the strong imperial loyalties that moved most of the volunteers. Patriotism is proposed as simple and generous. Self-sacrifice is something like an opportunity for the highest boy-scout badge attainable; there is nothing of the gleeful anticipation of blood and guts and the desire to kill that much of the memorabilia of Anzac letters and diaries suggest. As Amanda Lohrey points out,

> The Australians were used as shock troops on the Western Front in recognition of their staying powers and their appetite for a fight, and described repeatedly by contemporary observers as among the most savage and brutal of all Imperial troops. Undeniably there were elements of mateship that went to make up this brutal effectiveness but there were clearly other and less appetising elements as well.[5]

The British made the blunder and the film uses their culpability to offload the guilty strangeness of Australian volunteers invading Turkey. In Cairo, the film depicts the boys as playful rather than aggressively racist, avoiding historical evidence of the behaviour of Australian troops there.[6] As Lohrey says, 'It's interesting to imagine a Moslem version of the Gallipoli myth: racist infidel aggressor gets come-uppance'.[7] There is, however, some evidence that mutual admiration developed between Australian and Turkish troops as the campaign wore on.

Some scenes in *Breaker Morant* are structured around verbal capping in the way we have observed as common to male ensemble films, but it never really strays from inexorable forward movement through court case to execution. *Gallipoli* tends to confine the remnants of this pattern to the group of three mates which at one point includes Frank as a fourth. He, however, moves on to the higher destiny of paired friendship. The wit, like Snowy's line to the doctor who looks critically at his teeth, 'We're supposed to shoot the enemy, not bite them!', does not significantly touch the Archy-Frank dyad. It is as though with this film Williamson begins to separate the moralising from the satire in his work. The movement from contemporary Australia to the enshrined moments of its past has evidently broken the tension between the two impulses that mark his earlier writing, making work like *Phar Lap* and *The Last Bastion* seem a little inert.

So Frank and especially Archy are emptied of history, in order that they might be filled with myth. Frank has a father in Perth, with a hint of working-class background and Irish accent. Archy's father, harsh and materialistic, is rarely glimpsed; his 'true' father is the uncle (Bill Kerr) who trains him for running, reads to the children, and is uncorrupted by his quiet wealth of masculine experience. The uncle rather than the father is the progenitor. The displacement of father by uncle sidesteps the problem of adult masculinity and its lines of descent and command: its brute face is carefully turned away from the camera.

Bill Hunter's Major Barton is another kindly but helpless uncle figure who tries to find a way out of the suicidal order for his men to charge at the Nek. The night before the battle, he is glimpsed in his tent with champagne, listening to a recording of the male duet from Bizet's *The Pearl Fishers*. This scene is in perfect accord with the vision of the film in its two most powerful mythic moments. The first is the parting of the mists as the darkened ships move the troops towards Gallipoli, revealing the bizarre spectacle of lights spread over the hill and across the water, like the approach to Luna Park by night ferry on Sydney Harbour, all set to Albinoni's familiar, funereal *Adagio in G*. The second moment is even stronger: the slightly surreal underwater swimming scene off the beach at Anzac Cove, where the naked bodies are suspended in time, vulnerable and intimate. It is a scene that produces sounds and images completely alien to those of a battlefield. Bizet's *Pearl Fishers* and the Major's cultured taste for it, rich with nostalgia, comes together in this scene with Compton McKenzie's 'rose brown flesh burnt by the sun' and Peter Weir's necrophiliac taste for golden girls and boys who must 'like chimney sweepers, come to dust'. It gives a strange pre-Raphaelite cast to the myth.

Gallipoli's success shows how far characteristic deft, sardonic mockery and self-awareness can be replaced by a simple kind of Baden-Powell 'proud' view of the Anzac legend, simplified for family entertainment. And it indicates that the pulse of nationalist sentiment was at that moment fluttering so susceptibly that audiences could more than tolerate an account of the story completely lacking in irony. The Gallipoli campaign, a bungled military disaster, has become the key heroic drama around which national consciousness, under the imagined gaze of the rest of the world, has been organised. A richer ground for serious and complex irony, one that would entertain all of the elements, the romance, the epic, the tragic, and the small, stubborn sticking-points of the historic, could scarcely be imagined. But Australian popular taste in 1981 swallowed the gall of a song as bitter as Eric Bogle's 'And the Band Played Waltzing Matilda', a ballad that traces the fall of a heroic Anzac volunteer into the bitter satire of his return as a politely ignored basket case. It was adopted as a patriotic anthem, regarded as completely above irony, in great demand at ex-servicemen's clubs.

Breaker Morant is a shade more equivocal, incorporating Handcock's scepticism into the passion of a nationalistic martyrdom. But *Gallipoli* is only a mystery play. Williamson's sharp wit is confined to a small chorus of mates relegated to the margin. The tenor is religious, not conversational; it rejects the profane secularity in which Williamson developed his voice. Rapture, rather than a fresh alertness, is what the film tries to evoke. It moves inevitably towards Archy's appointment with death until his image freezes in a run that rhymes beginning and end. There is none of the dark metaphysical wit of Donne's sonnet, 'I run to death and Death meets me as fast'. Rather there is a sense of predestination, an element totally out of place in a film which purports to be historical. Archy's appointment with the highest honour is presented as something preternatural, equivalent to Miranda's appointment with the Rock: two ineffable transubstantiations of golden youth.

The television mini-series *A Town Like Alice* (1980), made by Henry Crawford and David Stevens, also participated in the surge of Australian nationalism for local, but also, eventually, American and British consumption. Like *Breaker Morant* the crucial cultural icon is Bryan Brown, this time in the central role of Joe Harmon, the heart of the romance, 'Australia'. As in *Breaker*, Brown's Australianness is composed against a background of Britishness in the form of his love interest, Helen Morse's Jean; the avuncular guardian solicitor of Jean's inheritance (Gordon Jackson); and England itself, which Joe visits in search of Jean. Jean's Englishness is part of the complexity of their love affair; consequently the treatment of Englishness is gentler than in *Breaker* or *Gallipoli*. Nevertheless, it is still used as the background which defines otherness. Jean must choose love, Australia and Joe within the imperatives of the narrative to form, at long last, a couple.

As in *Breaker* and *Gallipoli*, there is the mythos of the Australian bushman at war, articulated this time literally as the larrikin suffering crucifixion. Joe is crucified by the Japanese prison guards for his theft of poultry to feed the starving, displaced women and children on their endless forced march. Miraculously, he survives, unbeknown to the audience and Jean, so that eventually we may see his resurrection. His act of mateship is made, notably, on behalf of women, and in particular Jean, to whom this act is also a declaration of love.

Once more, Bryan Brown's persona is posited as a loner, an ingenious improvisor, the lean and laconic object of the narrative's desire. He bends rules on behalf of human impulse. The wartime backdrop which colours the first two episodes in Malaya, in this case, is less important in itself than as the first of two major voyages of endurance that make Jean's rite of passage towards Joe; for his very Australianness already qualifies him as a survivor. But in this love affair between Britain and Australia, Jean has gradually to face a destiny not in cosy English village life, nor in an air-conditioned colonial office, but in harsh, masculine, unbounded outback Australia. She has to survive the tests of Malaya and Willstown; she also has to survive the rigours of almost perversely delayed gratification. It takes several years, and several transcontinental searches, before they come together in Australia to marry. Even that desire is further tested in the extended final

Treeless landscape: the start of a family tree. Bryan Brown and Helen Morse looking just off screen to the mythic future in *A Town Like Alice*.

episode in which the characters run through a narrative obstacle course, an episode that shows how strongly Neville Shute's original novel imprinted the mini-series with the theme of 'populate or perish', a post-war concern which seems somewhat superfluous in the 1980s.[8]

The end of the long narrative march is the black-and-white family album snaps of Joe and Jean seen full-frame at the end. They smile zestfully, the ideal fifties' family, as they hold aloft their two small children. Archetypically, Joe holds the slightly older son, Jean carries the smaller daughter. Their wedding fulfills our desire, after so much titillation, to see them as a formal couple; but this shot, from some unspecified moment in the happily ever after, past that end-point, is a glimpse of the story's true investment in our fascination with the immediate pre-history of our time. Here is where we have come from. Here's the post-war baby boom which was, after all, in the terms of 'populate or perish', the whole point of the war.

Here, too, the lightly buried sub-theme of the novel is unearthed: the need to populate 'the empty north' against 'the Asian threat'. Much of the obstacle course that is the final part of the narrative, in which the couple is reunited in outback Australia but not yet fully at ease, is created by Jean's desire to alter life and customs in Willstown. It's 'a crook place for a woman, no mistake', but it could be 'a town like Alice'. She develops, with her inherited money, a ladies' shoe factory which employs local girls, and an ice-cream parlour as an alternative social amenity to the all-male pub. Jean brings a 'civilizing' influence which draws women out of their social invisibility and into the marriage market. The curt forewoman she imports from Britain for the factory is actually a curious echo of the penal colony notion of the female factory as a curb to female licence, and a means of channelling it into socially useful purposes. The factory brings the girls in to Willstown and fulfills the defined post-war needs of a decentralised, developing manufacturing sector, while the ice-cream parlour draws them into the light of marriageability.

Jean meets with resistance, even from Joe: 'You can't just come in here and change everything'. However, she eventually succeeds in bringing her modest portion of British capital and 'civilising' values to this obscure township at the ends of the earth. Meanwhile, the accident that befalls Joe's neighbour while 'poddy dodging' Joe's unbranded calves, provides a final rite of passage for Jean's acceptance by the community and her acceptance of it and its harshness. She survives the rigours of an epic ride for help across rising rivers. She both returns the act of self-sacrifice made by Joe in Malaya and proves herself to be his mate in both senses. Interestingly, the event ends with a scene in the Willstown hospital where she is treated for exhaustion. Joe visits her, a trifle sheepishly, and is unwilling to kiss her in public. Jean talks wryly of being saddle-sore. The scene prefigures her future confinement during childbirth and the essentially boyish public role that Joe will play then as he hedges shyly around such 'women's business'. Similarly, consider how Annie's illegitimate pregnancy is treated: the men are in on a secret which they encourage the women to keep from them.

So a fable of Australian-British relations is told in terms of man and woman. It is the story of the transit of the female to the territory of the male, and the fruitfulness of their union. They have 'everyman' names: an 'ordinary Joe' and Jean, a feminisation of John. The demands of a protracted love-story shape their romance as grand and exotic, within the epic of Malaya, then turn it slowly into the ordinary by making it drive towards family within conservative, male-dominated Australian rural life. The mini-series foregrounds the character of Noel, Jean's financial guardian and the narrator. It casts him, with his gentlemanly chivalry, as a potential rival to Joe in finally inadequate contrast to the charm of Joe's laconic directness. In Malaya, Joe is a daring larrikin romantic; back in Australia those qualities are hidden by the practicalities and reserve of outback station life; in England he is seen as a man's man, unperturbed by the class intricacies of English life, his essential Australianness undiluted. Jean has to bow to these qualities, sympathise with them and love them. She does not expect them to change; they are already perfectly adapted to their place of origin. If the chivalry is missing from the surface of an ordinary Australian 'joe', it was written large in Malaya, where he displayed a cheeky but genuinely chivalrous 'natural' duty towards women in distress. The ordinary family snapshot, finally presented as the mythic destiny of the narrative, demands the long stretch of the third and fourth parts in order to convert grand passion to everyday productivity; a conversion that so much 'women's fiction' enjoins us to acknowledge as necessary and dignified.

The cusp of the second phase is marked by the release of five films with strong commercial success in the summer of 1981-2: *Gallipoli, Winter of Our Dreams, Puberty Blues, Mad Max 2*, and the summer was capped by the release of *The Man from Snowy River* (discussed as the leading film of the third phase, below). All were financed and made before 10B(a) took effect. Each took a very different set of soundings of popular taste. *Winter* and *Puberty Blues* were firm local successes, quite regionalist in their primary address to an audience, but different in genre and tone. *Mad Max 2* was a runaway success in Australia and a considerable success overseas as *The Road Warrior*; it is at once candid and careless about its Australianness, which is a bonus to the way that it works as an action thriller, with more romance and less horror than *Mad Max*, despite even more *outre* art design.

Winter of Our Dreams is a quiet film, about a too-quiescent conscience. It is John Duigan's first Sydney film — he had been well-established in Melbourne — and it was made on a spectacularly low budget for a feature that skilfully packaged Bryan Brown and Judy Davis as romantic leads. Sydney's beauty is used to play up the drift towards moral and emotional desolation; it is not an insider's Sydney, but one highly responsive to the airy, maritime and sandstone qualities of the place at changing moments of the day. Bryan Brown (Rob) and Judy Davis (Lou) are used, against the grain of their previous roles, to portray an atypical film romance that leads to nothing. That is, unless you count the bleak, unwanted moments of self-perception for Rob, a one-time student radical ten years further down the track of a prosperous, easy life; or the slim chance Lou has of climbing out of the grind of her heroin habit supported by prostitution. Rob doesn't do much to open up her narrow hope of escape, beyond being contact with somebody 'outside', somebody at least partly responsive, uncritical, and almost fearsomely attractive to her. One of the best things in the film is this sense of her strong, frustrated desire for him which has to do with loneliness, lust, weakness, the contrariness of fate, and nothing at all to do with the conventions of male sexual fantasy. Contrast might be drawn with *Petersen*, for example.

Lou hopes to be liked by Rob. His ability to pretend not to notice this, nor its enormous consequences for her, is the risky business at the heart of the film. It is the device through which the lapse of political commitment is exposed for our contemplation: it looks at what happened to the political muscles and reflexes developed by the characters in their twenties, under the impact of material comfort and an 'open marriage' in their thirties. Duigan's 'Melbourneness' shows up in this moral drama. There is a sense of subtle unease towards easy-going Sydney, whose sixties' libertarianism has, by Melbourne standards, been simplified to seventies' hedonism.

Lou is attracted equally to Rob as he is described in his younger days in the diary of her friend Lisa, who has died of an overdose. The pattern repeats itself: Rob held back from Lisa; now he holds back from Lou, for all the 'openness' of his marriage and view of the world. Through Lisa's eyes, Lou sees and admires the earlier Rob in heroic moments of political action during the Vietnam moratorium movement. Rob now is the ironic, diffident owner of a radical bookshop. His wife, Gretel (Cathy Downes), is an academic who takes full advantage of her supply of sexually available students and the open arrangement she has with Rob.

Lou, the street prostitute, is shocked by what she discovers of their marriage and misreads Rob's encouragement of their mutual friendship as the sexual interest of an unattached male. When she stays the night and suffers a lonely, agonising heroin withdrawal in their guestroom, Rob and Gretel are slightly repelled. The more abstract sense of Rob and Gretel's moral and emotional withdrawal becomes concrete as they avert their gaze while helping Lou through the crisis. In the last analysis, Lou would not be a likely sexual partner or serious friend for Rob. The gap of education and material circumstances amounts to a class difference which causes him to withdraw, just as he withdraws from Lou's desire for him and her vulnerability.

The historic resonances of Lou's domain, King's Cross and Potts Point, and the inner-city harbour suburb of Balmain which is Rob's, are well treated. They are two peninsulas into the harbour with the city in between, a pink dream of the Sydney dusk. In another sense, they are two bohemias gone to seed in different ways: Potts Point and the Cross went to seed after one war, and were ploughed under to become the Vietnam era rest and recreation facilities for American servicemen. They soon flowered into a bed of prostitution, heroin and booze. Rob's bookshop, which uses the once-famous Exiles Bookshop as its location, is just outside the Cross, just as his life is tangential to the political history which physically and economically transformed the area. Balmain was once an inner-city, working-class bastion; through the sixties and seventies it became gentrified by the invading middle class and a section of its intelligentsia. Rob and Gretel's beautifully situated old terrace house above the harbour has been transformed inside into a split-level middle-class dream, just as the suburb has changed beyond the dreams and means of most of its original residents. New residents like Rob and Gretel can, however, maintain their radical credentials by living in a 'working-class' suburb. This knowledge is a bonus for Sydney viewers, neither essential to the film nor heavily relied upon by it; but the cultural and geographical conformation of the place is more scrupulously attended to than in the films that use Sydney merely as a striking backdrop, in which the Opera House, the Harbour Bridge and the harbour itself so frequently feature. Even a highly Sydney-oriented film like *Heatwave* 'cheated' freely with its locations.

To visit Rob, Lou comes by ferry over the dark water. He meets the boat, brings her back, in a sense, to the land of the living, the 'clean and well-lit space' of his house. They explore each other's worlds a little, then Rob pulls back. At the end of her visit, Lou goes back, 'cold turkey', into her own difficult world. At the end of the film, she joins — for company, and safety from herself — the anti-uranium vigil on the Woolloomooloo wharves, at the foot of those old McElhone steps which once connected the rich and the poor of Sydney. Her name is linked to 'the Loo': Woolloomooloo, and the old euphemism for toilet. It is also an abbreviated, masculinised female name.

Lou's addiction, and Rob's withdrawal and lack of sexual feeling in their love affair are proposed almost as two forms of the same condition. Both are exiled from themselves and both glimpse this briefly in each other, although Lou moves shakily but more emphatically to act on this realisation than Rob does. In this asynchronous meeting of worlds, decades and politiques, Lou on her precipice is closer to living in the real present of her life than Rob is, for all his advantages.

Bryan Brown and Judy Davis work beautifully together in their roles as emotional and intellectual poles of this highly controlled moral encounter. Bryan Brown received some reviews implying that he didn't possess the intellectual resonance demanded by the character; but his ability to deliver intellectually complex characterisations is well-demonstrated in *Third Person Plural*. In *Winter* he is an intellectual frozen in attitude and response, and he presents this face of anomie extremely well. At the same time, he can provide enough of the likeability and self-aware, but unselfconscious, attractiveness of his typical persona, to make Lou's emotional addiction to him credible. Until *High Tide*, Lou remained Judy Davis' best role. It is a marvellous emotional essay on the layers of abrasiveness, and near-fatal vulnerability, in Lou's pitifully defenceless, uninformed quest for self-knowledge. The two crowning, related scenes of their stillborn relationship are silent, private, brief reaction scenes: Lou sits alone behind her door in Lisa's old room with the makings of the lunch she was to have with Rob, after he has told her he's sorry, he can't come, he has a long-standing friendly cricket-match with a bunch of other prosperous lefties; and Rob, alone in the locker room, reluctant to join the match, allowing himself a moment of sharp self-distaste at the belated realisation of his own callousness.

Bryan Brown's Rob marks a point from which the distance between *Winter of Our Dreams* and films constructed around male Australianness can be measured. This film contains a moral argument far more fully worked out than the courtroom drama of *Breaker Morant*. It is a film of ideas despite the fact that it is constructed as a series of emotional possibilities and choices. Its Australianness, though beyond doubt, is never part of its pitch to an audience. It inhabits a winter of discontent, and even if the Australian winter is fairly mild, there isn't a single whiff of sweaty nationalism. Perhaps a case could be made for 'cool' versus 'hot' Australianness, aligned with distinctions between the critical versus the promotional, and the regionalist versus the 'naive' nationalist.

Puberty Blues recalls *Palm Beach* with its partly regional surfing-culture emphasis, but it is a straighter narrative, centred this time on two girls rather than boys who submit themselves with gusto to their rites of passage, both sexual and social. Debbie (Nell Schofield) and Sue (Jad Capelja) are credible, ordinary girls from the southern suburbs of Sydney, which are substantially prosperous without strong class or cultural pretensions. What lifts the film above more typical teenage sub-genres is the intimate portrayal of the two as they help each other elude parents, guard secret lives, undergo and survive their humble initiation into the dubious privileges of a surfie gang, and finally shrug it off to pass on to better things — like taking to the surf themselves instead of just loyally watching. The occasional use of cheeky, confidential voice-over gives character and authority to the film's address. Equally, the use of specific Cronulla locales and references enhances the sly wit of the film. It became a cult movie in those southern suburbs.

The girls worm their way into the Greenhills gang, and confine themselves with masochistic relish to its prescribed female roles; waiting, watching, getting food, being motherly, and having sex as required. It is, perhaps, the way the film teases this masochistic impulse to conform and be accepted, that won it such a strong audience; it relishes the moment with irony from the security of experience beyond it. Again, the past tense of the voice-over helps to establish this safe but sympathetic vantage.

But even the virtually silent scenes create a sense both of rapturous submission and ironic distance. The cake-making scene is a nice example. While the boys play cards through a boring wet day, refusing to 'do anything', the girls make a packet cake, decorate it and present it with a small flourish. The boys jab their hands into it and shovel it into their mouths as they play on. They barely acknowledge the cake's makers. The girls look at each other. No cake remains for them. Only a certain realisation.

In the end they decide to have their cake — and wait, almost without interest, to see if they can eat it too. They buy a surfboard and take it down to the beach, to the loud derision of the gang, the girls as well as the boys. Through the day, they work at it. By late afternoon they're managing to stay on and even, tentatively, to stand for a moment. The gang watches more silently; the girls are now impressed. At the end of the day, they walk away from the beach, jointly carrying their surfboard after their first really *great* beach day. Not only has their task been absorbing, they have broken with the confining desire to please: a truly radical break for ex-Greenhills girls.

Debbie and Sue are loyal mates without constant overt gestures proclaiming their mateship in the male style. It is interesting how little time is devoted to the males of the gang and their interaction in a film directed by that refiner of ockerdom, Bruce

Beresford. But Margaret Kelly's script, from Gabriel Carey and Kathy Lette's book of loose, provocative reminiscences, strongly proposes the girls, however passive, as subjects, and the boys as merely their temporary adornments, of little individual importance or character. It's a pleasant turning of tables, a line of female resistance in a wry, well-judged moral comedy.

George Miller and Byron Kennedy's *Mad Max 2* is a more refined, story-conscious sequel to *Mad Max*. Once again we are in a landscape in which petrol is scarce and cars are a fetish, but this time the traces of urban reality and identifiable vehicles have been obliterated. The country is dry, abstract and the means of transport fantastic. It is more decisive about its romantic form: the alienated hero is impelled to act on behalf of the civilised good by his own code of honour, despite his reluctance and asocial position. Like the original, the sequel is strongly, intuitively genre-based, but the hybrid, even mutant, forms of genre used, the powerful invention within convention, have no simple description. *Mad Max* built its blockbuster success out of dubious elements: fascination with violence, particularly that generated by people and machinery against other people, especially women; and the machinery of the car-crash and motorbike gang films. These were crossed with stray elements of samurai, ninja and futuristic fantasy films.

Mad Max 2 uses similar elements, but greatly increases the adventure and romance. There is a consciousness of the formation and trial of the hero incipient at the end of the first *Mad Max*, when, out of nihilistic revenge, he emerges as invincible arbiter of wild justice. So in *Mad Max 2* there are obvious elements of the western: the outpost besieged by barbarians, the intervention of the maverick hero, the extended chase-battle sequence *a la Stagecoach*. There are also echoes of Roman gladiatorial and Viking siege epics, after *Ben Hur*, *The Vikings* and *The Warlord*, for example. This much stronger and more decisive element of romance almost negates that of the anti-romantic, late movie creepshow. The highly charged, grotesque imagery of Hummungus' world is identifiably demonic, and can thus be clearly opposed in a way that a creeping anarchy which threatens to spill over and saturate the entire world cannot.

Max (Mel Gibson) by now is

> ... the kind of character that is doomed to wander, always serving other things, serving a greater order. He himself will not be the leader of that new order ... he does everything with a code of honour. He wouldn't kill unnecessarily. But it is just him and the world. And like all those heroes, inadvertently, they go on to serve a greater purpose.[9]

In this film he is not a lone hero; he sharing that function to some extent with the Gyro Captain (Bruce Spence) and the Feral Kid (Emil Minty).

Bruce Spence's character is somewhat similar to Steve Bisley's role as Goose in *Mad Max*; the Captain and Max form a male couple in which he is the helper who provides a comic foil. Like Goose, he traces his origins to the natural world. He is characterised by his leap out of the earth, his snakes, the hyperbolic gangling posture perfected by Spence in *Stork*, and the gyrocopter, which seems to fly more by intuition than technology. But this time, he is not a sacrifice to the violence Max must meet; he is a survivor, even a hero, and in the end a leader of the White Tribe to the promised land.

The Feral Kid is closely linked to Max also: his child in a way, he is in the process of crossing from animal wildness to socialisation. The narrative voice-over turns out to belong to the child grown old and become the leader of the White Tribe, as he looks back on the turning point in his life, the brief entry and exit of the maverick Max, like the kid who once knew Shane. Max's gift to the child, the musical toy that plays 'Happy Birthday', is not a casual one. Max's child died in the first film. The Feral Kid is not a helpless being in need of protection; he is a primitive animal being in need of something that will recruit him to the social group. Max gives him music to initiate his birth into the group by relating him to Max as mentor and father. In the last movement of the narrative, the child stows away on the oil tanker driven by Max as decoy to outwit Hummungus' tribe. He and Max survive the chase, battle and wreckage. When the dust clears, they are reborn from their close encounter with death together, the child lying across Max's stomach in his arms, like a newborn babe with its mother. But Max must be left behind like all maverick heroes, fast receding into the darkness as the White

The delirium of speed and the ecstatic threat of violent death. Machines of destruction in *Mad Max 2*: *Ben Hur* and *Stagecoach* collide head-on with futurism.

The hyperbolic, gangling posture, perfected by Bruce Spence in *Stork*, is amplified by his mad machinery in the role of the Gyro Captain in *Mad Max 2*.

Tribe takes the road to the coast. He can give social birth to the child, but cannot be part of society himself — or not in this film, at this stage of the cyclical generation of the hero.

The setting is the dry outback (near Broken Hill), the heartland of Australian mythology. It is presented as a harsh moral landscape that could as easily be Arizona, or the badlands in general, with the dryness of a moral drought as well as a post-apocalyptic petrol drought. But even if the landscape is not invested with the virtues of essential Australianness, and the words are spoken with only some sort of future-world accent, there are more moments of privileged recognition available here than in the original *Mad Max*. The character of the narrative, perhaps the genre, and certainly the hero or heroes, are all more Australian.

These moments include things like Max's Australian blue cattle dog — perhaps another Goose substitute — with its grinning, alert anarchic face. Others are the can of Bonza dog food, the silver boomerang of the Feral Kid and the bit of business in which the mechanics assess needed repairs on the tanker. More importantly, there is a stronger, less easily pinpointed sense in this sequel that Miller's intuitive generic fiction comes as much from this culture as from international, that is, U.S. derived, popular narrative traditions. If Max is a warrior-hero, he's a reluctant one, with something of the Bryan Brown persona's quality of being 'on to himself'. There's no outrage in Max when he finds sand and not oil in the tanker at the end. He smiles. He knew, or might have known, that the 'civilised' White Tribe would talk of honour, but not tell *him* the whole story; and this is a profoundly reserved character who rarely pulls a smile. Another example: when Max captures the Gyro Captain, he toys for a while with the notion of making him a captive slave. He sets up a bow contraption in the car trained at the Captain's neck, with the dog entrusted with the decision whether or not to release the bow. The dog flinches as he spots a rabbit from the car window and Spence's eyes bulge with terror. Later, it transpires that the bow wasn't loaded. The Gyro Captain once pulled a gun on Max, and this is just Max's laconic idea of a useful black joke which would keep him quiet until it is safe to release him. Bruce Spence is, of course, a character actor who is himself an icon, and this quality is fully used in the role, making the Captain the most likeable character. The admirable qualities are reserved for Max.

It is also worth noting that the Feral Kid first appears in animal skins, holding aloft a razor-sharp steel boomerang, against old stock rails near the White Tribe's fortress. The connotations are of a latter-day white Aboriginality crossed with technology.

The Hummungus, leader of the barbarians who have lain siege to the White Tribe's oil refinery compound, is even more a blend of technology and demonic, rather than primitive, Nature. His face is masked by metal grafted to the bone, his voice is electronically assisted, his obsessions are those of the relentless automaton, beyond reason. His chief warrior, Wez, is by comparison the embodiment of pure athletic barbaric power in his Ninja-like leaps and somersaults. The names are not incidental. The latinised Hummungus suggests a blend of human and fungoid qualities. 'Pappagallo' (Mike Preston), leader of the White Tribe, means 'parrot' in Italian, and his speechifying proves empty, matching the impotence signalled by his crippling leg wound. The play with names suggests the morality play which is never far below the surface, and points to the free association in the storytelling. The Gyro Captain is a reincarnation of Gyro Gearloose; Jim Goose struts like a goose; kundalini is a socially repressed and potentially metamorphic energy of the body. And so on.

With the shift towards this form of adventure romance, women become even less important in themselves than they were as objects of mesmeric violence in *Mad Max*. Jessie in *Mad Max* is set up as a ten-pin for the violence that will fell her. Although she delivers the castrating kick in the balls to the Toecutter, this one desperate but semi-liberated act, with its symbolic power, is merely a trigger for what the narrative has ready and set to go off. There is at the outset a suspicion that women and children will fall victim, which creates an obscene audience desire to have the threat to Jessie resolved by having the threat of Jessie removed; then the audience can quickly identify with Max's loss. The complexity of this creates a space for Jessie as a character; she is even given odd distinguishing characteristics, like playing a trombone.

But in *Mad Max 2*, the feminine is extremely marginal. The warrior girl of the White Tribe has a relatively unimportant role before her death in battle, and she does not really tempt Max romantically. The other White women are familiarly feminine in the terms of the western: obstructions to action, uninfluential voices pleading for peace, or soft instinctual things who need protection, and can thus win proto-heroes like the Gryo Captain to civilisation. The more interesting aspect of the feminine can be uncovered in various masculine shadings and guises across the heroes and villains. The Hummungus has an almost albino, androgynous lover on a chain who is killed by the Feral Kid's whizzing, lethal metal boomerang. The Kid himself is a touch androgynous, with long wild hair and animal furs; he is essentially the child of the male couple, Max and the gentler, more 'feminine' Gyro Captain, who can be fooled, his snake captured and his independence forfeited.

Above all, the entire tribe of Hummungus, even with its small scattering of female members, together with the perennial outsider, Max, constitutes a violent, perversely attractive male principle pitted against the more passive, captive female principle of the White Tribe. The imagery is of leather and metal against soft flowing home-spun material, relentless nomads against settlers with domestic animals, promiscuity against domesticity, action against words. The White Tribe is not purely good, of course. They are foolish and hypocritical, and furthermore they possess the technology of oil; they carry with them the infection of the old civilisation. Max does not trust or like them, except for his brief affection for the Feral Kid, who is their future, not their present; so we do not entrust them with too much identification. And of course, to be a warrior, Max must remain outside the feminine of civilisation and move on alone, to the next stage of his evolution as hero in the third film in the sequence.

7

The Third Phase (1981-?): Middle-Aged Spread?

In the boom year of 1982-3, following the tax-induced restructuring of the industry, the pattern of cycles, genres and types momentarily wavered and blurred in the rush. Gradually, as we have argued, the pattern of loyalties and assumptions of Industry-1 and Industry-2 emerged, and many of those films of transition can be interpreted in the light of these tendencies. By 1984-5, a sense of aesthetic stagnation had become increasingly difficult to ignore; we discuss this in the Epilogue to this volume. However, the real work of sorting symptomatically the plethora of quickly-mounted films beyond the mid-eighties cannot begin until a greater historical distance is achieved, and the nature of the commercial and cultural lives of these films can be assessed beyond the fairly crude identification of two industries, shadowing each other after the break in the established pattern of funding.

By the mid-eighties, of course, there has been a partial reversion to the use of government investment as a means to control the character of the industry and its films. The progressive symbiosis of the feature film and television mini-series industries continues, encouraged by the fact that they share the same government funding mechanisms. So the interpenetration of genres, styles, narrative cycles, as well as personnel and finance of the two forms can be expected to increase. This is not just a matter of, for example, the AFC genre, somewhat adapted, coming home to roost in the mini-series. As *The Man from Snowy River*

Cultural energy of the American musical teamed with judiciously overstated Australianness. John O'May, Jo Kennedy, Ross O'Donovan, Ned Lander and cast in *Starstruck*.

Glorious, repetitive, redundant 'proof' of male potency. Tom Burlinson as *The Man From Snowy River*.

The Third Phase (1981-?): Middle-Aged Spread? 181

demonstrates, it can also be a matter of finding a means of transferring that which pleases the diverse television audience to the big screen and writing it large, creating an even more extreme caricature, turning the Australian landscape into a widescreen panorama populated by simple, conservative heroic versions of ourselves, winners all, lucky again.

> For me, *Snowy* is a love letter to Australia, and for Geoff, a love letter to the mountains. We can't understand why any filmmaker would want to depress an audience. If you want to get depressed, turn on the television and watch the news.
>
> George Miller and Geoff Burrowes,
> interview in *Cinema Papers*,
> June 1982.

The Man from Snowy River, made by 'the other' George Miller (not of Kennedy-Miller), and Geoff Burrowes, marketed by showbusiness entrepreneur, Michael Edgley, both capped the nationalistic trend of the second phase and stimulated the strenuous commercialism that strongly marks the present, post-tax-incentive phase of the industry. *Snowy River* was not just the most successful *Australian* film to that date, but was the most successful film in Australia overall until overtaken by *Crocodile Dundee* in 1986. It revised many conventional wisdoms about the limits of the local marketplace and its appetite for an heroic Australian fiction drawn in the broad strokes of melodrama, the likes of which had not been seen since Ken G. Hall's Cinesound films of the thirties, such as *The Squatter's Daughter*, *Tall Timbers* or *The Silence of Dean Maitland*.

The title and climax are based on a famous school-anthology bush ballad by A.B. 'Banjo' Paterson. The melodrama is constructed to frame the poem's story of a boy's ride into manhood by bringing back, against all odds, a valuable colt from a mob of brumbies. It is a passionate, old-fashioned and romantic portrayal of the rite of passage in which a lad 'gains his spurs' and masters colts, stallions, brood-mares, mountains, women and male respect. The film is a boldly schematic, almost emblematic narrative, with an unashamedly clear-cut hero (Tom Burlinson), who is nevertheless bland enough for any viewer to identify with. It embellishes all this with surpassing Marlboro-Country imagery, and editing that varies between that of serviceable television drama for dialogue, and pyrotechnic television-advertising for action. The project was backed by detailed research into late-nineteenth-century mountain-man horsemanship, tackle and lore.

The film is structured around a number of symmetries, exemplified most strongly by Kirk Douglas's two roles as brothers. His performances, unlike those of the rest of the cast, are themselves strongly melodramatic. The pattern emerges: two brothers, Harrison and Spur, one a rich cattle king on the lowlands, one a poor miner in the mountains; two romances, past and present, in which Spur rivals Harrison for Matilda, and Jim rivals Harrison for Matilda's and Harrison's daughter Jessica; Spur as Jim's substitute father following the death of his true father, which makes Jim and Jessica virtual cousins.[1]

Then there is the recurrent story of the horses, laden with symbolism and moments of symmetry. The colt that got away in the story of fraternal rivalry over Matilda is now king of the brumbies, albeit a rather ancient one, if you do the maths. Jim's father's death is in part due to the rogue brumby's success in wooing away their valued mare, Bess. It was Jim who stopped his father from killing that rearing male symbol in the moonlight; so Jim is unwittingly responsible. He must leave the mountains until he has earned his place in them: his manhood. His entry into the world of Harrison and Jessica takes place when he 'masters' the new expensive colt just as Jessica seems to be losing control of it. Breaking the colt begins their romance. The rebellious brumby again disrupts this idyll; Jim incurs Harrison's wrath for riding the colt, and is dispatched to the mountains to recover lost stock. In this first high-country mission, he saves Jessica and restores her to Harrison. Jessica may be strong and wilful on low ground, but 'up there' she quickly finds herself in dire feminine need of rescue. When the colt is cut loose by Jim's jealous rival to join the brumby mob, Jim's second high-country mission is to recover him, and this becomes his rite of passage from stripling lad to man.

Harrison never had Matilda or her colt under complete control, and his weakness is symbolised by the freedom of the rogue brumby stallion which rampages through two generations of romance, as well as the castrating wound he inflicted on his brother — that is, himself. But Jim alone, under the gaze of another legend, Clancy of the Overflow, defies death and takes the plunge into legend that allows him to retrieve and tame not only the colt,

The Third Phase (1981-?): Middle-Aged Spread? 183

but the whole brumby mob, including the stallion, Bess, and lots of other good brood mares.

The music swells and the final scene overflows in the manner necessary to mark out this making of a man: it begins as Jessica runs to the stockrails to see the returning men, but where's Jim? Far behind them, dead-pan, single-handed, silent except for the cracking of his stock whip, Jim gloriously appears, in command of the entire mob of brumbies, colt, stallion, brood mares and all. His hat is pulled low and the shadow masks his eyes. His face, set in a scornful look, and his mastery of the subdued mob with a whip, are almost sinister, suggesting violence held in check by discipline alone. At first Jessica smiles, relieved to see him victorious; then in a second reaction shot she registers awe and even a shade of fear. Defeated, Harrison offers this new dominant male a cash reward, which Jim rejects. He will instead come back for his 'ten good brood mares in the mob'. His eyes shift coolly to Jessica: '. . . And whatever else is mine'. Jessica, the spirited girl who earlier accused her father's marriage plans of being 'a breeding programme for your daughter', now passively and gratefully accepts her place among the fertile brood claimed by the newly and rightfully arrogant Jim. His look to her may be a question, whether she is his, but it also asserts his dominance to such a degree that she can only watch in silence. Harrison gruffly concedes the lad his due. 'He's not a lad, brother', says Spur, 'he's a man'. And Clancy pronounces the handle to the new-born legend, 'The Man from Snowy River'. Jessica watches the new Jim ride out. At last he softens and smiles at her before urging his wonder-horse, the magical gift from Spur, into a gallop back home to the mountains, to a full symphonic rendition of 'Waltzing Matilda', the 'real' national anthem.

What emblematic meanings emerge from this story, with its symmetrical past which gradually resolves in the present? The strongest link is between horses, mountains and sexuality. Mounted on a single horse, after the rescue and its idyllic conclusion, Jim and Jessica are framed by the mountain-top vista. Just before they kiss, Jim says that the mountains are like a high-spirited horse: you can never take them for granted. Jessica adds: 'It's the same with people, too', meaning that, as a man takes care with a spirited horse or an unpredictable high-country climate, so he must take care in handling that other elemental, blindly wilful force, the feminine. It is a plea for mastery, sympathetic, even humble though it may be.

> Geoff looked after the authenticity of the mountain men while I looked after the overlay of character, the historical authenticity. This is why Jim is a very sexist person. It is historically accurate.
>
> That brumby stallion is not meant to be a lovable character — otherwise, how the hell would you sustain the end of the film, which is a kid removing horses from their native freedom? You would alienate your audience altogether if the final scene is Jim locking up a bunch of nice horses that are going to end up as glue.
>
> *Cinema Papers* interview, *op.cit.*

Jim's innate conservative sexism must be just as defensible, in emotional terms, as his revenge against and conquest of the wild horses, although the interview doesn't attend to this point. The film is not a recreation of the 1890s, but a recreation in the 1980s, and Jim's sexism must be incorporated into something honourable, like the natural, dramatic birth of a hero and a man. For a man to come forward, a woman must fall back in silent appreciation. Jessica and her aunt's female, 'feminist' stroppiness pays the audience in advance for the heavy interest exacted by the final, crucial, witnessed ceremony, of Jim's passage to manhood. Jessica has no corresponding initiation, only stages of subjection into a passionate acquiescence by the mountains, her need for rescue and the sight of Jim's unmatchable display. The film does not explore 'personhood', but rather a process which is specifically male. It is laboured almost hysterically by the narrative as though to compensate for some unnamed fear that there may after all be no male rite equivalent to the precise and weighty flesh-and-blood matter of giving birth. In this sense, male sexual potency is constantly tested but never finally proven, while female sexuality has its own magical, living proof. The film circles around this fact without confronting it, and instead constructs glorious, repetitive, redundant 'proof' of male potency.

The closest it gets to discussing this unarticulated central concern are the contemptuous or possessive discussions of brood-mares and breeding programmes, bloodlines of horses and gentry, and the 'mongrel mountain-men'. Jessica's spiritedness can be tolerated and negotiated, even valued, like that of the best horses or the challenging high country, as long as it can be seen as a phase that will pass into an acceptance of her place and biological destiny under a man's regime. In the best tradition of Mills and Boon, her rebelliousness never mocks the hero, but serves to provide a little fire for the romance. Only an old maid, like her aunt, denied her womanly potency, can be expected to continue as the sounding-brass of mild, feminist rebelliousness, so long after her time. The conservative narrative structure will negate Jessica's potency by defining her as future mother, suitably mated woman and necessary part of Jim's horse-breeding establishment in the high country. Her mother, Matilda, is misunderstood as a deceitful woman, a Jezebel like the whimsical gold mine that withholds its riches until it chooses. She had to die in childbirth. Such potency could not be allowed to survive; it had already 'castrated' Spur with a gun-shot blast to the leg, and ensured that the true manhood of Harrison was stillborn, over-determined by his doubts and jealousies.

The errant, rearing brumby stallion receives from the narrative Harrison's mark of Cain. It appears as harbinger of catastrophe and trial for Jim: it 'kills' his father and, together with the new, valuable colt, sets Jim two of his three tasks. Its appearances gradually bring the repressed story of the older generation to the surface, and its eventual capture by Jim resolves both stories, present and past. With this act, Jim publicly achieves a faultless, 'true' manhood, displaces the tyrant Harrison and wins the hand of the princess, who, as in any fairytale quest, is the king's most precious possession surrendered to the conquering prince. Jim is now unimpeded by fathers: one is dead, one displaced, and Spur is, as he emphasises, more of a partner. In fairytale terms, he is the wizard who presents the magical gift, an ordinary-looking horse which turns the ordinary-looking Jim into a hero.

The fairytale is subsumed with relative ease into the slightly crankier and more excessive structure of melodrama in which there are two opposing brothers, a buried rivalry and feud, the discovery of a lost uncle, and a temporarily obscured patrimony for Jessica. This last element seems less gratuitous in view of the imbalance between male and female rites of passage that are so important as the unconscious source of the narrative's meanings. It illustrates the male problem for which Jim's triumph is an attempted solution. But the other elements seem to exist as part of the melodrama itself, stylised and excessive embroidery of the moral pattern.

The gears of the melodrama grind a little too audibly in the scenes that bring the past and present love stories together, such as the confrontation between Jim and Harrison. Harrison enters Jessica's bedroom by a second door. 'Forgive me?' he asks, as though he were himself her lover. It is only then that he becomes aware of Jim's presence. 'It's time we had a talk', he tells Jim, and takes him to the library. There Harrison turns on him and questions him about the length of time he and Jessica spent in the mountains together. He is unaware that Spur is in the house with Jessica. Harrison accuses Jim of fortune-hunting, forces him to recognise his lack of capital and manhood, and that his suit is premature. Spur enters 'stage left', to intercede for Jim. 'I didn't recognise you without the gun.' 'Gun?' cries Jessica as she bursts in. Next the aunt enters, to recount yet another episode in the buried story, the misunderstanding over the colt. The clumsiness of this corresponds to the staginess of its entrances and exits, its succession of timely overheard or overseen incidents which prod the melodrama past this sticking-point.

Melodrama has rarely been laid on to such an extent in Australian films since the early sound period; it is, however, familiar in television 'soaps', and in the rare mini-series descendants of *Snowy River*, like *All the Rivers Run* and even *Return to Eden*, despite its contemporary setting. *Snowy River* was the first to risk using this form when writing large on the wide screen in a spectacular action adventure. It was the first to deal romantically with bush skills, horsemanship and stock work. It worked in the specialised lore of the mountain men, cleverly blending it with the universal mythos of high mountains as places of trial and transcendence. But the Australian bush, as such, is not so much romanticised as plainly spectacular, a worthy destination for bush-tourism.

> The significations are not those of the nostalgia film. Its time is not that of a lost, irretrievable communal past, but of a present. The bush is not alien, foreign, mysterious, uncolonisable, predatory or revengeful; it is a 'commercial, ecological, desirable, traversable and indeed acquirable space'.
> Tom O'Regan, '*The Man from Snowy River* and Australian Popular Culture', *Film News*, September, 1982.

The Third Phase (1981-?): Middle-Aged Spread? 187

Australia is celebrated, but without any specific history, save for the anthem-like ending and the ride-on appearances of Clancy, a literary folk legend. Two slightly surprising American characters are introduced: Harrison from some *Bonanza*-like chaparral, and Spur out of some folksy version of the Tennessee backwoods, as though a pair of American brothers might be justifiable in the nineties as left-overs from the fifties' goldrush. They do little to heighten the Australianness of the surrounding characters or history. In the dinner-party scene, when Harrison entertains Clancy and argues with Jim about mountain men, he invokes their long-standing resistance to the coming of railways, development and 'progress'. It is as though that familiar conflict between sheepmen and cattlemen over enclosures, agriculture and the railways, derived from the American Western, were overlaid on the Australian rural past for a brief, inconsequential moment. It is one that comes simply with the Kirk Douglas persona and his practised, prefabricated ham acting. Jack Thompson's performance as 'the legend', Clancy of the Overflow, is dead-pan, lit by the glow of the sunset, a portrayal of a man used to an audience of men who want to 'meet a legend'. It is deliberately iconic. He gets the 'look' right, keeps his speech dry and sparse; but the part is almost as generalised as the swagman on the old Billy Tea packet. He is not a character, but an image of what Jim will be, the laconic Australian hero in his prime. As we have noted, Jim himself is not a character rich in detail. Rather he is another image in which we can invest approval and identification. His looks, his gaze, his values, are clean and open. No one in the film is strongly marked by specific class, region, or ethnicity. The demands of melodrama do not include historically inflected vernacular.

There is no nostalgia because there is no real sense of the past, or even of period drama being used to dramatise innocence and loss. The concentration on heroes, winning and action as moral drama removes this film from the ambit of the AFC genre, even if it does retain familiar visual traces of bush picturesque, with costume and set-dressing as quiet spectacle. The film is informed, as O'Regan argues, by a confident sense of current Australian popular culture, based on a good working knowledge of television drama, and not by any duty towards 'culture'. *Snowy River* struck it rich in 1982 by creating an old-fashioned melodrama about making heroes out of ordinary blokes, and cutting down rich old tyrants (American, at that) to ordinary size.

Gallipoli and *A Town like Alice* mark a shift to a simplified and strongly partisan nationalism. *The Man from Snowy River* took advantage of that shift and struck an obvious chord with audiences for a time. But the melodrama pulled the film away from the vernacular and iconic elements that were part of those films, usually invested in male speech and demeanour. The nationalism of *Snowy River* is its folkloric source, its hero who wins on our behalf, its anthem-like ending and its spin-off bush clothing lines. It is interesting to see that, on one hand, the male-centred vernacular tradition of Australianness, with its scores of male character-actors, has largely moved to television mini-series like *The Dismissal, Waterfront, Bodyline* and *The Last Bastion*; while the out-and-out melodrama, more familiar from television soap, that succeeded so spectacularly for *Snowy River*, has had little influence on subsequent films.

One might construct a genealogy for *Snowy River's* melodrama. There are distant relatives in *Far East* (1982) and *Careful, He Might Hear You* (1983); *Razorback* is the mongrel off-spring of the melodrama in *Mad Max 2, Mad Max* and the much earlier *Wake in Fright. Phar Lap* is, of course, a film closely related to the pattern of *Snowy River*. It is a second Edgley horse film, again with Tom Burlinson and with an even bigger merchandising campaign tied to its vigorous promotion. But the melodrama of *Phar Lap*, written by David Williamson, is thoroughly subordinated to other elements that are to do with the vernacular and AFC-genre traditions of the second phase; besides, it is the story of the most famous horse in Australian folklore. It is a hero, to be sure, and a winner, but also martyr in the great Australian tradition.

So the story of the 'birth of a hero' in *Snowy River*, with its fairytale and melodramatic layers, has only really been risked once so far, despite its great success. It is possible that the moment in which idealised, partisan nationalism was acceptable in such a generalised form so lacking in irony was a brief one that has already passed. Certainly, the search for a way of 'speaking Australianness' that was the unconscious goal of so many of the films of the first two phases, and which finally found a commercially

The Third Phase (1981-?): Middle-Aged Spread? 189

successful answer, seems now to have lost much of its urgency. This may be related as much to the changes in film financing as to a decline in the plausibility of simplistic nationalist discourse. But whatever the reasons, there is an increasing hollowness in simplistically nationalist rhetoric in Australian film that dates from shortly after it was so successfully commercialised. There is either indecision about exactly what new direction will give impetus to the kind of modest aesthetic change and experimentation the Australian film industry allows itself; or else there is insufficient distance from which to clearly see the dynamic of the present phase. There are some memorable eccentric films from 1982, and one or two small subsequent trends, such as a returning interest in Australian Gothic; but the overriding impression after 1982 has been one of exhaustion, reiteration, and absence of nerve.

In 1982, two films used Asian settings and submerged versions of the plot of the famous forties' standard, *Casablanca*. Australians abroad were given a colourful, politically volatile setting for romance, or its sublimation. John Duigan's film, *Far East*, cast Bryan Brown and Helen Morse, making some capital from their belated coupling in *A Town Like Alice*.

Here the *Casablanca* homage is close to the surface, providing a gesture towards involvement with history and politics: Jo (Helen Morse) accompanies her political journalist husband, Peter, played by the theatre actor and director John Bell. The country they visit is not specified, but the para-military terror and corrupt military regime he uncovers strongly suggest the Phillipines. While he gets caught up in the endangered lives of his informants, Jo rekindles her old attraction to Morgan O'Keefe (Bryan Brown), somebody she knew intimately during the Vietnam War. Morgan now runs a nightclub that brings the exotic east to white, male tourists. Bryan Brown's character, like its Humphrey Bogart predecessor, is poised between amoral cynicism and a deeper, 'truer' loyalty to a private and unshakeable moral code. True to the earlier film, he finally acts to save his rival, her husband, at the risk of his own life. The truly ambivalent character played by Claud Rains in *Casablanca* is missing in *Far East*, and there is therefore no foil for O'Keefe's native, instinctive honour. Instead, the questionable nature of his income, and his exploitation of dancing girls as casual prostitutes, implies someone several shades more corrupt.

Similarly, Peter Weir's film from Christopher Koch's novel, *The Year of Living Dangerously*, uses the fall of Sukarno and the massacre of the country's potentially insurgent communist party members in 1965 to give moral *frisson* to a brief, passionate affair between an Australian journalist Guy Hamilton (Mel Gibson) and Jill, a British Embassy secretary (Sigourney Weaver). The time and place are specified, and events are interpreted for Hamilton and us by his cameraman, an Australian-Chinese dwarf called Billy Kwan (Linda Hunt), who projects his passionate nationalistic dreams on to President Sukarno.

Yet the real political and moral crunch for Australia, represented by Sukarno's proclaimed Year of Living Dangerously, is ignored. Mel Gibson's Australian identity colours him as a flawed hero, but he is not implicated in events. The moral dilemma that belatedly concerns him has more to do with journalistic ethics than the consequences of that violent eruption for the history of Indonesia, Australia and South-East Asia. Should privileged British Embassy information, divulged in intimate trust by Jill, be used by Guy to write an article that might precipitate the violence it warns of? Is the scoop of a lifetime more important than an affair of the heart?

Neither Australia's diplomatic silence on the massacre, the support which Australia gave to the new Suharto government with American approval, nor the ironies that multiplied from this deepening of our own anxious submission to American desires, live or breathe in the film. This violent and complex event is finally diminished to a colourful background for a love affair abroad. Guy Hamilton's temporary blindness is caused by an action so foolhardy it is almost self-inflicted. Confined to his bed with a detached retina that needs complete immobility, he nevertheless risks permanent injury in order to join Jill on the flight out of Jakarta to London. His affliction is symbolic of the character's blindness at many levels. He is insensible to the real danger around him; to the responsibilities of another's love and trust; to the political events from which he constructs a scoop that will transform his career in journalism. But his real blindness is never explored by the film. Billy Kwan talks about the *wayang*, the Javanese shadow-puppet drama, suggesting to the uncomprehending Guy that there is another, unseen dimension, a mystical source, of the intricate shadow imagery of Indonesian politics that so fascinates Billy.

The Third Phase (1981-?): Middle-Aged Spread?   191

Billy Kwan's powerful role in the novel is that of a creature of his own invention, a victim as well as hero of his political imagination, and strange third party to the love affair between Jill and Guy. Weir's film, however, is most interested in the last of these aspects of the character; and so Kwan's act of suicide as an appeal to the heart of his falling idol, Sukarno, makes little sense. It merely confirms his oddity and tragi-comic failure. Guy Hamilton/Mel Gibson is restored to honour as the wounded hero who finally chooses love. The moral parallels and divergences between his life and that of the crazy, passionate, dwarfed Billy Kwan could have been made at least as vivid as the more ordinary story of Guy and Jill in which Billy is a kind of Cyrano de Bergerac, taking vicarious pleasure in Guy's success with the woman who is beyond his own reach. Instead, the film proposes love as the moral cap-stone. Guy's limited moral perspective is forgiven. In fact, he does violence to the meaning of events in the film when he 'comes to his senses' and makes an almost suicidal dash to the airport in the name of love.

Admittedly, there is a credible sexual tension between Mel Gibson and Sigourney Weaver in scenes like the moment in the car after the cloudburst, or when Guy seeks Jill out at the embassy party and leads her from the room without a word. These are worth mentioning because there is so little erotic intensity in Australian film, despite the frequency of love scenes, sex scenes, sex comedies and ocker comedies. Does the poverty of erotic imagination reflect the relative scarcity of love stories for this cinema; or is sexuality still too much of a danger-zone for a fundamentally prudish Australia, which still hedges the subject with crude misogynist humour, still subjects it to group ridicule, or keeps a sociological distance? Certainly, as Meaghan Morris pointed out in 1979, 'there is little or no glorification of full-blown romantic love, for example, and none of the heightened respect for the eternal drama of the couple that defines the themes of so much European and American cinema.'[2]

The exceptions begin to dot the field towards the end of the second phase and into the present one; but they still seem like exceptions. John Duigan achieves a minor triumph of this kind with the non-couple formed by Judy Davis and Bryan Brown in *Winter of Our Dreams*. By contrast, Bryan Brown and Helen Morse are brought together in a rather cliched attempt at the full-blown drama of the eternal couple. They remain cardboard quotations from American and European romance and embody nothing more substantial from their own culture than its receptivity to outside influence. As we have noted, Judy Davis and Sam Neill have some moments that approach eroticism in *My Brilliant Career*; Tom Burlinson and Sigrid Thornton's romance is rinsed clean of any erotic stain that might have blemished the essentially teenage concerns of *The Man from Snowy River*. *Monkey Grip* is one later example of erotic passion taken seriously. It is treated as a form of addiction in the relationship between Noni Hazlehurst and Colin Friels — a relationship that founders on addiction of a more literal kind. There is also *Careful, He Might Hear You*; and the more recent Paul Cox films that explore sexual passion; and period projects like Stephen Wallace's *For Love Alone*. There was a stunted, deformed eroticism in his early short feature, *Love Letters From Teralba Road*, between Bryan Brown and Kris McQuade. In *Third Person Plural*, Brown was a character whose abjection is finely constructed around erotic tension springing from philosophical uncertainty. The original romance between Bryan Brown and Helen Morse in *A Town Like Alice* did achieve some romantic, sexual intensity, if only through the sheer privation enforced by the narrative.

But it is still a curiously short list of restrained examples which seems to indicate a conviction on the part of the industry that romance does not spell financial success. Perhaps Bryan Brown's frequent appearances in these films indicates something about why his persona is in such demand. Nevertheless, it is interesting in *Far East* that the sensuous pans that slide over the Brown torso are not genuinely erotic; the romance is too 'cooked'. Helen Morse's character, her very presence, is almost extraneous as the camera conducts its slightly fatuous affair with the beefcake male body.

Both *Far East* and *The Year of Living Dangerously* are about Australians adrift, making themselves relatively at home in Asian tourist society. *Year* uses this social melange as a way of explaining the casting decisions insisted upon by Metro-Goldwyn Mayer who fully financed the film. *Far East* creates a greater sense of a fragment of Australian society transplanted with its national character intact, especially around Morgan O'Keefe and the Koala Klub. It is both an impediment and an advantage in the moral action of the story.

The Third Phase (1981-?): Middle-Aged Spread? 193

Like Bogart, Bryan Brown comes good and brings his seedy demimonde contacts to bear on the problem of getting Peter (John Bell) and his contact Rosita (Raina McKeon) out of a para-military bunkhouse and on to a departing fishing trawler. There is a slight but definite trace of Australia's ignoble Vietnam involvement: Morgan O'Keefe's nightclub and its pot-bellied Australian regulars are remnants of that Australian expeditionary adventure, left behind with their small commercial ventures and a little money to spend on prostitutes in a buyer's market. It is not enough to undo the eventual heroism of Morgan O'Keefe; just enough to maintain intimacy with its Australian audience. By contrast, *The Year of Living Dangerously* is addressed to the world, with Weir and Gibson as two marketable Australian elements in an international package.

Heatwave, Phil Noyce's second feature, and Don Crombie and Tony Buckley's *The Killing of Angel Street*, both released in 1982, form another pair at work in similar narrative territories, though more local. Underworld involvement in Sydney's real estate development has been part of the Sydney view of politics since the disappearance of Juanita Neilsen, a King's Cross community newspaper editor, in 1975. So has the idea of political and police corruption and illegal silencing of local community dissidents. Both films deal with Juanita Neilson's murder and the residents' battle to save Victoria Street, King's Cross, from rapacious development.

Both films take the populist view of white folks' land rights against thinly disguised big business crime and corruption. But the two films take very different approaches. *Angel Street* follows its central character Jessica Simmonds (Liz Alexander) step by step through a brutally accelerated 'getting of wisdom', in which 'goodies' and 'baddies' are defined with almost cartoon simplicity. *Heatwave*, by contrast, attempts to mirror the complexity of its conspiracy and paranoia in its editing and the relative obliqueness of its story. In *Angel Street* a heroine emerges, although the odds are against her changing anything; in *Heatwave*, no one is without compromise, some impurity of motive. The two main characters, played by Richard Moir and Judy Davis, are finally left under the same cloud of scepticism that covers all the others; audience investment in them and the love interest between them remains slight.

Angel Street tries to be a simple, warm-hearted story of little people's resistance to the forces of greed, money and power. *Heatwave* tries to be a maze of meanings within a baroque display of cinematic technique. Its vision of the people and channels through which power moves in Sydney feels like one more alluring embellishment in the shimmering fabrication of the film, rather than a fundamental political impulse. In the end, a new vista of meaning is suddenly, fleetingly glimpsed in the style of the cool, slightly removed horror of a film like Polanski's *Chinatown*. But a cinematic bravura that seems to belong more to the unresolvable delirium of Sirk's *Tarnished Angels* too often overwhelms this delicate process of discovering meaning.

Also, the climax of *Chinatown* delivers a doubly significant revelation, in which the intimacy of incest is uncovered at the heart of what had seemed like a play of fraud and corruption exclusively at the public level. But *Heatwave* has only one hand to play, however complicated its strategy and stylish its mise en scene. No one is exactly as they seem in *Heatwave*, but there is never the sense of the floor suddenly giving way into the profound personal abyss that *Chinatown* reveals in its closing moments. The two main characters of *Heatwave* are forced to bear witness to the true horror of Sydney's corruption, greed and violence, but they seem to remain untouched both physically and emotionally by what they see. Richard Moir's character changes. The young, idealistic architect is forced gradually to compromise his design for the disputed building site that might have set new standard for inner-city re-housing. In doing so he descends by degrees into the reality of the violent, unscrupulous struggle. The changes are slow. He loses his bearings and sensitivity as a creeping paralysis overwhelms all feeling. Even when Kate decides to shoot the crime boss she is defeated (or saved) by a night-club junkie motivated by sexual ordinary jealousy, who kills him instead.

The final image is briefly glimpsed at the end of a long, extremely self-conscious forward track: the body of the missing Juanita Nielsen surrogate bursts free from the storm-water drain and rises into view on the rain-sodden building site. This is the last of a series of extended forward tracks that runs through the last movement of the film; each one makes its way, with gliding certainty, through densely elaborated spaces of milling people, New Year's Eve debris, or the mud and clutter of a construction

The Third Phase (1981-?): Middle-Aged Spread? 195

site. The final tracking movement which answers the question, 'What has been blocking the drains?' is at once portentous and ironic, even detached. It neatly caps the *mise en scene* that develops from the time that Kate (Judy Davis) leaves her flat with the gun, and draws attention to itself as an impressively 'cinematic' means of unfolding the narrative. Yet there is an uneasy sense of disproportion. So much is done to deliver nothing more powerful than a coolly ironic footnote to the story. Perhaps the image is in part a signal to a Sydney audience that everything in the Juanita Neilsen case will one day come to the surface; the cover-up will crack open. Perhaps also, more generally, it is meant to suggest purgation: after the wave of heat comes the cold wet change; after the two main characters' 'trial by fire' comes the killing of Mr Big and the system, unblocked, in the end clears itself.

The ABC television mini-series *Scales of Justice* provides another view of the intricacies of corruption and crime. It deals with complicity of police and petty crime, upper-echelon crime and high-ranking police officers, and the unassailably respectable Mr Bigs and senior politicians. *Scales* gradually builds a grim edifice from tiny details, links, tactics and snares; nothing is elaborated, style is functional, not allusive, and the demands on the viewer are fairly high. But the connections and implications are knitted together into a persuasive explanation of the way corruption might function inside a police force, judiciary and government. By contrast, *Heatwave* pays heavy dues to cinema. Whole scenes like the discovery of the lawyer's blood-soaked body in bed have more to do with *The Godfather* and *The Conversation* than with the subject matter of *Heatwave*. Because of this and its preference for alluding to things rather than showing them, the parts of the case finally drift apart, rather than interconnect.

Of obvious interest, however, is the way *Heatwave* breaks with the generally tepid style in Australian film, and how much it clearly risks by making such demands upon its audience. The musical soundtrack, by Cameron Allen, also breaks with tradition. Constant, sometimes subliminal electronic music and snatches of radio and insect noise are part of a soundtrack that does not restrict itself to emotional cues and lyrical fillers. *Heatwave* is a Sydney film without really being a regional one. It serves up the city on a plate, garnished with snippets of strong Sydney mythology, but it is still a tourist's Sydney, composed of its most striking views of water, heat, light and strident architecture, and remains vague about the spatial and semantic relations between its parts. *Heatwave* attempts to portray the subtleties of class in Sydney — or, rather, the different voices with which money speaks — but, by and large, observed differences collapse too quickly into the safety of journalistic truisms.

Starstruck (1982) was another markedly Sydney film. It is the second feature of Gillian Armstrong, and the first musical since *Oz*. *Starstruck* is especially interesting for the way that it combines confident, energetic musical comedy with cheerful vulgar enthusiasm for Sydney-side Australiana. Kangaroo suits, Sydney-Harbour-Bridge imagery (in the year of its fiftieth anniversary celebration), and the Opera House were brought together in a kitsch homage to Sydney in advance of a short-lived but intense wave of interest in 'I love Sydney' tee-shirt art.

Starstruck has been applauded as an impressive achievement for the way it yokes together the promiscuous cultural energy of the American musical comedy and a judiciously overstated Australianness; and also for 'a resilient matriarchal order', even an 'ocker matriarchy' at its centre while being in a genre 'so sexist that (the fact) is rarely ever mentioned'.[3] It follows the story of Jackie Mullins (Jo Kennedy), 'managed' by her Puckish fourteen-year-old cousin Angus (Ross O'Donovan), who rises by obscure means to fame at a New Year's Eve rock concert. In winning the contest at the Opera House she saves the family pub from its creditors; and so her success unites her two worlds: crazy ambition and her working-class life as a barmaid in the old Sydney Rocks area, at the foot of the southern pylons of the Harbour Bridge.

All of the genre's old-fashioned expectations are dutifully fulfilled; the 'backstage' musical comedy form is treated with as much reverence as the Sydney icons. Angus, at least, tries to direct the narrative and to 'manage' his cousin, but she always exceeds and escapes his fourteen-year-old efforts. Angus is a shrimp, an affectionate comic butt for jokes; and it could be said that the charm of the narrative is the way that the two, equally persistent, discords of Jackie and Angus combine to create a wry and likeable concordance. The 'ocker matriarchy' (if that is not a contradiction

The Third Phase (1981-?): Middle-Aged Spread? 197

in terms) of Jackie's mother Pearl (Margo Lee) and her grandmother Nana (Pat Evison), back home in the endangered Harbour View Hotel, is another layer in the story of difficulties that life presents for Jackie, yet it also somehow harmonises, at last, with her anarchic desires. In fact, it may well be the root of all her strength. Pearl is brassy, lusty and authoritative, passing off the lover who has shot through with the small change as 'a good root'; Pat Evison's Nana is a huge source of good faith and gentle sentiment, silly as a chook, reliable as a rock. Both are worthy additions to Australian film's very small gallery of iconic female characters.

They are the background against which many articulations of gender are read. For example, Jackie's tight-rope outfit, complete with lampoonish false breasts, and the rest of her armoury of 'things a girl must do for fame'; the comatose, ne'er-do-well or fly-by-night male figures who come and go from the pub menagerie; Angus' pip-squeak efforts to stay in control of 'his' story and Jackie's destiny and his occasional freakish success; and the parody of tough Australian masculinity performed by the gay life savers in the roof-top pool. There is certainly a case at least for seeing the film as subjecting ockerism to warm-hearted feminine ridicule.

Jo Kennedy does well with her part, which really is a tight-rope walk, inviting the voyeurism which is a reflex in this genre, and simultaneously rebuffing it good-naturedly through comic self-consciousness, exaggeration and lampoon. The weakest moments in the film, in fact, are the production numbers which often assert, rather than demonstrate, that they are all about crazy good fun. Confidence only really falters in the staging and cutting of these numbers, which do not seem genuinely spontaneous; an edge of compulsory good fun creeps into them, and the rhythm marks time instead of accelerating throughout.

Starstruck bears comparison with *Shirley Thompson Versus the Aliens*, made ten years earlier. *Shirley* blended genres, including the rock musical, to produce a dark, anarchic, Gothic vision of retro-style Australiana, and Shirley went mad (in order to stay herself) in the process. *Starstruck* adheres much more closely to its comic, rock-musical genre, intuitively using the New Wave fashion of the early eighties and its tolerance for popularised Australiana. Its heroine is never really in the slightest doubt of a happy ending in the comic tradition. Furthermore, she is at home in the world in a way that is unimaginable for Shirley. But that is not simply because popular feminism is confident enough to shift masculinity to the comic margins of its Australianness; it is also because of the malleable simplicity of Jackie Mullins, compared to the kind of stuff that Shirley Thompson is made of.

Another eccentric film of 1982 which energetically proposes an Australianness that is not merely male self-justification is Haydn Keenan's extremely low-budget *Going Down*. Nationality, of course, isn't a conscious priority in the film. Where genre enabled *Starstruck* to camp up its Australianness, the playful uses of genre in *Going Down* allow this element to be negotiated without being pursued. But in any case, *Going Down* is, once more, a Sydney film, a midsummer night's dream of an upside-down inner-city netherworld, in which planned departures to New York, forays to buy large quantities of cough medicine, music, fixes, surreal car trips, inexplicable awakenings on Bondi Beach (beneath a cardboard cut-out palm tree), epic drunken journeys on roller skates, and a final car chase to the airport in the manner of a Jacques Tati vacation are intermingled. The filmmakers' own headline-like synopsis does it better justice: 'Zany mums-to-be survive depressed drinkie, druggie cash cult romp'.

Four actresses generate the strength and vitality of *Going Down*: the late Vera Plevnik (Jane), Tracy Mann (Karli), Moira Maclaine-Cross (Ellen) and Julie Barry (Jackie). The last two are also credited with the screenplay; Vera Plevnik is especially striking for both the strength and the negativity that she projects as the manic-depressive Jane. Karli is on her way to New York, the metropolis which was fashionably the object of all urban desires that exceeded Sydney in the early eighties. (A couple of years it would be Tokyo.) Ellen is a retiring, mothering, innocent abroad. Around the four women revolve a galaxy of male hangers-on, mostly played by the brilliant, funny David Argue in four roles, including that of a four-eyed roller-skate freak with double vision, perpetually rolling helplessly backward out of frame, around furniture or negotiating the steps down to the underground railway. In fact, where the female characters are, for once, strong and differentiated, the male characters are literally interchangeable at this level, distinguished only by a comic exaggeration based in stereotype.

It is as if the *mise en scene* deliberately stumbles in its pursuit of the haphazard narrative events, adventures and collisions of the night. The style is funky *cinema-verite* which just keeps up with all the changes of narrative tack and new declarations of generic direction, from comedy through social realism to musical comedy and even comic action film. *Going Down* has antecedents in *Shirley Thompson*, Bert Deling's 1977 *Pure Shit* (a one-night ride through the Melbourne drug scene), *Mouth to Mouth*, *Palm Beach*, and Haydn Keenan and Esben Storm's *27A* (1973), which follows the final, institutionalised months of a metho derelict, played movingly by Robert Darra. It also shows eccentric traces of Jacques Tati, Jerry Lewis, Henry Jaglom and Jon Jost. The direct, confident style of the film owes much to its position outside the mainstream narrow-mindedness of the industry proper; and just as much to its position within the cheaper, rougher and ruder traditions that run at a tangent to that mainstream.

The relatively strong, plain voice of the film is used to speak a precise regional subculture, an exact *milieu*, that feels as if it belongs at least in part to the filmmakers themselves — including director, writers and actors. Like *Palm Beach*, the film has a genuinely comic sympathy with its *milieu*; it demonstrates that prized quality of 'being on to yourself', wry, wise and funny, but with feeling.

Monkey Grip, directed by Ken Cameron, adapted from a 1977 novel by Helen Garner, is another subculturally precise film. This time, however, the *milieu* is not scenic Sydney but Melbourne's inner-city Carlton, its life centred on art, music, theatre and drugs, in communal households in which single-parent children are reaching primary-school age while their parents reluctantly nudge the lower boundaries of middle age. Helen Garner's book about a year in the life of Nora, a woman in her thirties with a twelve-year-old daughter, is written from within that *milieu* almost in the style of a journal, with the late sixties still apparent. The slight, undeclared time-lapse in the film makes it different from *Going Down*, which talks on the run from the chaotic moments of its production in the eighties.

Two further qualities distinguish Ken Cameron's style of social realism: at its best it has a mellow, ironic Eastern European flavour; and a deliberate formlessness like that of the original novel, which

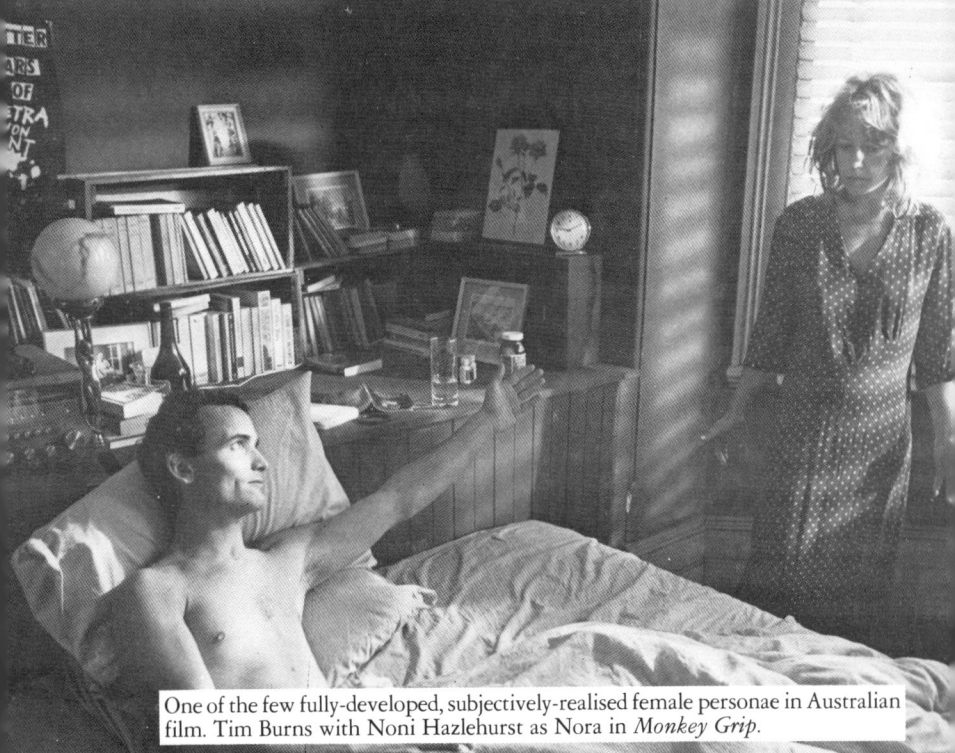

Max, the perennial outsider, a violent, perversely attractive male principle. Mel Gibson in *Mad Max 2*.

One of the few fully-developed, subjectively-realised female personae in Australian film. Tim Burns with Noni Hazlehurst as Nora in *Monkey Grip*.

is written in an unshaped, confessional style, dependent upon small sharp verities of character and feeling, or telling detail. These two aspects of Cameron's style do not readily accommodate each other, or provide immediately recognisable, structured, mainstream viewing. Cameron's earlier work had been low-budget and non-mainstream, including films like *Out of It* and *Temperament Unsuited*. He had tended to specialise in the school film subgenre found in different forms in both Australian mainstream and dramatised documentary. In mainstream film, it is an AFC subgenre, which deals with expensive private schools; in documentary, it is generally dedicated to the 'problem' of government schools and their spirited, unwilling inmates. How could this style cohere with the carefully textured prose and minimal, repetitious incident of a novel tracing a year's progress in a love affair suspended between two kinds of addiction?

The solution lies in a middle ground in which the intimacy of Nora's diary becomes a reflective, rather than narrative, voice-over, and the year is shaped into the space between two summers, two swims at a Melbourne public baths, in which the 'Deep Water/ Aqua Profunda' sign takes on a metaphoric significance. The affair between Nora (Noni Hazlehurst) and Javo (Colin Friels) still runs its intense, dislocated course, and the artless functionalism of Ken Cameron's social-realist style is well attuned to it. But the film is a rather more densely symbolic and plotted work than the novel, moving from deep water to dance, from making music to making love, from laughing to weeping — lightly shaped by its movement from one narrative incident to another, all with a slightly more frequent use of metaphor than is usual in social realism.

What is most interesting, by contrast with the boyishness of so many earlier films, is the way *Monkey Grip* makes erotic yearning the core of its romance, and the feeling between mother and child, Nora and Grace (Alice Garner, Helen Garner's daughter), the second source of the film's romance. Social realism is put in the service not of issues but of feelings, documented in their natural, banal condition. When this intense process is centred on Nora and mediated by Noni Hazlehurst's extraordinarily natural, emotionally rich performance, one begins to see what a telling exception *Monkey Grip* is in the Australian context, and what a risk it was as a result.

Essentially, it tells no story other than that of the fading in, the strengthening, loosening and fading out of the connection between Nora and Javo, against the background of the fluctuating affairs and household arrangements of the other women and men in her environment. It also tells of the steady, wise, helpful relationship between Nora and Grace. The three or four lovemaking scenes are beautifully lit (by David Gribble) and managed so that they are about eroticism and addiction, rather than pornography, titillation or 'sexploitation'. This is a minor miracle in a cinema of which it was said in 1979:

> An unsympathetic soul watching a quick succession of raunchy comedies and realist dramas might be forgiven for concluding that Australia is dominated either by a race of unattractively puritan adolescents obsessed with 'getting it' (people who see sex, like excretion and vomiting, as something lewd or grotesquely comic), or by a race of misogynist psychotics for whom sexuality in general is a danger zone, with hatred, fear and contempt ever-present and prone to erupt into violence.[4]

Monkey Grip makes a telling comparison with the issue-based sexual dramas of, say, *Petersen*, *Duet for Four*, even *Maybe This Time*; one could almost argue that Hazelhurst's role as Nora is one of the few fully developed, subjectively realised female personae in Australian film, in which it is possible to appreciate a mixture of roughness, tenderness, intelligence, foolishness, irony and passion, and from which it is possible to develop an affectionate sense of cultural exactitude.

Goodbye Paradise, directed by Carl Schultz, is another eccentric film in that bumper crop of 1982. Its distribution was long in doubt, despite the awards for its screenplay by Denny Lawrence and Bob Ellis, and for its well-judged central performance by Ray Barrett as Michael Stacey, O.B.E., living in enforced and seedy retirement in Surfer's Paradise, 'Australia's version of the afterlife', a little Miami on the coast of Southern Queensland. *Goodbye Paradise* has become a cult film of sorts. It is perhaps the talkiest of Australian films, an extremely local version of the wise-cracking forties' American detective genre. It has too much plot, too many endings, is excessive in almost every way; but it is very easy to indulge a script with such affection for cinema, such a witty and evocative use of a place as wildly over-determined as Surfers, and such a local *and* genre-conscious piece of casting and characterisation as Ray Barrett's Stacey.

He is as over-determined as Surfers itself, and the relationship between them is so strong that it is hard to imagine the sequel, '*Goodbye Adelaide*', which was at one stage planned. In a landscape of gaudy nightclubs, neon and real estate, Stacey is a former Deputy Police Commissioner, retired early not for the usual dishonourable reasons but for inexcusable candour born of drunkenness. He confesses in long, self-conscious voice-overs, strewn with occasionally brilliant one-liners that flow in and out of the competing mordant repartee of his dialogue. The effect is similar to Tom Waites' talking blues. Lawrence and Ellis' sensitivity towards the question of cultural distinctiveness ensures that the use of such a thoroughly American genre as the seedy private-eye film, set in a place of suitably freakish extravagance, is made to speak with strong local and ironic inflection. *Goodbye Paradise* makes the same rich use of place in the narrative as does *Puberty Blues*, or, even more so, *Palm Beach*. (It is worth noting that all these films are set on or near the beach.)

The opening movement follows Stacey through his first night of falling hard off the wagon, after learning that his publisher is cancelling the contract for his expose of the police force, which has been too long in the writing. Stacey is sure that the contents have leaked and that pressure has been applied. He shambles off into the endless night of Surfers. In a sequence which both establishes the film and disorients the viewer, placing us inside Stacey's alcoholic haze and occasional blackouts, Carl Schultz displays a sympathetically florid directorial style. Next morning, Stacey is called out to see a former friend, and present local member of parliament, who had cut him short in one of the many bars of the previous night. The scene juxtaposes plot development — the request to quietly find a missing daughter — with an apology rich and pithy in its cultural accuracy: 'Sorry about last night — Trades Hall, the Labor Party, my preselection, what can I say?' The scene is a nice example of the way an imported genre can be made to speak a local tongue ('You're still as mean as a beach full of blue bottles.') and, even more, local history and folklore.

It turns out that a few old cronies from another expeditionary force in the early sixties who kept the communist menace at bay in the jungle of Malaya are planning a military coup under cover of the separatist new-state movement on the Gold Coast. True to the genre, finding Cathy is just a means of stumbling into the real action. But the dark forces turn out to be slightly ludicrous, greying good old boys who still boyishly believe that might is right — for them. One, played by Jack Clancy, presides over a post-hippy commune called 'Eden', with a style that is too intellectually dim to include irony; but none of this gets in the way of his ambition to rule the world. The coup doesn't quite come off. ASIO, in the form of a good-time girl played with customary astringency by Kris McQuade, has been on the trail all along. Stacey witnesses mayhem among the rainforest and plexiglass rhubarb hothouses of Eden, after which, in a state of drunken disorientation that recalls and surpasses the binge which opens the film, 'normal' life resumes in Paradise. In the process, he has lost his best friend and lover, Kate (Robyn Nevin) to a car bomb set for him; this is a misjudged narrative economy, since Robyn Nevin plays a lovely and wise character who deserves to survive into sequels in a more foreground role. But Stacey retains his dog, and together they walk up the beach and into the salty haze of morning, 'signing off' with the last of his melancholic voice-overs: 'Now is the time for all good men to come to the aid of their home towns . . .'

Goodbye Paradise is not one of the more disciplined Australian films: the florid, melancholically witty verbal style of Bob Ellis is augmented, some might say outdone, by Schultz's cluttered, dense visual style: puns like the sign, 'Fantasia Macabre' which lights the dim place where Stacey is beaten up by police goons, or the peripatetic sequence shots that trail and mimic his alcoholic, stumbling course. But the perpetual *mise en scene* of Surfers itself always outdoes them both with countless tawdry occasions for wonder. Ray Barrett's performance manages to pull these three excessive elements into some kind of working relationship.

Underlying this achievement is the use of genre, both to avoid the unforgivably obvious in the search for a voice for Australian film, and to explore the genre itself as a medium that might carry that voice. As with *Mad Max 2*, genre is re-tuned to local conditions. Of course the detective genre is even more subject to self-conscious and ironic pastiche than the adventure romance, so the question of an authentic, home-grown hybrid is not simple.

The Third Phase (1981-?): Middle-Aged Spread? 205

But there is a vast difference between *Goodbye Paradise* and the coldly external, crudely-worked and unsympathetic uses of genre in films like, say, *Raw Deal* (1977), *Snapshot* (1979), and *Turkey Shoot* (1981), even were it possible to argue some contorted case for regarding the *oeuvre* of Tony Ginnane as a southern or mid-Pacific version of Corman's New World Pictures, or its misjudged calculations as judicious post-modern delirium. The immediate and glaring difference between these films and *Paradise* is the disregard of the local. No matter how mythical or stylised, *Paradise* remains within the limits of what things are actually like, here and now, and therefore stands a chance of some intimacy with truth.

If *Goodbye Paradise* didn't make a killing at the box office, it certainly gave life to the environment in which stories are dreamt and risks taken in the industry. And unlike so many of the 1982 cold films and their internationalist forerunners, it does not willingly accept cultural subordination, but rather steals a genre from the dominant culture with which to demonstrate insubordination, and subtle, vital difference. Yet is does so without the heroic nationalist martyrdoms of *Gallipoli, Breaker Morant* or *Phar Lap* (1983), or the guileless nationalist heartiness that afflicts some aspects of otherwise estimable films such as *Buddies* (1983).

We of the Never-Never (Igor Auzins, 1982) has things in common with *The Chant of Jimmy Blacksmith*. It is something of a show-pony film, though with the handicap of high expectation; a big-budget, period outback panorama which essays some of the knotty contradictions of race and gender. But it does so with AFC-genre gentility; it is middle-brow and somewhat high-flown. In fact, *Never-Never* is something of a dinosaur, surviving some time after the species had generally evolved into the mini-series.

Never-Never's cinematographer, the late Gary Hansen, begins the film with an extraordinary, low, sweeping aerial shot. It is a gesture equal to the magnificence of the space it traverses: the Northern Territory flood plains when the ground cover is high. The camera picks up a galloping horseman racing to tell his mates news big enough to fill and change this magnificent, generous, changeable space: the boss is stabbing them all in the back. He's bringing a wife to The Elsey.

Jeannie Gunn (Angela Punch McGregor) courts the company of local Aboriginal women in *We of the Never Never*.

Ray Barrett, as ex-Deputy Police Commissioner Michael Stacey, abandons his getaway bus in the last stages of his boozy odyssey in *Goodbye Paradise*.

The Third Phase (1981-?): Middle-Aged Spread? 207

So begins a study of the social in microcosm: the isolation of an early twentieth-century Territorian cattle station. The stockmen react with fear and contempt at the idea of a white woman owned by the boss on The Elsey, threatening the foundations of their kingdom, disturbing the simple privileges of being white males. Little of this is verbally articulated; the film captures beautifully, as if in a time-warp, the laconic conservative shyness, especially around women of higher status, of those of our grandfathers who were rural labourers. For example, while Aeneas Gunn (Arthur Dignam) lies dying, Jack (Lewis Fitz-Gerald) and Jeannie Gunn (Angela Punch-McGregor) have an agonising exchange on the verandah. Jack is desperate but utterly unable to speak his feelings to the boss's wife even then.

Mrs Aeneas Gunn, the quaintly-named author of the book *We of the Never-Never*, is a 'plucky little woman', and Jeannie in the film is more so. She responds to the challenge of being a creature apart, a virtual alien in a place of endemic loneliness and beauty, with a courage that only occasionally wavers into tears. The film is a serious attempt to transform the original story of an Edwardian lady of Adelaide put in charge of primitive, childlike natives, into one in which a brave white woman stands as the civiliser of male racism; of privileged woman uniting with women of an alien culture on the grounds of their universal condition as women; of woman made great through adversity to produce Woman, the eternal mediator.

What this late-twentieth-century vision damaged most is the truth about Aboriginal women in the Territory in areas like The Elsey. Diane Bell's research shows how drastically the first appearance of white women on cattle stations curtailed the traditional independence of Aboriginal women, redefining their business as domestic rather than stock work. They lost prestige in the eyes of their men and were cast in a new anglicised mould of sexual difference that meant the decline of their power and the degradation of their culture.[5]

Nevertheless the film contains a truly classic scene of Australian racism, a blend of empire loyalty and white supremacy precisely true to the period. After a time of inhuman isolation as lady of her rough and meagre house, Jeannie begins to venture among the Aboriginal women, learn their language and beliefs and break down the barrier between mistress and servant. Her style of dress becomes more informal; she wears brighter, looser clothes and walks arm-in-arm in pastoral accord with the laughing black women. Friction develops between Jeannie and Aeneas over this loss of social demeanour, and even more, over her fury at the stubborn refusal of the men to accept her as a human being. Then Jeannie and Aeneas come as guests to a ceremonial dance. The light dawns fairly readily upon the gentle, bookish man, Aeneas, and he encourages the white stockmen to attend too, as a mark of respect. The boys (John Jarrett, Tony Barry, Lewis Fitz-Gerald and head stockman Martin Vaughan) watch moodily until suddenly they can take no more. The youngest leap up, fire pistols in the air and feel impelled to shout 'God save the King!' It is an extraordinary moment, in which the contradictions of their time and place seem to burst through them.

But the main thesis — than Jeannie can transform attitudes and bring a dawn of enlightenment to Northern Territory racism — is not borne out even in the film's terms. The aesthetic values of the scenic and picturesque are given priority, and Jeannie, in her crinolines amid the bush, is the centrepiece of that aesthetic. There is a clear attempt to update the gently patronising rhetoric of the original; but the book's position, a conscious demonstration of greater tolerance, remains central. The Aboriginal characters are little more than extras; they remain passive objects of white interest. Does their silence, their background anonymity, signify gratitude? The plot instructs us at the end that the Aboriginal people are replying to this kindness, the extension to them of human status, by according the dead Aeneas the honour of a corroboree. 'Jeannie's loneliness is abated by the closeness of her "family" of black and white people who provide comfort and warmth.'[6] 'But even this closing gesture leaves these people out entirely, casting them as the dignified, simple, generous ones, the traditional (and of course pitiable) victims of racist subordination. They never speak as characters, let alone answer back; their role is essentially mute. They are spoken for, even if it is by the most careful, ideologically correct voices of tolerance.

If Jeannie herself were more perceptibly complex and less a splash of contrast setting off the epically picturesque, then her interaction with real Aboriginal people and her attempt to overcome the sexual and economic obstacles of racism might have lifted the film above the bravura of the visuals. Angela

An honourable attempt to re-open the recent past, but a little too close to the waxworks? The cast of *The Dismissal* on the set of the House of Representatives, including Bill Hunter, Max Phipps, John Meillon and John Stanton.

High country landscape as sign of alienated, paranoid human relations: Richard Moir in *Plains of Heaven*.

Punch-McGregor does her best to put strong feeling into the role, but, either as written or as she emerges from the editing, she is continually, harmoniously posed, rather than positioned genuinely as the element that throws contradictions of gender, race and morality into relief. And so the film remains a goodly gesture against racism; no risks are taken and exploration is restricted to the picturesque brief of the AFC genre. In its way, Charles Chauvel's 1957 film *Jedda* touches more painful racist nerves today than this one, because at least it takes aesthetic risks with a cranky combination of tragic melodrama and epic and exotic blends of Aboriginal and European mythologies. But the bland 'we' this film speaks for is that of an ideological never-never.

The filmmakers went to the trouble and expense of going to the real remote Elsey Station, and certainly made a feast of its special country; but the style remains illustrative of the place, never seeking out its real history or symbolism. By contrast, the 1983 low-budget film by Ian Pringle and John Cruthers, *The Plains of Heaven*, takes the Bogong High Plains country of Victoria and makes the story of two men in a satellite tracking station grow from the distinct physical significance of the place. Richard Moir plays a technical, city person; Reg Evans plays an eccentric stoat fancier, painfully tuned to the high plains country. One whiles away the time rigging the apparatus to tune into American West Coast television game shows, the other is so receptive to the strange transmissions and emanations of the bleak, beautiful place that he is a little mad. The younger man gradually comes to understand the sanity of the other's madness, an understanding that grows as he walks and drives through the night streets of Melbourne, the lovely contrast of an urban landscape. *Plains* is an interesting attempt at a poetic essay on landscape and environment, within a form on the margins of the mainstream.

Careful, He Might Hear You, directed by Carl Schultz in 1983, was a big-budget melodrama of class and sexuality, based on the novel by Sumner Locke Elliott. The thirties' Sydney decor and John Seale's lush lighting and cinematography combined with Schultz's extravagant style give the film a strong familial resemblance to the AFC genre, but its heart is not set on the prestige of period Australiana. Produced towards the end of that

The Third Phase (1981-?): Middle-Aged Spread? 211

cycle, *Careful* has more in common with 'The Child' segment of *Libido* than with *Breaker Morant, Kitty and the Bagman* or *We of the Never-Never*; it makes more sense to compare it on one hand with the women's melodramas of Sirk, Curtiz and Borzage of earlier American cinema, and on the other with European art cinema. The only other film to risk using such an excessive form as high melodrama is *The Man From Snowy River*, but the two have utterly different themes. The latter deals with the external rites of manhood and dominance, while the former is concerned with inward, hysterical sublimations of threatening female sexuality.

For all its bush picturesque and period lyricism, Australian film has never ventured far into the territory of romantic art, which has little to do with narcissistic prettiness and 'innocence'. Rather, Australian film has engaged in an unconscious search for a position counter to the rude, early ocker comedies; taste versus gesture. Perhaps the ocker comedies actually came closer to romanticism, with their sense of the extravagant and marvellous, than the dutiful AFC genre films of the seventies do; although this may overestimate the willingness of *Stork*, *Bazza* and their audiences to submit to passion and imagination. Nevertheless, the ocker lives closer to the brink than his respectable alternatives, and the films touched by Australian Gothic are closer still, because of their determination to overstate.

Very few Australian films have trusted the instincts of a genuinely popular culture and its romantic dictates: that the world, and everything in it, can be transformed at will. The ocker comedies, the films of Australian Gothic, to some extent the urban road movies, the few subculture regional films, the locally-inflected genre pieces, and the tiny handful of full-blown melodramas are the limited areas of mainstream Australian cinema that have welcomed the imprint of popular culture, and in turn admitted something of its close kinship with romantic art.

Where *The Man From Snowy River* is naive, sentimental melodrama, the highly-wrought sentiment of *Careful* is much more ironic, self-conscious, even faintly camp. It is a fifties-style melodrama in the vein of Douglas Sirk, dressed in thirties' garb and decor. Repressed sexuality and differences in wealth within a family spill out as degrees of excess in decor, dress, textures, gesture, lighting, 'atmosphere' (the ceaseless drift of smoke, leaves, petals and thistledown across the exterior shots), music and *mise en scene*. The excess of the form is simply a proper response to the excess of the story.

As Peter Brooks argues, this strained relationship between means and ends produces formal qualities that are strained, exaggerated, excessive, over-the-top. There is a sense that the overloaded signifiers make 'large but unsubstantiable claims on meaning'[7]. So the normal process of toning things down in favour of realism is abandoned to a greater or lesser extent. The melodrama then proceeds to overflow with large and volatile meanings.

The carefully overwrought melodrama influences the story of Vanessa in *Careful*; it has a weaker influence over the enveloping story of P.S., the small boy who is the bone of contention between his two aunts. For a time the two stories are entangled as Vanessa demands that they share the raising of the boy.

Vanessa (Wendy Hughes) appears to the boy P.S. at first like a dream, a fairy princess in the state room of a steamship from Europe. Gradually she assumes an increasingly restrictive and distorting role in his life, her attentions full of a strange intensity somehow linked to the fact that he is the child of her brother-in-law, whose casual interest once gave her the most erotic moment of her life. P.S. (Nicholas Gledhill) enters into an almost sexual intimacy with Vanessa's refined masochism when he spends time in her grand house. Finally he rebels, and Vanessa, Lila (Robyn Nevin) and P.S. battle for control of his destiny. His name is P.S. because his dead mother regarded him as a postscript to her life. At the end he claims a name. 'I'm Bill!', he cries, and runs to proclaim it to the big gardens of the house that Vanessa once occupied, as if 'Bill' were another word for freedom.

The child's life with Lila in working-class Balmain is cosy and comfortable; Vanessa takes him across the harbour to a Mosman waterfront mansion, dresses him stiffly, supplies him with toys that must not be damaged, and lessons that must be taken. The careful contrasts between exquisite wealth and genteel poverty, north and south sides of the harbour, refined and cheery forms of repression, are all part of the contrived formality. So is the motif of travel across water as the harbour takes on the significance of the River Styx, and increasingly separates P.S. from an authentic life on either side of it. He soon resists Vanessa's relentless, rigid

The refined masochism of classic female melodrama: Wendy Hughes as the snow queen Vanessa in *Careful, He Might Hear You*.

'kindness', even torments her in turn. In the end she drowns in an historical disaster in which a ferry was sliced in two by a liner on the fog-shrouded harbour. P.S. has learnt enough to grieve her loss. His grief redeems her slightly from her fate as the Snow Queen: beautiful, hysterically frigid and virginal.

The alternatives for female sexuality offered are fixed by class imagery: the mousy, domestic genteel poverty of loyal, warm, conventional Lila, her sexuality submerged beneath respectability, is opposed to Vanessa, wealthy and refined; the ice-bound image of the feminine. There is a third possibility: the probably perfect, and therefore deceased, third sister, the mother of P.S. The film leaves hints that she had the exquisite taste of a Vanessa, the emotional warmth of a Lila, and yet possessed a sexual earthiness equal to that of P.S.'s father (John Hargreaves). She is a true male fantasy, whose imaginary presence forces wrong decisions and perpetual inadequacy on all the women in her shadow. Her perfection apparently extended even to a loving tolerance of her husband's womanising, including his sexual provocation of her sister; and her extremely sentimental death has turned him into the drunken ne'er-do-well she had once saved him from being.

Vanessa is trapped by this construction, which magnifies her refinements of manner and money into a frigidity on all levels, and her lust for her brother-in-law into a perverse obsession which must deny itself in order to flourish. What option has she but a doomed ferry ride late on a foggy night? The logic of the melodrama is that the woman charged with an excess of desire must go mad or die. Vanessa's problem, her deathly, frozen, excessive desire, is a staple of romantic art. It is pleasing that the narrative thaws at least enough to accord her some moments of wisdom and insight, and allows us some sense of loss when its conservative economy requires her death.

Careful, with its elegant period setting, its first-person narrative centred in the child, the theatricality of its *mise en scene*, is much more intentionally an art film than the AFC genre films before it. Three other films of the post-tax-incentive period with such a European art-film feeling about them that they have rendered even Melbourne as a slightly angst-tinged European city are Paul Cox's *Lonely Hearts* (1982), *Man of Flowers* (1983) and *My First Wife* (1984). They are worth treating as three variations on the theme of the personal, although their differences are as plain as their common points. They make a striking set, because they establish the possibility for the first time in mainstream Australian film of making strongly 'authorial', subjective films; for a filmmaker to be treated as an artist whose *oeuvre* is part of the art-film end of the commercial sector. There is a sense that the film-investment incentives did momentarily encourage the production of riskier films, which included a small but significant growth in the art-film area with the entry of new and successful entrepreneurs, like Ronin Films, into Melbourne, Canberra and Sydney distribution and exhibition. Paul Cox's films have progressively established him as that rare thing in the Australian scene, the *auteur*.

To distinguish between the three fairly crudely, *Lonely Hearts* (co-written with John Clarke, alias Fred Dagg) is a somewhat dark, but not bleak, comedy of the emotions, which deals with a middle-aged piano-tuner (played excellently by Norman Kaye), who has lived with his mother until her death and now attempts to find happiness with a shy and lonely younger woman (Wendy Hughes) whom he meets through an introduction agency. *Man of Flowers* makes a surreal, subterranean exploration of the gentle but perverse changes of a similar, over-mothered character (again played by Norman Kaye), and centres on the aesthetic contemplation of flowers, art, young nude girls, and music. *Lonely Hearts* has a beautifully-made 'commercial' style, modulated to a subtle and, by Australian standards, muted tone. By comparison, *Man of Flowers*, made on a shoestring, is a defiant and anarchic film, smuggled across the mainstream border in the guise of an extremely beautiful art film. The tone is bleaker than *Lonely Hearts*, but the humour (co-written this time by Bob Ellis) stings against the mordancy of the story. *My First Wife* is different again. Cox takes subjectivity to an even more intense, angst-ridden level as he follows the emotional and mental breakdown of a musician (John Hargreaves) under the sudden collapse of his marriage, and the loss of both his wife (Wendy Hughes) and child. This is a film of late-afternoon Melbourne light, low skies, and private pain becoming public as a man tears himself apart in the manner of a Greek tragedy.

The continuities between the films of cast, crew and place are stronger than usual in the industry; and in each film there is a suffering male sensibility under a particularly intimate scrutiny very different from that of the *Petersen*-style films of the seventies. The first and third could almost be 'male weepies' in the European art-film tradition, although the Australianness of the setting and idiom is never in doubt in either. The middle film is the wild card, but even it could be shuffled into this category on some counts, although it is closer to Bunuel than to Bergman. As distant or unexpected relatives of the male weepie, each centres on male sexuality and male feeling in a way rare in the local context.

The down-to-earth Fred-Dagg-like humour of *Lonely Hearts* lightens the austerity and alienation to a genuinely comic pathos. Close to the beginning of the film, Peter (Norman Kaye) is fitted for a new toupee from Hong Kong, something to shield him and his patch of baldness during the coming encounter with Patricia (Wendy Hughes). He can hardly believe that someone so young and good-looking could have agreed to meet him, and he is alarmed and excited under his customary gentle courtesy. The catty salesman deflates and browbeats him into buying an overpriced, youthful hairpiece. Much later, as his love affair runs aground on sexual inexperience, Peter has a brief dizzy spell of kleptomania in the local supermarket and is arrested. Embarrassed beyond belief, he returns to the sanctuary of his mother's house and tells her dog, 'They humiliate you, and send you back to your miserable little life . . .' He takes off the wretched hair-piece as Patricia knocks at the window. In a lovely series of half-mimed exclamations and explanations, Patricia expresses complete acceptance through the window before Peter rushes to the door. 'You look terrible! What's happened to your little fur hat?' The story declares the couple united. A tender comic affection is felt for each character which annulls the cruelty of whatever pathos they might have in the eyes of the world.

The process of the story is strengthened by small cameos and Tati-esque gaucheries along the way. It is impossible not to sense the hand of John Clarke in this; for example, the way Peter's car, the only one following the hearse in his mother's funeral procession, is caught by changing traffic-lights and then kangaroo-hops forward in a cloud of exhaust. Another example is the scene in which a fellow customer in the pizza shop confides with surprising vehemence, 'You can't beat a good bang, can you?'. Peter's virginity is giving him a painfully hard time, and he replies

'Fuckin' oath!' in a way at once entirely consistent with the needs of the situation and his heart, *and* entirely out of character. Best of all, he says it with simple, considered seriousness, and the incongruity with his usual behaviour is the measure of his progress towards worldliness. The line works craftily on many levels of comedy and pathos, and epitomises the graceful balance of writing, acting and staging.

In *Man of Flowers*, Norman Kaye shifts register, towards a Flemish absurd surrealism blended with Australian Gothic. The final tableau shot of Kaye and several other unmoving, anonymous, dark-suited figures, looking out on a small green rise over the grey waters of Port Phillip Bay, directly alludes to Magritte. They are set there like monuments to the accommodating Europeanness of which Melbourne is capable. As in *Lonely Hearts*, there is a deliberate, affectionate *frisson* set up between European culture, vision, and look, and a resolutely antipodean geography, idiom and abrasiveness. Nonsense erupts periodically into the gentle but serious absurdity of a man who arranges flowers in massive quantity, writes letters accounting for himself to his dead mother, pays a young girl to strip slowly, at a discreet distance, to a Donizetti aria, and then, overcome, rushes across the road to the church where he plays tumultuous Bach fugues on his organ. How can further nonsense erupt into a story of this kind? It does so in florid, Ellis-style set pieces belonging to cameo characters like the postman, the psychoanalyst (played by Bob Ellis) and the sculptor. The story is not well wrought. It tends to fall into bits around the anti-aesthetic, angry young action painter (Chris Haywood) who lives with the girl who does the languorous strips. Her experimental affair with a lesbian friend is also a structural problem. The strongest part of the film is its sympathetic, non-exploitative treatment of bizarre sexuality, explored through Yuri Sokol's marvellous imagery of the man of flowers, his childhood memories of repression (by the law-of-the-father) and sensual awakening (by the ravishing image and touch of the mother) all conveyed in richly reprocessed images recalling home movies, and 'starring' Werner Herzog as the father.

Finally, *My First Wife* is a drama of family and sexuality, the same territory explored in Wim Wenders' *Paris, Texas*. But this is a condensed, dream-like film set wholly in Melbourne. Again it is a place of wintry southern light, of exultant and poignant

Monuments to the accommodating Europeanness of which Melbourne is capable. Norman Kaye is the *Man of Flowers*.

classical music, and suburban train journeys laced with the rapid passage of bare trees past the window. John Hargreaves' role as emotional shipwreck tentatively salvaged is finely played. It confirms his ability, prefigured as early as *Don's Party* and as late as *Careful, He Might Hear You*, to find the genuinely pathetic and moving edge of the larrikin male, the tears and weaknesses that go with the 'shit-eating' grin. If the narrative fails to prepare us for Helen's (Wendy Hughes) announcement that the marriage has been over for years, this has to do with its subjective proximity to John (John Hargreaves); his position is that women are mysterious, fundamentally inexplicable. Helen's motivation is never clear and her emotional and sexual desertion, and the departure that deprives John also of their mutually beloved child, Lucy, becomes difficult to forgive. But the film works to establish Auden's dictum, 'We must love one another or die', and its discovery of powerful dream-like imagery drawn from suburban Melbourne in support of its emotional claims on the audience, is welcome indeed. In the seventies one might have expected a film like this to gravitate helplessly to television-like social realism. In the eighties its eccentricities can not only be accommodated but positively flaunted.

> (*Buddies* is) the first Queensland film to be accepted by Queensland without any cultural cringe.
>
> (John Dingwall, writer
> and producer, *Buddies*,
> Rockhampton
> *Morning Bulletin*,
> August 3, 1983.)

Perhaps in trying so hard and, for the most part, successfully, to be a defiant, celebration of a region, *Buddies* didn't notice the effect of substituting 'have-a-go' Australian zealotry for cringing self-apology. Like *Undercover* (1983), the film resonates to the 1982 Advance Australia campaign, and to the lingering plausibility of that moment of dogmatic Australian nationalism; so some false notes are struck, especially in its theme song, 'Buddies'. They indicate a slightly incoherent attempt to 'target' the market-place nationalism of the period. This sits oddly with the film's fine comic regionalism; so much of it is 'honourable', as Bob Ellis might say, and infused with such admirable comic energy, that the advertising-style refrain, enjoining us to 'have a go', jingles tinnily. Perhaps the phrase 'have a go' is simply worn out now that almost every last cent has been milked from it; and perhaps this was already true when *Buddies* was belatedly released in 1983.

As in *Sunday Too Far Away*, John Dingwall's fine sense of narrative form in *Buddies* underlies the rough-as-guts speech and action. *Buddies* is again a slightly tinny word to Australian ears. Was 'mates' considered overdone, or unrecognisable for export purposes? It is set in the central Queensland gemfields, and follows a few months in the lives and inconsistent fortunes of two miners and their extended family of shanty-town neighbours. It is highly traditional comedy, working through obstacles to the formation of couples; and is also very much in the style of the springtime pastoral, like H.E. Bates' *The Darling Buds of May*. Those who come to the little collection of humpies, chook-runs and old buses, in which the spirit of freedom is alive, cannot resist it. They stay on, drinking it like a tonic, being transformed. Tax collectors don't wander into camp, but the twin-prop aeroplane salesman and a whole family do. Father, mother, daughter and prospective son-in-law arrive in a campmobile; and gradually they change, as though they were tax-collectors to whom the idea of collecting taxes has grown foreign. Dingwall transforms the rough and dusty gemfields into serendipity.

There is even an element of *Huckleberry Finn* in it, somewhere. Lisa Peers, as the daughter of the doctor (Norman Kaye) chooses between the two 'buddies' (Colin Friels and Harold Hopkins) and they finally see the end of their partnership in view. The Harold Hopkins character opts to head off into the deeper, more remote sapphire country, as though the frontiers of freedom have receded. This is not just because bigger, sharkier operators are moving in and rigging the game, obliterating the hopes and efforts of self-employed miners like Mike and Johnny, although this is dramatised in the battle between the two dinosaurean bulldozers. It is also because love, in the archaic terms of comedy, is seen as the natural limit of freedom, a kind of tender, civilising trap. Mike is claimed by it, and so the male couple must dissolve and its lone survivor, Johnny, must take the path of the eternal boy and light out for the shrinking territories that are always elsewhere.

Obedient to the conventions of comedy, the hard-drinking, rough-talking Kris McQuade character also falls in love — with the twin-prop salesman who comes to deliver the plane that Mike

The Third Phase (1981-?): Middle-Aged Spread? 221

and Johnny have never learnt to fly. Somehow he stays on. He extends to her the soft, civilising trap, as Lisa Peers' character does to Mike (Colin Friels). It simply can't be helped. Love eases the way from freedom to submission to Nature's demands. Comedy exacts its sacrifices in the form of obligatory couples, just as melodrama exacts its deaths. But there is a real loss in seeing that rare thing, a strong, free, even iconic female character like Kris McQuade's, bow low to her generic fate. She becomes a soft, romantic and unlikely thing who boards a bus for the city, perhaps forever. Colin Friels does not change character or revert to a more old-fashioned stereotype with the approach of 'love'. Only Kris McQuade un-makes herself and goes completely against her own grain. It is as though we are really in the Forest of Arden and *As You Like It*, and Kris McQuade is a kind of male impersonator, like Rosalind, who is released by love back into her female self. And Norman Kaye's enraptured, gentle soul, that so often gives rise to the exclamation, 'Wonderful! *Won*derful!' is really speaking Celia's famous 'Wonderful, wonderful, and most wonderful, wonderful, and yet again, wonderful . . .'. Better this, perhaps, than the too-familiar 'taming of the shrew' that Kris McQuade's conversion recalls with uncomfortable clarity, though modulated by Simon Chilvers' quirky 'Petruchio'.

But these reservations are slight beside the achievement of *Buddies* in finding a natural, graceful, larrikin voice, with which it speaks so lovingly of a Queensland place. It is a place so removed from the dictates and decorums of the dollar that it is possible to offer your guest your television antenna coat-hanger for his jacket as a mark of courtesy.

Another eccentric comedy of 1983, impressive for its toughness in dealing almost educationally with a range of sexual issues, albeit pre-AIDS, is *The Clinic*, directed by David Stevens from a screenplay by a doctor, Greg Millins. It follows a day in the life of a clinic for venereal disease with a comic rhythm not far removed from that of a British *Carry On . . .* film. The striking difference is the lack of prurience, and the genuine sense of a work place developing through its crisis-crossing, case-based structure. *The Clinic* is interesting also for the way it unselfconsciously depicts Australian city culture. Chris Haywood's role as the main doctor on duty, with Pat Evison as the social worker, for instance, are amply 'Australian' without a single sign of effort. The film's attention is trained on the almost pedagogical problem of getting its audience into a particular state of mind on sexual issues. It is at once properly fascinated, and properly pragmatic. In the main it succeeds, and *The Clinic* is that thing of wonder: an Australian film whose main protagonist (Chris Haywood) is *incidentally* gay, without this affecting either his viability as a protagonist, or the clarity of his masculinity.

Phar Lap (1983), written by David Williamson, directed by Simon Wincer, produced by John Sexton and strenuously promoted by Michael Edgely, is a horse film that follows the path blazed by *The Man From Snowy River*. A more direct lineage can be traced to *Breaker Morant*, *Gallipoli* and the marriage of the male-ensemble film and the AFC genre. Its obvious siblings are television mini-series, like *The Dismissal* (1983), *Bodyline* (1984), *Waterfront* (1984) to a point, and *The Last Bastion* (1984). *Phar Lap* is more in the business of national martyrs than heroes, and the list of mythic figures not yet 'done' is growing shorter. There is still Les Darcy, of course, the great boxer who, according to the Australian myth, was 'done in' by the Americans. It is a story along the lines of *Phar Lap*, and is probably in the pipeline by now.

The other striking thing about *Phar Lap* is that it is a carefully-aimed and judicious big-budget missile, targeted at a broad general audience. The money is almost tangibly weighed and placed in every scene. Horse-racing is still a national passion, with very broad working-class interest. The myth of Phar Lap, the greatest Australian galloper of all time, who never let down his multitude of working-class backers when the Depression was biting most deeply, is a museum-piece that didn't need a great deal of dusting-off to be recirculated as popular memory. The film is carefully worthy and tasteful enough to secure a middle-brow audience similar to that of the AFC genre, and the resonance of a great Aussie winner — and martyr — is, fifty years later, sufficiently palatable and coincident with new economic hard times to work well.

Interestingly, the Australian version is offered as a requiem. It begins with news of the horse's death in America, possibly by poisoning at the hands of the American mob, and flashes back to the story of his rise to glory and tragic end. The U.S.

The Third Phase (1981-?): Middle-Aged Spread? 223

version is chronological, so that the horse's fate has surprise value only, and the elegaic 'lest we forget' is removed completely. A ritual of popular memory (tinged, of course, by the sacred grief of martyrdom) is changed into a period horse story.

By cutting to the past from the wintry reverie of Phar Lap's trainer (Martin Vaughan), the Australian version also centred the story very much on one man's parallel fight against the odds. Their story is thus suspended between two wharfside arrivals. The first, at the start of the flashback, is that of the ungainly, unpromising gelding from New Zealand as he is unloaded, anxiously watched by the Vaughan character who has staked his small savings on this horse because of its champion bloodlines. The second, at the end of the film, is that of the horse's corpse; the world champion is dead in his prime because, in this version, the American mob could not afford to have an unstoppable outsider come in and destroy the delicate balance of the rigged tracks. In between comes the glorious story of the horse who was 'all heart', a hero of the working class, who couldn't be stopped even by the killing handicap weights he was forced to bear by that prime class enemy, the Victorian Turf Club, in his third victorious Melbourne Cup. Alongside runs the story of his trainer and handler (Tom Burlinson in a role that in many ways recalls *Snowy River*). They have to survive doubts, the contempt of other owners, and the idiosyncrasies of the animal himself. Both roles are well-filled; Martin Vaughan's drawn face and hunched figure make a powerful icon of the Depression era, otherwise signified in the film mainly by bleakness, grey clothes and hundreds of men's hats, almost as if the whole era was one long winter. In the teeth of bleakness and austerity comes a *winning* story.

In *Phar Lap*, as in the mini-series which are its siblings (with the partial exceptions of *Waterfront* and *The Dismissal*), we see the earnestness of the AFC genre partly transposed from picturesque period values to encompass a populist, nationalist reading of history. The populism is in the address to a common 'humanity' that is somehow beyond class, yet is figured forth strongly in imagery of 'the little man' and his champion; and to a sense of history as popular memory of small victories amid larger defeats, a gesture that soothes the historical sense even while seeming politically to arouse it.

'The little woman', if she sneaks into a scene or two in all

Hundreds of men's hats and a famous horse: the iconography of nostalgia in *Phar Lap*.

The Third Phase (1981-?): Middle-Aged Spread? 225

this, is there in quite a different sense: not as everywoman, but as the supportive or decorative wife, or, ideally, both. Judy Morris, as the wife of an American member of Phar Lap's syndicate (Ron Leibman), has one brief moment of modest defiance. Celia de Burgh, however, who plays the sweetheart and then wife of Tom Burlinson, is limited to little sweet gestures and an almost mute rendition of womanly virtues. Populist Australian history, it seems, congeals around piercing martyrdoms of the male spirit, from the bitter-sweet defeats of convict days through Ned Kelly to those of war and sport. Australianness, it seems, inheres in women hardly at all. And when you hear the moving, collective, populist voice of the crowd at the race-track chanting 'Phar Lap! Phar Lap!', that voice is exclusively male.

The original Phar Lap was stuffed and mounted after his death, and the art of taxidermy for years preserved his memory until this latter-day resurrection. That fact irresistibly recalls Pauline Kael's description of Australian film as taxidermy. The mini-series *Bodyline* recreated the infamous visit of the English cricket side to contest the Ashes in 1932. Gary Sweet, as Don Bradman, is obliged to spend a great deal of his time simply 'incarnating' the original hero, raising his arms and slowly turning his body to face the sweep of the crowd — who all wear those same hats, by the hundreds, from the *Phar Lap* crowd scenes. It was as if his presentation was thought of as a celluloid version of taxidermy; he didn't represent Bradman, he displayed him, often mutely. This is not to underrate the compelling ten hours of viewing that the series managed to create from cricket, the characterization of the English captain Jardine (Hugo Weaving), and antagonism between Australia and the British, especially as manifest in the 'bodyline' bowling introduced by the British against the unbeatable Australian side. Nevertheless, the iconic process of representing Australianness, established so early and powerfully in *Sunday Too Far Away*, and subsequently characteristic of all male-ensemble films, is intensified or rigidified in *Phar Lap* and the related mini-series to a monumental art form, not unlike taxidermy.

The Dismissal, in 1983, led the way for *Bodyline* and *The Last Bastion* in 1984. The two Kennedy-Miller productions (*Dismissal* and *Bodyline*) made extensive use of a contemplative voice-over to narrate the story and set the tone of the series.

The huge success of the contemporary British mini-series *Brideshead Revisited*, with its cultivated and seductive voice-over by Jeremy Irons, seems to influence *The Dismissal* to a new infusion of awe for the intonement (interment?) of memory. But this is not a memorial fantasy about the refinement and decay of sensibility amid extremes of class and wealth; it is *the* television docu-drama, erected in memory of the real, deposed Labor Government of 1972-5, dismissed by the then Governor General ('Queen's man'), Sir John Kerr, in an act that tore many veils from the face of real power in this country at that moment. To many eyes, what was exposed was not just the relentless born-to-rule ideology of the old Australian establishment, but the deliberate, destabilising intervention of American secret intelligence activities in the affairs of this supposedly sovereign state.

What would be the effect of writing for *The Dismissal* a voice-over of the poignant, fluted kind so affecting in that grave ballet of class moves, slowed almost to the point of absurdity, *Brideshead*?

> The narrative is crucial: it knows the truth, and thus marks the limit of our knowledge; it locks its historical material into the inexorable fall of the tragic hero; and its present anterior tense sonorously combines immediacy and seriousness... This persistent narrative determinism, saturated with dramatic irony, serves a profoundly teleological conception of history, one which hardly encourages political action.
> Stuart Cunningham and Stephen Crofts, in *Film News*, April/May, 1983.

Instead of unpicking the complex web of factors that connected personalities, intentions, impulses, actions and the wider forces of Australian and world history, *The Dismissal* concentrates economically on backroom drama and careful, polished impersonations of the key politicians. These impersonations, however, do not become representations or interpretations of character and event. The voice-over erects its monumental style in honour of 'understanding': 'But maybe now we can begin to understand, and to understand is to forgive'. But a pageant of re-enactments of 'the scenes we never saw', presided over by a canny, sorrowful, educated voice-over, necessarily excludes the advice and commentary of people and institutions that played such intricate roles in the story: government bureaucracies, the

The Third Phase (1981-?): Middle-Aged Spread? 227

media and their bosses, and public opinion.[8]

The series dignifies itself with the suggestion that it dares to re-open a wound, a Pandora's box of private knowledge, in order to refresh the memory. But this mortuary art is no more dedicated to historical understanding than are the thousands of public war memorials erected in Australian country towns to other casualties of history. Like those monuments, it offers a place to the genuine need to remember. The short film *Exits* (1981) which deals with how the events of November, 1975, affected a few people in Melbourne, is far more painful and complex than *The Dismissal*. And in another way, Max Gillies' just-over-the-top impersonations of Hawke, Fraser, Peacock, Reagan and others also probes much harder for the political bone. For Gillies, impersonation is the means by which to produce, not solemn wax works, but deadly serious caricature.

As the post-tax-incentive period has gone on, there is much more evidence of staidness than of inventiveness. The tastes and styles of the middle years have been replayed and played out in the later years, possibly because of the partial re-inclusion of AFC approval as an essential ingredient since the tax incentive for investors has been reduced. Possibly, too, the lapse of that moment when it was possible, on film, loudly and euphorically to proclaim Australianness, has left a period of indecision. Certainly, in 1983-4 there was very little evidence of confident inventiveness; the exceptions might include the two later Paul Cox films discussed above, *Man of Flowers* and *My First Wife*, and possibly *Strikebound* (directed by Richard Lowenstein), although *Strikebound* is primarily a re-production of certain British history dramas of the early seventies such as *Days of Hope* and *Culloden* in the Australian context. But it is the first attempt at the subject of strikes and labour relations — a very large theme in Australian culture — on the big screen since *Sunday Too Far Away*, although the mini-series *Waterfront* precedes it on television.

Nevertheless, some of 1984's examples of much earlier trends are praiseworthy. *Fast Talking*, written and directed by Ken Cameron, for example, is perhaps the most masterly example of Australian social realism thus far. Rod Zuanick is excellent as the 'con artist' Steve, a fast-talking, slippery eel of a kid who squirms his way through the centre of the story. There are lovely

A conventional romance with a sharp sense of the migrant experience. Ivar Kants Steve Bisley, Annie Byron, Gosia Dobrowolska, Halina Abramovicz and Dennis Miller in *Silver City*.

One of the rare direct engagements with class and capital, the labour history film *Strikebound*, with leading players Carol Burns and Chris Haywood.

The Third Phase (1981-?): Middle-Aged Spread? 229

scenes in which the poetic power of the genre is tapped: for example, when his mother's things are moved violently out of the house, Steve watches as the moving men let one full drawer of underwear slip and spill from the chest they are carrying. His eye catches their slightly derisive distaste for this evidence of the feminine as they try to jam it back in. Another is the moment when Steve first ventures into Redback's (Steve Bisley's) motorcycle wreckers' yard, a surreal, magic place under Redback's presiding genius.

Michael Pattinson's *Street Hero* tries to energise and expand a similar social realist domain with rock music. It is another story of a kid — read 'boy' — who flirts with trouble as his family breaks up around him. It uses brightly-lit, larger-than-life sets to signify the intense night-life of the teenage urge for freedom, and relentlessly applies heavy, elaborately mixed rock music and some techniques of rock-clip editing. It works, in fits and starts, but it doesn't cohere. It is difficult to maintain one's patience with the literally 'supporting' role of Sigrid Thornton as Gloria, an ever-available listening or leaning post for Vinnie (Vince Colossimo), the rebel without a cause.

Silver City, Sophia Turkiewicz's first feature, produced by Joan Long, is a late entry in the respectable AFC genre, a curiously old-fashioned, undemanding story which follows the arrival in Australia of a young Polish migrant, Nina (Gosia Dobrowolska) in 1949. She has formed friendships on the boat with an educated married man, Julian (Ivar Kants) and his wife, Anna (Anna Jemison). In the 'silver city' of the corrugated-iron migrant camp, an affair between Nina and Julian develops for a while. The story is sandwiched as a flashback between two moments of their meeting on a train, years later. Nina, still single, a teacher rising on her career ladder, wistfully watches Julian arrive to the welcome of his wife and grown children. The tone of *Women's Weekly* romance creeps in too often, distracting the film from the emotional and erotic pulls between people. Rather, it explores safer, more sunlit grounds, in which Julian is something of a poor specimen, pulled in contradictory directions, and finally forced to satisy the unyielding moral framework of the genre. This is not to deny the sympathetic care with which the migrant experience of the post-war period is re-created 'from inside'. From this perspective Australians seem as dense and ludicrous as they first judged the non-English speaking migrants to be. And the lovely central performance of Gosia Dobrowolska, a Polish actress who had, herself, recently migrated to Australia should not be overlooked.

The big-budget *Razorback*, directed by rock-clip maker, Russell Mulcahy, promised to be the most shamelessly exploitationist film of the time. A wild pig (curiously called a 'razorback', as though that were common Australian parlance, rather than American) roams the outback, devouring female ecologists, ripping homes apart and seizing babies from their cradles. The 'pig rampant' motif clearly spills over from, and into the human world. Benny and Dicko (Chris Haywood and David Argue) are two caricatured porcine males whose kangaroo-pet-food factory, a foul, marvellous, Dickensian place of carcasses and steam, is the prime symbol of the fallen state of man and his rapaciousness. Nature breeds her revenge in the form of giant pigs who feed off the offal of apparently ceaseless kangaroo slaughter that somehow goes on despite a landscape almost completely bare of vegetation. An obscure smoke drifts across every frame with no apparent source (probably traceable to its real origins in Mulcahy's rock clips). Perhaps it can be recuperated by the viewer as an emanation from the hell that is mankind; *Razorback* is *Wake in Fright* revisited, but with the theme of the male as pig writ large and Gothic. Yet it falls back on the usual old stories of woman as victim, and man as eventual hero, in a saga of man against beast. The scenes between Benny and Dicko remain as if part of another, more interesting, film of pure Australian Gothic, with wit and deliberate grotesquerie.

But it was still possible in the same year for a film like *Fantasy Man* to be produced. It is a very low-budget film, written and directed by John Meagher, which is an even more curious throwback. It recalls the fumbling aesthetic of, say, Tim Burstall's *Two Thousand Weeks* in 1968, made in a complete vacuum of past practice and audience demand. In *Fantasy Man*, Harold Hopkins plays a man in a cliche of a mid-life crisis. Jeannie Drynan plays his zombie-like wife with an existence so inexplicably vacant that she must, it seems, either signify, or spring from a mind in the cast of the very early sixties. Eerily, the film never declares its strange oscillation through twenty years as something of which it is conscious, and yet this remains the only striking thing about it. A film like this makes one rub one's eyes and wonder if one and a half decades of industry history really did take place.

8

Epilogue: Famous Last Words

I await the end of the cinema with optimism.[1]

It's been a very honorable industry. Sometimes it's been dull, but by God it's been decent! . . . There are films that the entire industry knew before the first frame was shot should never be made, but made they were. But basically, it's been an astonishingly thrilling experience.[2]

I don't think anyone with eyes or ears could seriously call *Indiana Jones and the Temple of Doom* or *The Cotton Club* or *Dune* the films of free men. . .[3]

The unique capacity of video is to make the work mortal and immortal at the same time, a form of survival through mutation — or death through embalmment.[4]

Sometimes freedom at the production level can be translated into commercial success only when distributors and/or exhibitors decide to nurse an unusual film through a difficult period until it achieves box-office health.[5]

The middle of the road is a very dead end.[6]

Taking the most pessimistic view, this has been a peculiarly inhibited cinema, enclosed by its second-world, second-cinema contradictions. It is organised into a restrictive force field of aesthetic choices by its government patronage, its mythos of commerciality, and the dictum that the cinema shall be the philosopher's stone in Australia's quest for national identity.

The social imaginary that animates this cinema has been the desire *for* a social imaginary, a desire largely unfulfilled because of the double bind of our construction within 'dependency', both cultural and economic. We have tried to hold our pessimism in check, to explore the relative richness of variation that has arisen under the regime of such a desire. But our interest, at this final stage of the argument, is in signs of any possible escape from this prism of opposing mirrors to a cinema that can articulate 'cinema' more confidently and 'identity' less obsessively, and far more richly and critically.

Apart from the short, freakish run of eccentrics which got through in the boom year of 1981-2 among the many 'commercial' films that escape the memory because they never reached the screen, the third and present phase of the industry could not be said to have fostered the production of very many 'unusual' films. The cinema of what has been called 'still the easiest country in the world to make a feature film' seems to be mired in an endless reiteration of its own middle past.

An impression of exhaustion, replication and *deja-vu* which afflicts mainstream cinema throughout the world in the middle eighties. As Jonathan Rosenbaum puts it, 'When one hears that firms in Seattle and Toronto are planning to colour in old black and white classics on image processors and release these coloured versions on videocassette, it certainly feels as though we're at the end of something.'[7] But Australian cinema seems particularly restricted. The greater commercialisation of its base has not liberated its filmmakers, or thrown open its field of aesthetic possibilities. On the contrary, the tension between 'honourable' and 'commercial' has merely constricted the field further, and 1984 and 1985 have continued the stale and increasingly bland pattern of repetition.

The present industry was born again in rhetoric about film as the most important, mass industrial artform at a moment when television had long assumed this mantle. Now, as the advent of video threatens further displacement, putting cinema on the shelf and under electronic control, the restoration of an Australian cinema feels increasingly late, and its efflorescence in talk and movies seems more and more like a sunset effect.

We have explored the ways in which this cinema has entrapped itself in a restrictive field of aesthetic choices. It has done so under two regimes of virtually self-imposed censorship: one is the desire to be acceptable to official culture which flows from the industry's dependence on government patronage. The other is the anxious, always mysterious demographics of the box office, audience and markets which determine the requirement of a pre-sale as early as the first moves of project development. And, of course, both of these are modified by the ambivalent demand, explored in Chapter One, that a second cinema be like, but not too much like, Hollywood. This false choice between the devil of worthiness and the deep blue sea of crassness, between the AFC genre/social realism and cold commercialism, does not allow much freedom. It encourages the safe, middlebrow, middle-of-the-road attitude that characterises Industry-1 at its worst, and opposes it not with the films of free people, but with the cable-fodder or instant video of Industry-2.

As we have seen, the most striking development of the second phase, which otherwise oversaw the consolidation of these narrow polarities, is the evolution of a way of speaking Australianness through a blending of the AFC genre's period and 'taste' with the male ensemble film's 'offensively Australian' vigour and strong repertoire of male iconography. *Breaker Morant* paved the way to *Gallipoli* and beyond, into the realm of period mini-series like *Bodyline, The Last Bastion, Anzacs*. At last, it seemed, the right chord was struck and resonated through large audiences and optimistic box-office figures. The industry was speaking Australianness in a way that the people wanted to hear, and that governments could feel proud of and broadcast abroad.

The Man from Snowy River is the high-water mark of this tide of approval for a shamelessly partisan nationalism, romantically cleared of any residue of wryness or irony, and consequently losing the likeable quality of 'being on to yourself' that balances the best of Bryan Brown's embodiments of what it is to be Australian. David Williamson's work was important in finding and shaping the male-ensemble form; his own transition from the ironic to the romantic influenced the evolution of a successful way to screen Australia. But equally important have been the iconic definitions offered in the work of actors like Bryan Brown, Jack Thompson, Mel Gibson and Paul Hogan, supported by a rich gallery of character actors like Bill Hunter, Steve Bisley, Max Cullen and Tony Barry, who have intricately inflected and refined an articulation of male Australian vernacular. They continue a long-standing Australian tradition established in the twenties by actors like Arthur Tauchert and Tal Ordell, and developed in the thirties and forties by Peter Finch, Pat Hanna and Chips Rafferty.

Of course the merging of these two tendencies of the first and second phases to satisfy, on the verge of the third phase, the wave of public desire for a positive representation of Australianness on film, is in complete response to the double bind of the social imaginary of this cinema, explored in Chapter One, that centres on the equivocal nature of our declaration of ourselves. Boyishly positive as the enunciation of Australianness so often is, in the films and series concerned, the 'rub' that creates all of the stories is the simultaneous embrace and rejection of our dependence. The other (Britain or America) is the source of meaning, of readable difference. And the desire of these texts is to be part of the ritual of recognition and refamiliarisation; however deft the handling of the ritual becomes, the underlying anxiety that the answer to the question of identity can never be found remains. It is there in the choice of stories, the shaping of heroes, all of the deft provocations to self-love. The posture of accommodating dependence, both economic and cultural, forces us to endlessly repeat the pattern of assertion and rejection of an identity that can never be truly afforded, or taken for granted. *The Man from Snowy River*'s rite of passage is, therefore, also enacted for the 'young nation' in search of the legend from which they can read the 'difference' that might otherwise go unnoticed.

But in the third phase there is not even this degree of aesthetic adaptation, even though this adaptation was confined to the closed terms of a social imaginary turned in upon the problem of itself. There is of course, the new benchmark set by the huge box-office success of Paul Hogan's *Crocodile Dundee* in 1986, surpassing the previous record set in Australia by *E.T.*. But this event is curiously separate from the trends that surround it, and its success does not seem to provide any clear augury for the health of the industry, economically or aesthetically. From this perhaps too recent vantage, the film, like its huge success, is a curiosity, a well-timed and well-aimed capitalisation upon Hogan's immense

Paul Hogan comes to town (New York) in *Crocodile Dundee*.

popularity, both at home and abroad, particularly in America. He is the representative of casual, self-deprecating, likeable Australianness, inviting the world to come and relax in Australia, and Australians to tour in their own country. Hogan has a decade of popularity behind him in Australia as a wry, but never really satiric stand-up comic from television talk shows and advertising. *Crocodile Dundee* has some elements of story, but never enough to disturb these strong foundations, or the associations with Paul Hogan's existing popularity; the rhythm is as slow, and the jokes as pleasurably telegraphed, as in a television talk show. The tourist-board-style promotion is never far away.

The storyline borrows from a variety of thirties American comedies, with a mix of Tarzan and Peter Pan sitting easily with Hogan's television persona which carries Australian casualness to something like an art form. The idea of a naif abroad, a post-industrial noble savage set loose in the big city, in this case the skills of the Northern Territory buffalo hunter applied to New York, is a pleasantly familiar one; Capra's *Mr Deeds Goes to Town*, or La Cava's *My Man Godfrey* (both 1936) come to mind at once. *Mr Deeds* also has the motif of the newspaper woman (Jean Arthur in *Mr Deeds*, Linda Kozlowski in *Crocodile*) from the big city who comes to the provinces and can't resist bringing back alive an extraordinary specimen of primitive virtue (Gary Cooper and Paul Hogan respectively). And virtue it proves to be: the heroine finally sees that there is an irresistible and quite unconscious moral superiority in the genuine article, and she chooses him over her sophisticated big-city fiancee.

In both cases — 1936 and 1986 — a simple, appealing and conservative populism sets up this choice and gives approval to the 'silly' man, in the original sense as 'innocent', unspoiled by knowledge. The city breeds human complexity, competition, corruption; people don't really know each other, but are burdened by 'useless' ambitions and opinions. The wilderness breeds wise fools like Mick 'Crocodile' Dundee, who says, when asked about the arms race, 'It's none of my business'. Nor does he really have 'opinions' about the mindless kangaroo shooters who blunder drunkenly through the bush with spotlights; he has no 'opinion', but after a moment's thought he does have a simple and effective counter-action that easily scares them off. Implicitly, this populist scorn for the 'myth' of knowledge reassures us in our powerlessness and our sense of never being able to know enough to overcome it. Our simplicity is our virtue, the film tells us, and if we can't avoid our planned extinction, we can at least be more confident about dealing with New York muggers. In both 1936 and 1986, we seem to be getting simple stories for scary times. Hogan has called the film 'a feelgood movie', revealing how close it comes to familiar categories of television advertising.[8] Capra's film embodies far more complex desires, including a conscious attempt to criticise and counter New Deal government interventionism. Hogan's film is probably far less politically conscious in its appeal to the desire to retreat from the vast problems of the eighties.

There are no real baddies in the film, no real dangers, not even the danger of sexuality. Hogan has the perpetual, incorruptible boyishness of Peter Pan, even if his outfit is bushland brown, not woodland green. There is even a moment in which he points to 'his' territory in the northern outback: 'There it is: the Never Never country'. His practiced simplicity is a long way from the primitive gesture that was *Barry McKenzie*, early in the first phase. Both films involve an unapologetically Australian hero abroad, although the metropolis to conquer shifts from London to New York. But with Mick Dundee there is absolutely no offence intended, nor is he ever really a comic butt, as poor Barry is. Mick is, in fact, a winner in all the small and unassuming ways, and cannot possibly offend anyone, Australian or American. Where *Barry McKenzie* satirised each of its target audiences for the other, *Crocodile Dundee* flatters both. The Tourist Board couldn't be better served.

Otherwise, the most noteworthy development of the third phase has been a small re-flowering of the Australian Gothic tendency which began as the darker side of ebullient ockerism, itself in part a mask for the severe lack of confidence of the first phase. *Bliss* (1985) has been the box-office high-point of this resurfaced tendency; the film's distributors had no confidence in the film, and its producer, Tony Buckley, was obliged to 'four-wall' it for a period to prove its potential as an art-house film with a relatively large and steady audience. In fact, the cold feet of the distributors became the central drama of the film's publicity campaign, along with quite violently mixed reviews. In such a stagnant aesthetic climate, *Bliss* looks like a breakthrough, with its 'fresh' surrealism, its blurring of reality and dream, life and after-life, and the bizarre

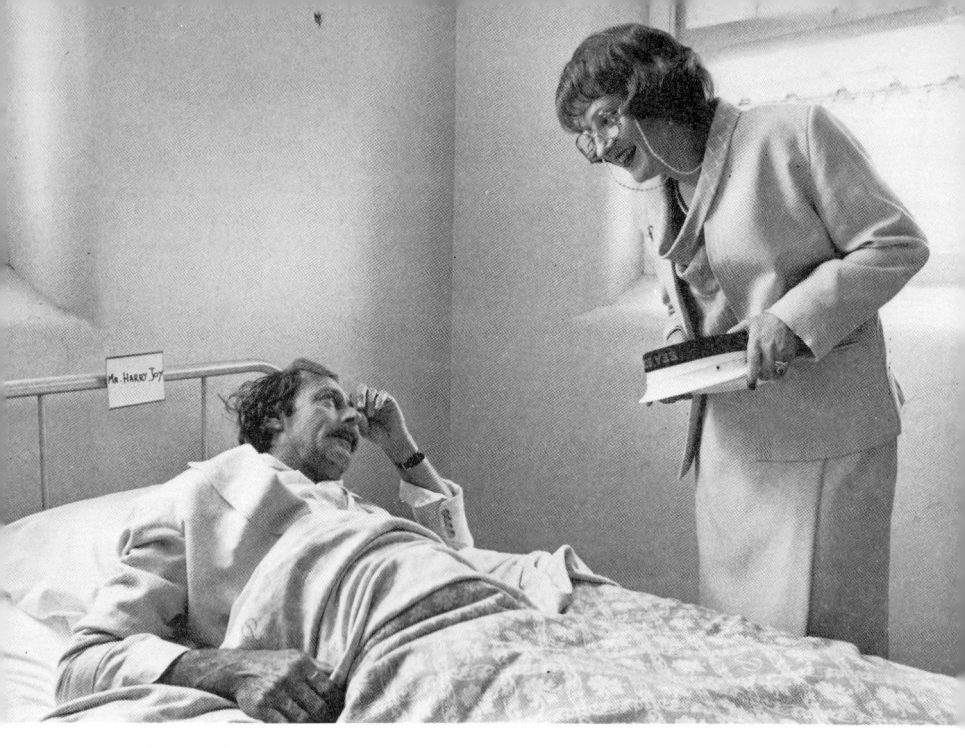

Life or after-life? Matron (Kerry Walker) assures Harry (Barry Otto) he is not himself, in *Bliss*.

The Gothic 'underworld' of Bartertown in *Mad Max: Beyond Thunderdome*.

texture it creates with its black, Gothic view of Australian life. But its formal experimentation is anticipated as early as Fellini's work in the sixties, or even in eccentric seventies mainstream American films like *Slaughterhouse Five*. Still, its success is heartening, to the extent that it gives credibility to an impulse off-centre to, if not quite outside, the tight forcefield of aesthetic possibilities.

The long-awaited 'Mad Max 3', *Mad Max: Beyond Thunderdome*, in 1985, which pressure-cooked anticipation by shooting on a closed set and swearing its crew to secrecy about the plot, finally feels a little too much like a film made by Spielberg: no longer the film of a 'free' man. The creation of two contrasting worlds, Bartertown and the lost children's valley, seems to draw off most of the film's energy; there is a lot of mythology, but little of the intuitive play with mythic archetype that made Mad Max 2 so rich. The third film has crowded sets and ingenious action to rival Spielberg, but there are no live ends to follow, and while Max has not yet surrendered the precious anomie that makes him a viable hero in the early stages of a romance cycle, he has lost much of it in the cooking.

The earlier films in the *Mad Max* cycle draw energy from Australian Gothic, which is a genuinely local aesthetic tendency, and one that has had some vitalising effects on the industry. They also make a typically eccentric use of a bizarre mix of genres. There is an enjoyable whiff of danger in this process. The films speak to an adult sense of 'the movies', and the risks that could be taken knowingly. *Beyond Thunderdome*, however, conforms too readily to the 'PGR' canon established by the *Star Wars* cycle: it moves fast but risks little.

Clearly, the two subsidiary groupings that seem to offer the greatest hope for anyone looking for a way out of the static forcefield between the dominant poles of worthiness and commerciality, are Australian Gothic and the eccentrics. In these we see the traces of small expeditions towards some of the major cinematic territories excluded from the present aesthetic force field. To appreciate how impoverished this cinema is, it is necessary to consider some of these exciting, shrinking possibilities if we are to proceed in a free spirit of speculation.

For a start, melodrama is a curiously stunted branch of film. We have noted some of the important exceptions, all of them

Secrets, confessions, rumours and politics: the Jesuitical, in the person of John Flaus, in *Traps*.

'successful' films: *Mad Max 2*, *The Man from Snowy River*, *Careful, He Might Hear You*. But despite the financial rewards for these ventures, Australian cinema shows a curious inability to deal with passion, dream, the marvellous, the play of extremes that belong to Romance and its mongrel offspring, melodrama. Outside the Gothic and eccentric films, and a few elements of the fantastic in the work of Peter Weir, Paul Cox, and, more recently, Jane Campion, there has been a marked unwillingness to join the games of popular culture and engage with such close accomplices of surrealism as pulp literature, horror comics, fairytales, true romance confessions, popular science, the unconscious, rituals and dreams. Few Australian filmmakers appear to understand Raymond Chandler's remark, 'It probably started in poetry, almost everything does'. Where in Australian film is the appetite and readiness for the marvellous, the appeal to exaltation, impatience with the sham of official public culture, insistence on emotions and ideas experienced to the hilt?

This is a cinema perilously short of films that explore territories in which opposites call each other into being, the shadow of the self is embraced and the sacred is acknowledged in a proper spirit of hopeful scepticism. Surely life is needed in the cinematic responses to what are perhaps our most dangerous times, despite a strictly-maintained veneer of normalcy. But melodrama, excess, passion are revamped in the most old-fashioned and conservative ways, harking back to the early thirties and Ken Hall's *Tall Timbers* and *Squatter's Daughter*. So *The Man from Snowy River* was remade by one of its producers as *Cool Change* (1986), in which 'mountain men' are set against the new enemy of the present, the 'townies' and 'greenies' who wish to curtail their right to exploit the high country. It is a veritable National Party romance. Alexander Kluge expresses a wish for a storytelling of the Left that could move into some of the traditional territories of the Right: myth, dream, a potent imaginary. Never was its absence more sorely felt. But perhaps the problem is more difficult and subtle, and the play of extremes, in forms close to the heart of popular culture, must inspire us to an understanding on a level one move on from violent opposites and their mutual dependence.

Which brings us to another aching gap in this cinema: political film. This should never, of course, be considered as dealing narrowly with politics, but, more profoundly, as dealing with history in order to clarify our position and our political strength in the present. The exceptions are quickly counted: *Newsfront, Strikebound, Exits, Traps. Newsfront* achieves many lovely and precise articulations of the past from which we are generated, but they are held within a melancholic sentimentality that finally limits their use in the present. *Strikebound* also retains an edge of melancholic contemplation as part of a tradition of labour history-telling in the style of Ken Loach. It exists to fill gaps, to throw light on other hidden or dismissed histories.

But we need history films that alter our sense of the present. *Traps* (1985) flirts with this possibility. It teasingly promises in part to explore the contradictions of the Hawke Labor Government. As Tim Rowse discusses, the film plays with the notion of 'secret history': '*Traps* is not so much an expose, more an essay on the rhetoric of telling secrets.'[9] The engagement with history remains teasing, playfully factitious, fascinated by the infinite regressions in the opposing mirrors of politics and media, and the way that the half-lit space between is rich in conspiracies, lies, confessions and secrets. 'The secret history is a special kind of symbolic capital; it includes, equally, both information and the possibility of information we might never have. The gaps give as much pleasure as the records, if not more.'[10] *Traps* is halfway between *Allies* (1984), an intelligent example of the expose documentary, and *Exits* (1980), an experimental, playful venture into the private and public debris around the sacking of the Whitlam Government. *Traps* is an interesting eccentric, but not a film as confident of its right to speak directly about things political as, say, Rosi's *Cadaveri Eccellenti*.

But, once again, a film need not be about politics to be 'political'. It can be argued that, in a second cinema, any film in a critical vernacular tradition qualified by precise local renderings of region, gender, class and race must be a 'history' film with political meaning in the present.

Kenneth Frampton has argued that a critical regionalist architecture is an architecture of resistance, of strategic counter-action to the impact of placeless, homogenising, technocratically formidable 'universal' civilisation; the elements of critical regionalism are derived indirectly from the peculiarities of a particular place and time.[11] Translated into the terms of a small local cinema, sharp local cultural detail in a film whose narrative

Crowded sets and ingenious action — but something lost in the cooking? *Mad Max: Beyond Thunderdome.*

is implicated with the place itself, and the network of meanings it has acquired, can mark the site of a true polar opposite to the limbo world of the cold commercial group of films. And whatever the story, whatever genre or generic mix may take us that step away from 'documentary reality' of a particular time and place, films which are alert to the demands of a critical vernacular will be alive to political meaning. They will also, of course, have their primary life before a domestic audience. Films posed in this way may not gratify a huge international audience, but may well fascinate a large audience abroad, as well as speaking directly to a particular cross-section of the home audience. The appeal is not national, nor is the impulse to gratify its audience, in contrast to the increasingly calculated 'innocence' which has embalmed the male-ensemble and AFC-genre versions of national identity. Nurturing certain film distributors, like Ronin in the Australian market, who seek out marginal, lower-budget films and promote and program them in a way that gradually contacts and builds a small but sufficient audience, are needed to offset the 'one-week-on-acid-test' model of the major distributors and exhibition chains. New modes of distribution on television and video, like the proposal of something on the model of Britain's Channel 4, are also essential ways of creating new audiences. Only these may guarantee the preservation of some small aesthetic freedom and permit such films to get through the bureaucratic decision-making process.

Such films would be critical rather than consensual in their address to an audience, particular rather than iconic in their characterisation, aimed at defamiliarisation rather than recognition. If we are to find the way out of the double-bind that 'fixes' the question of cultural identity and limits it to conservative, consensual national terms, it is probably through a whole-hearted embrace of the contradictions of dependency, a move impossible in films making a conscious nationalist appeal. Critical regionalism unpicks the threads that bind our cultural baggage; the male ensemble, AFC-genre film tries to knit them into the tidiest, most portable bundle possible, contradictions and all.

None of this is meant to imply that 'critical regionalist' films would necessarily be restricted to the aesthetic of social realism, despite that group's 'natural' affinity for small budgets and a socially critical posture. Social realist 'problem' films tend to make an

Wrong World, right kind of cinema? Jo Kennedy and Richard Moir just surviving at the edge of a doubtful future.

aesthetic virtue of the most quotidian realities; for them, reality is purely material, often bleak, cheap or cluttered, under the pallor of functionally low light levels; furthermore, the 'problem', with its essentially pessimistic connotations, generates and defines the world of the story; there is no story outside it, and understanding is folded in upon itself. A critical, regionalist eye for the particularity of a cultural time and place can be open to all formal playfulness, transgeneric mixes, sensual realities, and possibilities of the marvellous, for which we have been calling.

Does this kind of rumination seem like a manifesto in search of a cinema? Not entirely. As we have seen, the most interesting films among the eccentrics involve just such a mix; and they involve some blurring of the traditional distinction between the commercial mainstream and the low-budget independent. It is possible to connect, for example, *Shirley Thompson versus the Aliens*, *Palm Beach*, *Third Person Plural*, *Against the Grain*, *Going*

Down, *Starstruck*, *Man of Flowers*, *Traps* and *Wrong World*, and to see the makings of an antidote to a social imaginary caught by the riddle of 'national identity'; and to a cinema that is correspondingly stuck in the very dead end that is the middle of the road.

Notes

Chapter 1

1. For example, Joan Mellen, *The Waves at Genji's Door*, Pantheon Books, N.Y., 1976; Stuart M. Kaminsky, *American Film Genres*, Pflaum, Dayton Ohio, 1975; or Andrew Bergman, *We're in the Money*, New York U.P., 1970.
2. I am grateful to Stuart Cunningham for several stimulating recent works in which he turns over this question (and brings Elsaesser's important recent work to attention), especially 'The Text in Film History', *Australian Journal of Screen Theory*, 17/18, 1986.
3. Thomas Elsaesser, 'Film History and Visual Pleasure: Weimar Cinema', in *Cinema Histories, Cinema Practices*, eds. Patricia Mellencamp and Philip Rosen, American Film Institute Monograph IV, 1984.
4. *Ibid.*, p.77.
5. *Ibid.*, p.74.

   An interesting exposition of the political economy of dominion capitalism is in Philip Ehrensaft and Warwick Armstrong, 'Dominion Capitalism: a first statement', *Australian and New Zealand Journal of Sociology*, 14(3) Part 2, October 1978.
7. As late as March 3, 1986, we were still disengaging our legal structures from those of Britain in the Australia Act and the Australia (Request and Consent) Act.
8. Sylvia Lawson, 'Towards Decolonization: some problems and issues for film history in Australia', *Film Reader* 4, 1979.
9. This process is traced in Richard White, *Inventing Australia: Images and Identity*, Allen and Unwin, 1981.
10. See, for example, John Sinclair, 'From Modernisation to Cultural Dependence: Mass Communication Studies and the Third World', *Media Information Australia* 23, February 1982, and Malcolm Alexander, 'Dependency Theory and the Structural Analysis of Australian Society', Paper No. 41, La Trobe University Dept. of Sociology, August 1977.
11. Ross Gibson, *The Diminishing Paradise: literary perceptions of Australia*, Sirius Books, Sydney, 1984.

12. Bernard Smith, *Australian Painting 1788-1970*, Oxford U.P., 1971.
13. Australian Film Commission.
14. *See* the 'eccentric' grouping, Chapter 2.
15. *See* the 'eccentric' grouping, Chapter 2.
    See the 'AFC genre' and 'social realist' groupings, Chapter 2.
16. This is a concept with considerable heuristic efficiency, fundamental to all film theory since the early seventies, but notoriously difficult to demonstrate. It refers to styles of camera placement, editing, 'sutured' point-of-view, and the plausible diegetic 'reality' this creates in American narrative film roughly from the late silent or early sound period though to the decline of the studio system and its vertically integrated system of production and distribution in the late fifties.

Chapter 3

1. Tim Burstall, Tariff Board Hearings, Transcript (1973):971.
2. *Ibid.*
3. John Hinde, *Other People's Pictures*, Australian Broadcasting Commission, 1979, Chapter 5.
4. Meaghan Morris, 'Personal Relationships and Sexuality', in *The New Australian Cinema*, ed. Scott Murray, Nelson, Melbourne, 1980, p.148.
5. Cited by David Stratton, *The Last New Wave*, Angus and Robertson, 1980, p.171.
6. Stratton (*ibid.*) says that it earned $225,000 in film hire, on a $50,000 budget.
7. Sir Henry Bolte was a colourful, long-standing Victorian Liberal premier, abhored by the left with much the same horrified fascination that Sir Joh Bjelke-Petersen, of Queensland, so recently commanded.
8. The Sydney 'push' of the sixties' sceptical, existentialist style of libertarianism was strongly influenced by John Anderson, Professor of Philosophy at Sydney University, in the fifties and sixties.

Chapter 4

1. Quoted by David White in *Australian Movies to the World*, Fontana and Cinema Papers 1984.
2. *See* David Stratton's account of the post-production process

in Ken Hannam's absence, in *The Last New Wave*, Angus and Robertson, 1980.
3. Ian Hunter, 'Corsetway to Heaven', *Arena*, 41, 1976, p.10, reprinted in Albert Moran and Tom O'Regan (eds), *An Australian Film Reader*, Currency Press 1985, pp.190-3.
4. Meaghan Morris, in *The New Australian Cinema*, op.cit., p.143.
5. *Ibid*.

Chapter 5

1. Played by Graham Matters, the official Wizard employed by the University of N.S.W. Students Union for several years.
2. Gary Foley was a well-known black rights activist in the seventies who had considerable involvement in the writing of the script.
3. Except for the American co-production, *Wake in Fright*.
4. John Duigan, quoted in Sue Mathews, *35mm Dreams: Conversations with five directors about the Australian film revival*, Penguin, 1984, p.218.
5. 'Personal Relationships and Sexuality', in Scott Murray ed., *The New Australian Cinema*, Nelson, 1980, p.146.
6. For example, Brian McFarlane, *Words and Pictures*, Heinemann, Australia, pp.111-127.
7. Review of *Palm Beach*, *Cinema Papers* (24), December/January 1977- 8, p.660.

Chapter 6

1. Susan Gardner, 'From Murderer to Martyr: the legend of Breaker Morant', *Critical Arts Monograph*, 1 (July 1987). We are indebted to this excellent essay for alerting us to many sources on Morant.
2. Russel Ward, 'Another Perspective of Breaker Morant', *Metro Media and Education*, p.51.
3. 'Renar', *Bushman and Buccaneer: Harry Morant, His Ventures and Verses*, Sydney, H.T. Dunn, 1902.
4. August, 1980.
5. Amanda Lohrey, '*Gallipoli*: male innocence as marketable commodity', *Island Magazine*, 9/10 (March 1981), p.20.
6. Lohrey *ibid*:31, citing Bill Gammage, historical advisor on

Gallipoli.
7. *Ibid*.
8. We are indebted to an unpublished essay by Sue Gruszin, a student at the New South Wales Institute of Technology, for this insight.
9. George Miller interviewed by Pat Broeske, *Films in Review* 33(8), October, 1982, p.142.

Chapter 7

1. This last carries with it the faintest whiff of incest, something frequently entertained by, but seldom actualised in, melodrama. If Spur is Jim's adoptive, surrogate father, and if he really *were* Jessica's father, then. . . But in a brief scene at the gate, he dismisses Harrison's twenty years of suspicion.
2. Meaghan Morris, 'Personal Relationships and Sexuality', in Scott Murray (ed.), *The New Australian Cinema*, Nelson, 1980, pp. 134-5.
3. Stuart Cunningham and Tom O'Regan, 'Starstructures', *Filmnews*, March, 1983, which cites Charles Altman (ed.), *Genre: The Musical, A Reader*, Routledge and Kegan Paul, 1981, p. 175.
4. Meaghan Morris, *op.cit.*, p. 134.
5. Diane Bell, *Daughters of the Dreaming*.
6. AFI.1. Awards Screenings Credits List and Synopses, 1983.
7. Peter Brooks, *The Melodramatic Imagination: Balzac, Henry James, and the Mode of Excess*, Yale University Press, New Haven, 1976, p. 66.
8. Sylvia Lawson, '*The Dismissal*', *Filmnews*, April/May, 1983.

Chapter 8

1. Jean-Luc Godard, *Cahiers du cinema*, 1968.
2. Phillip Adams, quoted in David Stratton, *The Last New Wave*, Angus and Robertson, 1980, pp.294-5.
3. Jonathon Rosenbaum, 'How to live in air-conditioning', *Sight and Sound*, Summer 1985, 54(3), p.163.
4. *Ibid.*, p.166.
5. *Ibid.*, p.165.
6. The English title of Alexander Kluge's 1973 film.
7. Rosenbaum, *loc.cit.*, p.162.

8. Quoted in John Baxter, 'A fistful of Koalas', *Cinema Papers*, May 1986, p.29.
9. Tim Rowse, '*Traps*: a sympathetic joke on its audience', *Filmnews*, 16(1), February/March 1986, p.15.
10. *Ibid.*
11. Kenneth Frampton, 'Towards a Critical Regionalism: six points for an architecture of resistance', in Hal Foster (ed.), *The Anti-Aesthetic: Essays on Post-Modern Culture*, Bay Press, 1983.

A Select Filmography

ABC OF LOVE AND SEX AUSTRALIAN STYLE
Released 1978. Eastman colour, 35 mm, 85 minutes. director: John Lamond. producer: John Lamond. screenplay: Alan Finney and John Lamond. photography: Garry Whapshott (in Australia), Lasse Bjork (in Sweden). design: Stephen Walsh. editor: Russell Hurley. cast: Robyn Bartley, Leon Cosack, Katie Morgan, puppetry by Denis Nicholson.

ADVENTURES OF BARRY McKENZIE, THE
Released 1972, Melbourne. Colour, 35 mm, 114 minutes. director: Bruce Beresford. producer: Phillip Adams for Longford Productions. screenplay: Bruce Beresford and Barry Humphries, from comic strip written by Humphries. photography: Don McAlpine. design: John Stoddart. music: Peter Best. editors: William Anderson and John Scott. cast: Alexander Archdale, Dick Bentley, Paul Bertram, John Clarke, Peter Cook, Julie Covington, Barry Crocker, Judith Furse, Wilfred Grove, Jonathan Hardy, Barry Humphries, John Joyce, Avice Landon, Margo Lloyd, Chris Malcolm, Spike Milligan, Maria O'Brien, Dennis Price, William Rushton, Mary Ann Severne, Bernard Spear, Brian Tapply, Jenny Tomasin, Jack Watling.

AGAINST THE GRAIN
Released 1981. Eastman colour, 16 mm, 76 minutes. director: Tim Burns. producer: Tim Burns for Nightshift Films. screenplay: Tim Burns and Michael Callaghan. photography: Louis Irving. editors: Peter Bailey, Chris Cordaux, Melissa Woods. cast: Joy Burns, Letham Burns, Mary Burns, Michael Callaghan, Sandy Edwards, George Sutton.

ALVIN PURPLE
Released 1973. Colour, 97 minutes. director: Tim Burstall. producer: Tim Burstall for Hexagon Productions. screenplay: Alan Hopgood. photography: Robin Copping. cast: Abigail, Graeme Blundell, Sally Conabere, Noel Ferrier, Jon Finlayson, Alan Finney, Jill Forster, Penne Hackforth-Jones, Dina Mann, Kris McQuade, Dennis Miller, Debbie Nankervis, Anne Pendlebury, Jacki Weaver.

ALVIN RIDES AGAIN
Released 1974, Brisbane. Colour, 89 minutes. directors: David Bilcock and Robin Copping. producer: Tim Burstall for Hexagon Productions. screenplay: Alan Hopgood, with Tim Burstall and Alan Finney. photography: Robin Copping. cast: Abigail, Bryony Behets, Graeme Blundell, Chantal Contouri, Jon Finlayson, Noel Ferrier, Maurie Fields, Alan Finney, Reg Gorman, Penne Hackforth-Jones, Dina Mann, Kris McQuade, Debbie Nankervis, Candy Raymond, Frank Thring, Frank Wilson, Arna-Maria Winchester.

ANNIE'S COMING OUT
Released 1984. Eastman colour, 35 mm, 96 minutes. director: Gil Brealey. producer: Don Murray for Film Australia. screenplay: Chris Borthwick, John Patterson, from the book by Rosemary Crossley and Anne McDonald. photography: Mick von Bornemann. composer: Simon Walker. designer: Robbie Perkins. editor: Lindsey Frazer. cast: Tina Arhondis, Simon Chilvers, Wallas Eaton, Drew Forsythe, Ray Meagher, Monica Maughan, Angela Punch-McGregor.

ATTACK FORCE Z
Released 1980. Eastman colour, 35 mm, 110 minutes. director: Tim Burstall. producer: Lee Robinson for John MacCallum Productions and Central Motion Picture Corporation. screenplay: Roger Marshall. photography: Lin Hung-Chung. composer: Eric Jupp. design: Bernard Hides. editor: David Stiven. cast: Sylvia Chang, Mel Gibson, Chris Hayward, John Phillip Law, Koo Chuan Hsiang, Sam Neill, John Waters.

BACKLASH
Released 1986. Eastman colour, 35 mm, 89 minutes. director: Bill Bennett. producer: Bill Bennett for Mermaid Beach Productions. screenplay: Bill Bennett, with dialogue by the cast. photography: Tony Wilson. music: Michael Atkinson, Michael Spicer. editor: Denise Hunter. cast: David Argue, Gia Carides, Lydia Miller, Brian Syron.

BACKROADS
Released 1977, Sydney. Colour, 16 mm, 61 minutes. director: Phillip Noyce. producer: Phillip Noyce. screenplay: John Emery, Phillip Noyce and cast. photography: Russell Boyd. cast: Terry Camilleri, Gary Foley, Bill Hunter, Zac Martin, Julie McGregor.

BARNEY
Released 1976, Melbourne. Colour, 84 minutes.director: David S. Waddington. producers: David S. Waddington and John Williams for Columbia Pictures. screenplay: Colin Drake. photography: Richard Wallace. cast: Sean Kramer, Lionel Long, Brett Maxworthy, Spike Milligan, Colin Petersen, Robert Quilter, Mike Preston, Rob Steele, Al Thomas.

A Select Filmography 253

BEST OF FRIENDS, THE
Released 1982. Eastman colour, 35 mm, 96 minutes. director: Michael Robertson. producer: Tom Jeffrey for The Friendly Film Company. screenplay: Donald McDonald. photography: David Gribble. composer: Brian King. design: John Carroll. editor: Ron Williams. cast: Graeme Blundell, Ruth Cracknell, Les Foxcroft, Moya O'Sullivan, Angela Punch McGregor, Graham Rouse, Henri Szeps.

BETWEEN WARS
Released 1974. Technicolor, 35 mm, 100 minutes. director: Michael Thornhill. producer: Michael Thornhill. screenplay: Frank Moorhouse. photography: Russell Boyd. editor: Max Lemon. production design: Bill Hutchinson. costumes: Marilyn Kippax. sound: Ken Hammond. cast: Corin Redgrave, Arthur Dignam, Judy Morris, Patricia Leehy.

BLISS
Released 1985. Eastman colour, 35 mm, 115 minutes. director: Ray Lawrence. producer: Anthony Buckley for Window III Productions. screenplay: Peter Carey and Ray Lawrence from the novel by Peter Carey. photography: Paul Murphy. composer: Peter Best. design: Owen Patterson. editor: Wayne le Clos. cast: Lynette Curran, Helen Jones, Barry Otto, Tim Robertson.

BLOOD MONEY
Released 1980. Eastman colour, 16 mm, 72 minutes. director: Chris Fitchett. producers: Tom Broadbridge and Chris Oliver for Filmworks. screenplay: Chris Fitchett, John Ruane, Ellery Ryan. photography: Ellery Ryan. editor: Chris Oliver. cast: Bryan Brown, Peter Curtain, John Flaus, Chrissie James, Sue Jones, John Proper, Peter Stratford.

BMX BANDITS
Released 1984. Colour, 35 mm, 90 minutes. director: Brian Trenchard-Smith. producer: Tom Broadbridge, Paul Davies for Nilsen Premiere. screenplay: Patrick Edgeworth. photography: John Seale. production design: Ross Major. editor: Allan Lake. music: Colin Stead and Frank Strangio. cast: Angelo D'Angelo, Nicole Kidman, David Argue.

BOY WHO HAD EVERYTHING, THE
Released 1985. Colour, 35 mm, 94 minutes. producer: Richard Mason, Julia Overton for Alfred Road Films. director: Stephen Wallace. screenplay: Stephen Wallace. photography: Geoff Burton. production design: Ross Major. editor: Henry Dangar. music: Raph Schneider. cast: Jason Connery, Diane Cilento, Nique Needles, Laura Williams.

BREAK OF DAY
Released 1976, Melbourne. Colour, 35 mm, 112 minutes. director: Patricia Lovell. producer: Ken Hannam for Clare Beach Films. screenplay: Cliff Green. photography: Russell Boyd. design: Wendy Dickson. composer: George Dreyfus. editor: Max Lemon. cast: Tony Barry, John Bell, Eileen Chapman, Maurie Fields, Ben Gabriel, Sara Kestelmann, Ingrid Mason, Andrew McFarlane, Geraldine Turner.

BREAKER MORANT
Released 1980. Eastman colour, 35 mm, 90 minutes. director: Bruce Beresford. producer: Matt Carroll for South Australian Film Corporation. screenplay: Bruce Beresford, Jonathon Hardy, David Stevens from a play by Kenneth Ross. photography: Don McAlpine. musical arranger: Phil Cuneen. design: David Copping. editor: William Anderson. cast: Bryan Brown, Allan Cassell, Terry Donovan, Jack Thompson, Charles Tingwell, John Waters, Edward Woodward.

BREAKFAST IN PARIS
Released 1982. Eastman colour, 35 mm, 94 minutes. director: John Lamond. producer: John Lamond. screenplay: Morris Dalton. photography: Ross Berryman. composer: Brian May. design: Stephen Walsh. editor: Jill Rice. cast: Elspeth Ballantyne, Jack Lenoir, Rod Mullinar, Barbara Parkins.

BUDDIES
Released 1984. Eastman colour, 35 mm Panavision, 97 minutes. director: Arch Nicholson. producer: John Dingwall for JD Productions. screenplay: David Eggby. photography: David Eggby. design: Phillip Warner. editor: Martin Down. cast: Simon Chilvers, Colin Friels, Harold Hopkins, Norman Kaye, Kris McQuade, Dennis Miller, Lisa Peers.

CACTUS
Released 1986. Fuji colour, 35 mm, 90 minutes. director: Paul Cox. producers: Jane Ballantyne and Paul Cox for Dofine. screenplay: Paul Cox, Bob Ellis and Norman Kaye. photography: Yuri Sokol. design: Asher Bilou. editor: Tim Lewis. cast: Sheila Florance, Peter Aanensen, Isabelle Huppert, Norman Kaye, Bunduk Marika, Monica Maughan, Robert Menzies.

CADDIE
Released 1976, Sydney. Colour, 35 mm, 103 minutes. director: Donald Crombie. producer: Anthony Buckley. screenplay: Joan Long, from autobiography by 'Caddie'. photography: Peter James. design: Owen Williams. composer: Patrick Flynn. editor: Tim Wellburn. cast: Takis Emmanuel, Pat

Evison, John Ewart, Willie Fennell, Les Foxcroft, John Gaden, Melissa Jaffer, Helen Morse, Robyn Nevin, Kirrily Nolan, June Salter, Jack Thompson, Jacki Weaver.
CAREFUL, HE MIGHT HEAR YOU
Released 1983. Kodak colour. 35 mm widescreen, 111 minutes. director: Carl Schultz. producer: Jill Robb for Syme International Productions and New South Wales Film Corporation. screenplay: Michael Jenkins, from novel by Sumner Locke Elliott. photography: John Seale. composer: Ray Cook. design: John Carroll, John Stoddart, John Wingrove. editor: Richard Francis Bruce. cast: Isabelle Anderson, Nicholas Gledhill, John Hargreaves, Wendy Hughes, Robyn Nevin, Geraldine Turner, Peter Whitford.
CARS THAT ATE PARIS, THE
Released 1974, Melbourne. Colour, widescreen, 91 minutes. director: Peter Weir. producers: Hal McElroy and Jim McElroy for Royce Smeal Film Productions and Salt Pan Films. screenplay: Peter Weir, from story by Piers Davies, Keith Gow and Peter Weir. photography: John McLean. design: David Copping. composer: Bruce Smeaton. editor: Wayne Le Clos. cast: Deryck Barnes, Terry Camilleri, Max Gillies, Chris Haywood, Edward Howell, Melissa Jaffer, John Meillon, Charles Metcalfe, Kevin Miles, Tim Robertson, Bruce Spence.
CATHY'S CHILD
Released 1979. Eastman colour, 35 mm, 90 minutes. director: Donald Crombie. producers: Pom Oliver, Errol Sullivan and Dick Wordley for C. B. Films. screenplay: Ken Quinnell, from novel by Dick Wordley. photography: Gary Hansen. composer: William Motzing. design: Ross Major. editor: Tim Wellburn. cast: Bryan Brown, Alan Cassell, Arthur Dignam, Michele Fawdon, Willy Fennell.
CHAIN REACTION, THE
Released 1980. Eastman colour, 35 mm, 90 minutes. director: Ian Barry. producer: David Elfick for Palm Beach Pictures. screenplay: Ian Barry. photography: Russell Boyd. design: Graham Walker. editor: Tim Wellburn. cast: Stephen Bisley, Ralph Cotterill, Hugh Keays-Byrne, Richard Moir, Ross Thompson, Arna-Maria Winchester.
CHANT OF JIMMIE BLACKSMITH, THE
Released 1978. Eastman colour, 35 mm, wide-screen, 122 minutes. director: Fred Schepisi. producer: Fred Schepisi for Film House Australia. screenplay: Fred Schepisi, from novel by Thomas Keneally. photography: Ian Baker. composer: Bruce Smeaton. design: Wendy Dickson. editor: Brian Kavanagh. cast: Elizabeth Alexander, Ray Barrett, Ruth Cracknell, Don Crosby, Julie Dawson, Tommy Lewis, Robyn Nevin, Freddy Reynolds, Jack Thompson.
CITY'S CHILD, A
Released 1972. Colour, 35 mm from 16mm, 80 minutes. director: Brian Kavanagh. producer: Brian Kavanagh. screenplay: Don Battye. photography: Bruce McNaughton. composer: Peter Pinne. design: Trevor Ling. editor: Brian Kavanagh. cast: Monica Maughan, Sean Scully, Moira Carleton.
CITY'S EDGE, THE
Released 1983. Eastman colour, 35 mm, 91 minutes. director: Ken Quinnell. producers: Pom Oliver and Errol Sullivan for Eastcaps. screenplay: Robert Merritt and Ken Quinnell from novel by W. A. Harbinson. photography: Louis Irvin. design: Robert Dein. editor: Greg Ropert. cast: Tom Lewis, Hugo Weaving, Katrina Foster, Mark Lee, Ralph Cotterill.
CLINIC, THE
Released 1982. Eastman colour, 35 mm, 90 minutes. director: David Stevens. producers: Robert le Tet and Bob Weiss for the Film House and Generation Films. screenplay: Greg Millen. photography: Ian Baker. editor: Edward McQueen-Mason. design: Tracy Watt. cast: Simon Burke, Pat Evison, Chris Haywood, Rona McLeon, Gerda Nicholson, Suzanne Roylance.
CLUB, THE
Released 1980. Eastman colour, 35 mm, 90 minutes. director: Bruce Beresford. producer: Matt Carroll for South Australian Film Corporation. screenplay: David Williamson from his play. photography: Don McAlpine. design: David Copping. editor: William Anderson. cast: Alan Cassell, Margaret Doyle, Harold Hopkins, John Howard, Graham Kennedy, Jack Thompson, Frank Wilson.
COCA COLA KID, THE
Released 1985. Eastman colour, 35 mm, 97 minutes. director: Dusan Makavejev. producer: David Roe for Grand Bay Film International. screenplay: Frank Moorhouse, based on short stories by Frank Moorhouse. composer: Tim Finn, William Motzing. photography: Dean Semler. design: Graham Walker. editor: John Scott. cast: Bill Kerr, Eric Roberts, Greta Scacchi, Tim Finn, Max Gillies, Chris Haywood, Kris McQuade.
COOL CHANGE
Released 1985. Eastman colour, 35 mm, 93 minutes. director: George Miller. producer: Dennis Wright for Delatite Productions. screenplay: Patrick Edgeworth. photography: John Haddy. composer: Bruce

Rowlands. designer: Leslie Binns. editor: Phil Reid. cast: Lisa Armytage, John Blake, Wilbur Wilde, Alec Wilson.

COOLANGATTA GOLD, THE
Released 1984. Eastman colour, 35 mm widescreen, 120 minutes. director: Igor Auzins. producer: John Weiley for Angoloro Productions. screenplay: Peter Shreck. photography: Keith Wagstaff. design: Bob Hill. editor: Tim Wellburn. cast: Colin Friels, Joss McWilliam, Robyn Nevin, Josephine Smulders, Nick Tate.

CROCODILE DUNDEE
Released 1986. Eastman colour, 35 mm Panavision, 100 minutes. director: Peter Faiman. producer: John Cornell for Rimfire Films. screenplay: Paul Hogan and Ken Shadie. photography: Russell Boyd. editor: David Stiven. design: Graham Walker. Cast: Paul Hogan, Linda Kozlowski, John Meillen, David Gulpilil, Maggie Blinco, Steve Rackman, Gerry Skilton.

DALMAS
Released 1973, Melbourne. Colour, 16 mm, 103 minutes. director: Bert Deling. producer: Apogee Films. screenplay: Bert Deling. photography: Sasha Trikojus. music: Spectrum. cast: Peter Cummins, John Duigan, Max Gillies, Peter Whittle, Roger Ward.

DARK ROOM
Released 1982. Eastman colour, 35 mm, 96 minutes. director: Paul Harmon. producer: Tom Haydon for Nadira. screenplay: Michael Brindley, Paul Harmon. photography: Paul Onorato. composer: Cameron Allen. design: Richard Kent. editor: Rod Adamson. cast: Allen Cassell, Diana Davidson, Ric Hutton, Anna Jemison, Svet Kovich, Oriana Panozzo, Rowena Wallace.

DAWN!
Released 1979. Eastman colour, 35 mm, 115 minutes. director: Ken Hannam. producer: Joy Havill for Aquataurus Film Productions and South Australian Film Corporation. screenplay: Joy Cavill. photography: Russell Boyd. design: Ross Major. editor: Max Lemon. cast: Bunney Brooke, John Diedrich, Ron Haddrick, Gabrielle Hartley, Ivar Kants, Bronwyn Mackay-Payne, Tom Richards.

DEAD EASY
Released 1970. Colour, 16 mm. director: Nigel Buesst. producer: Nigel Buesst. screenplay: Nigel Buesst. photography: Vincent Monton. cast: Kurt Beimel, Peter Carmody, Peter Cummins, Brian Davies, Mark McManus, Anna Raknes, Bruce Spence.

DEAD KIDS
Released 1981. Eastman colour, 35mm, wide-screen, 97 minutes. director: Michael Laughlen. producers: Antony I Ginane and John Jarrett for Endeavour Productions and Bannon Glen. screenplay: William Condon and Michael Laughlin. Music: Tangerine Dream. design: Susanna Moore. photography: Louis Horvath. editor: Petra. cast: Michael Murphy, Louise Fletcher, Dan Shor, Fiona Lewis, Arthur Dignam.

DEATHCHEATERS
Released 1976. Eastman colour, 35 mm Panavision, 100 minutes. director: Brian Trenchard Smith. producer: Brian Trenchard Smith. screenplay: Brian Trenchard Smith. photography: John Seale. cast: Michael Aitkens, Noel Ferrier, Drew Forsythe, Margaret Gerard, John Hargreaves, Chris Haywood, Grant Page, Roger Ward, Judith Woodroffe.

DEMONSTRATOR
Released 1971, Canberra. Colour. director: Warwick Freeman. producers: David Brice and James Fishburn for Freeman-Fishburn International and Act One. screenplay: Kit Denton from novel by Elizabeth and Don Campbell. photography: John McLean. design: Sid Fort. composer: Bob Young. editor: Anthony Buckley. cast: Michael Aitkens, Slim de Grey, Noel Ferrier, Ken Goodlet, Harold Hopkins, Irene Inescourt, Joe James, Gerard Maguire, Max Meldrum, Kenneth Tsang, Doreen Warburton, John Warwick.

DESOLATION ANGELS
Released 1982. Eastman colour, 35 mm, 95 minutes. director: Chris Fitchett. producer: Chris Oliver for Winternight Productions. screenplay: Chris Fitchett, Ellery Ryan. photography: Ellery Ryan. composer: Mark MacSherry. musical performer: Josephine Ford. design: Josephine Ford. editor: Tony Stevens. cast: Nick Lathouris, Kerry Mack, Jay Mannering, Marie O'Laughlin, Kim Trengrove, Karen West.

DEVIL'S PLAYGROUND, THE
Released 1976, Melbourne. Colour, 35 mm, 107 minutes. director: Fred Schepisi. producer: Fred Schepisi for The Film House. screenplay: Fred Schepisi. photography: Ian Baker. design: Trevor Ling. composer: Bruce Smeaton. editor: Brian Kavanagh. cast: Simon Burke, John Diedrich, Arthur Dignam, Sheila Florance, John Frawley, Jonathan Hardy, Thomas Keneally, Charles McCallum, Nick Tate.

DIMBOOLA
Released 1979. Eastman colour, 35 mm, 94 minutes. director: John Duigan. producer: John Weiley for Pram Factory Pictures. screenplay: Jack Hibberd from his play.

photography: Tom Cowan. composer: George Dreyfus. musical performers: Captain Matchbox Whoopee Band. design: Larry Eastwood. editor: Tony Patterson. cast: Natalie Bate, Max Cullen, Max Gillies, Dick May, Chad Morgan, Tim Robertson, Bruce Spence.

DON'S PARTY
Released 1976, Canberra. Colour. director: Bruce Beresford. producer: Phillip Adams for Double Head Productions. screenplay: David Williamson from his play. photography: Don McAlpine. editor:William Anderson. cast: Ray Barrett, Clare Binney, Pat Bishop, Graeme Blundell, Jeanie Drynan, John Hargreaves, Harold Hopkins, Graham Kennedy, Veronica Lang, Candy Raymond, Kit Taylor.

DUET FOR FOUR
Released 1982. Eastman colour, 35 mm, 100 minutes. director: Tim Burstall. producers: Tim Burstall and Tom Burstall. screenplay: David Williamson. photography: Dan Burstall. composer: Peter Sullivan. design: Herbert Pinter. editor: Edward McQueen-Mason. cast: Diane Cilento, Gary Day, Wendy Hughes, Vanessa Lee, Mike Preston, Michael Pate, Sigrid Thornton.

EARLY FROST
Released 1982. Eastman colour, 35 mm, 90 minutes. director: anonymous. producers: Geoff Brown and David Hannay for David Hannay Productions. screenplay: Terry O'Connor. photography: David Eggby. composer: Mike Harvey. design: Bob Hilditch. editor: Tim Street. cast: Danny Adcock, Jon Blake, Daniel Cumerford, Guy Doleman, David Franklin, Janet Kingsbury, Diana McLean, Joanne Samuel, Kit Taylor.

EARTHLING, THE
Released 1980. Eastman colour, 35 mm, 100 minutes. director: Peter Collinson. producer: Elliot Schick for Earthling Productions. screenplay: Lanny Cotler. photography: Don McAlpine. composer: Bruce Smeaton. designer: Bernard Hides. editor: Mick Beauman. cast: William Holden, Ricky Schroder, Pat Evison, Olivia Hamnett, Jack Thompson, Alwyn Kurts.

ELIZA FRASER
Released 1976. Colour, 35 mm, 127 minutes. director: Tim Burstall. producer: Tim Burstall for Hexagon Productions. screenplay: David Williamson. photography: Robin Copping. design: Leslie Binns. composer: Bruce Smeaton. editor: Edward McQueen-Mason. cast: John Castle, Noel Ferrier, Martin Harris, Trevor Howard, Bill Hunter, Gerard Kennedy, Serge Lazareff, George Mallaby, Ingrid Mason, Grant Page, Sean Scully, Charles Tingwell, John Waters, Arna-Maria Winchester, Susannah York.

EMMA'S WAR
Released 1987. Eastman colour, 35 mm, 95 minutes. director: Clytie Jessop. producers: Andrina Finlay and Clytie Jessop for Belinon. screenplay: Clytie Jessop and Peter Smalley. photography: Tom Cowan. composer: John Williams. design: Jane Norris. editor: Sonia Hoffman. cast: Noeleen Brown, Terry Donovan, Pat Evison, Donal Gibson, Bridie Lee, Mark Lee, Maranda Otto, Lee Remick.

EMOH RUO
Released 1984. Eastman colour, 35 mm, 90 minutes. director: Denny Lawrence. producer: David Elfick for Palm Beach Pictures. screenplay: Paul Leadon and David Poltarak. photography: Andrew Lesnie. composer: Cameron Allen. designer: Robert Dein. editor: Ted Otton. cast: Martin Sacks, Joy Smithers.

EMPTY BEACH, THE
Released 1984. Kodak colour, 35 mm, 100 minutes. director: Chris Thomson. producer: John Edwards and Timothy Read for Jethro Films. screenplay: Keith Dewhurst from novel by Peter Corris. photography: John Seale. designer: Larry Eastwood. editor: Lindsay Frazer. cast: Ray Barrett, Bryan Brown, Peter Collingwood, Belinda Giblin, Kerry Mack, Anna Maria Monticelli, John Wood.

END PLAY
Released 1976, Melbourne and Sydney. Colour, 35 mm, 114 minutes. director: Tim Burstall. producer: Tim Burstall for Hexagon Productions. screenplay: Tim Burstall, from novel by Russell Braddon. photography: Robin Copping. design: Bill Hutchinson. composer: Peter Best. cast: Delvene Delaney, Sheila Florance, Belinda Giblin, Ken Goodlet, George Mallaby, Kevin Miles, Charles Tingwell, John Waters.

ESSAY ON PORNOGRAPHY, AN
Released 1973. Colour. director: Christopher Cary. producer: James Steiner. photography: Mike Franklin. cast: Glen Johnston, Helen Mason.

EXITS
Released 1980. Colour, 16 mm, 48 minutes. Production and direction: Paul Davies, Carolyn Howard, Pat Laughren. screenplay: Paul Davies. cast: Mary Anne Gray, Robert Antoniades, Carolyn Howard.

FANTASM
Released 1976. Colour. director: Richard Bruce (Richard Franklin). producer: Antony Ginnane. screenplay: Ross Dimsey from an

idea by Antony Ginnane. photography: Vincent Monton. cast: Maria Arnold, John Bluthal, Dee Dee Levitt, Bill Margold.
FANTASM COMES AGAIN
Released 1977, Melbourne. Colour. director: Eric Ram (Colin Eggleston). producer: Antony Ginnane. screenplay: Ross Dimsey (as Robert Derri re). photography: Vincent Monton. cast: Angela Menzies-Wills, Clive Hearne.
FANTASY MAN
Released 1984. Eastman colour, 35mm from 16 mm, 82 minutes. Director: John Maher. producer: Basil Appleby, Darrell Lass for Centaur Enterprises. screenplay: John Maher. photography: Tom Cowan. design: Darrell Lass. editor: Rod Hibberd. cast: Jeanie Drynan, Harold Hopkins, Terry Mack.
FAR EAST
Released 1982. Eastman colour, 35 mm, 100 minutes. director: John Duigan. producer: Richard Mason for Alfred Road Films. screenplay: John Duigan. photography: Brian Probyn. design: Ross Major. editor: Henry Dangar. cast: John Bell, Bryan Brown, John Clayton, Bill Hunter, Sinan Leon, Helen Morse, Raina McKeon.
FAST TALKING
Released 1984. Eastman colour, super 16 mm, 95 minutes. director: Ken Cameron. producer: Ross Matthews for Oldata Productions. screenplay: Ken Cameron. photography: David Gribble. composer: Sharon Calcraft. design: Neil Angwin. editor: David Huggett. cast: Toni Allaylis, Steve Bisley, Dave Godden, Peter Hehir, Gail Sweeney, Chris Truswell, Rod Zuanic.
FATTY FINN
Released 1980. Eastman colour, 35 mm, 90 minutes. director: Maurice Murphy. producer: Brian Rosen for Children's Film Corporation. screenplay: Bob Ellis and Chris McGill. photography: John Seale. composers: Grahame Bond, Rory O'Donohue. design: Lissa Coote.
FELICITY
Released 1979. Eastman colour, 35 mm, 90 minutes. director: John Lamond. producers: John Lamond and Russell Hurley for Krystal Motion Pictures. screenplay: Felicity Robinson. photography: Garry Wapshott. design: Stephen Walsh. editor: Russell Hurley. cast: Glory Amen, Joni Flynn, Jody Hansen, Chris Milne, Marilyn Rodgers.
FIGHTING BACK
Released 1982. Eastman colour, 35 mm, 100 minutes. director: Michael Caulfield. producers: Tom Jeffrey and Sue Milliken for Samson Productions. screenplay: Michael Cove and Tom Jeffrey. photography: John Seale. design: Christopher Webster. editor: Ron Williams. cast: Ben Gabriel, Caroline Gillmer, Lewis Fitzgerald, Kris McQuade, Wyn Roberts, Paul Smith, Catherine Wilkin.
FINAL CUT
Released 1980. Eastman colour, 35 mm, 98 minutes. director: Ross Dimsey. producer: Mike Williams for Wilgar. screenplay: Jonathon Dawson. photography: Ron Johanson. composer: Howard Davidson. design: James Penny. editor: Tony Patterson. cast: Lou Brown, Deanne Carsas, David Clendenning, Jennifer Cluff, Narelle Johnson, Amanda MacTaggart, Thaddeus Smith.
F.J. HOLDEN, THE
Released 1977. Eastman colour, 35 mm, 101 minutes. director: Michael Thornhill. producer: Michael Thornhill for F.J. Films. screenplay: Terry Larsen. photography: David Gribble. production design: Lissa Coote and Monte Fieguth. editor: Max Lemon. music: Jim Manzie. sound: Don Connolly. cast: Paul Couzens, Eva Dickinson.
FOR LOVE ALONE
Released 1985. Kodak colour, 35 mm, 102 minutes. director: Stephen Wallace. producer: Margaret Fink for Waranta. screenplay: Stephen Wallace, from novel by Christina Stead. photography: Alun Bollinger. composer: Nathan Waks. design: John Stoddart. editor: Henry Dangar. cast: Helen Buday, Judi Farr, Regina Gaigalas, Hugh Keays-Byrne, Sam Neill, John Polsen, Hugo Weaving.
FOURTH WISH, THE
Released 1976. Colour, 35 mm, 105 minutes. director: Don Chaffey. producer: John Morris for Galaxy Productions and South Australian Film Corporation. screenplay: Michael Craig, from his television serial. photography: Geoff Burton. designer: David Copping. composer: Tristan Carey. cast: Brian Anderson, Robert Bettles, Michael Craig, Cul Cullen, Julie Dawson, Les Foxcroft, Ron Haddrick, Ann Haddy, Brian James, John Meillon, Robyn Nevin.
FRAN
Released 1984. Eastman colour, 16 mm, 94 minutes. director: Glenda Hambly. producer: David Rapsey for Barron Films. screenplay: Glenda Hambly. photography: Jan Kenny. cast: Annie Byron, Noni Hazlehurst, Alan Fletcher, Rosie Logie, Narelle Simpson, Travis Ward.
FREEDOM
Released 1982. Eastman colour, 35 mm, 95 minutes. director: Scott Hicks. producer: Matt Carroll for South Australian Film Corporation and Endeavour Communications Corporation. screenplay: John Emery.

photography: Ron Johanson. composer: Don Walker. musical performers: Don Walker, Cold Chisel. design: Herbert Pinter. editor: Philip Reid. cast: John Blake, Jad Capelja, Max Cullen, Kati Edwards, Chris Haywood, Candy Raymond, Charles Tingwell.

FRINGE DWELLERS, THE
Released 1986. Kodak colour, 35 mm, 99 minutes. director: Bruce Beresford. producer: Sue Milliken for Fringe Dwellers Productions. screenplay: Bruce Beresford, from novel by Nene Gare. photography: Don McAlpine. design: Herbert Pinter. editor: Tim Wellburn. cast: Bob Maza, Justine Saunders, Kristina Nehm, Ernie Dingo, Malcolm Silva, Kylie Belling.

FUTURE SCHLOCK
Released 1983. Ektachrome colour, 16 mm, 72 minutes. directors: Barry Peake and Chris Kiely. producers: Barry Peake and Chris Kiely for Ultimate Show. screenplay: Barry Peake and Chris Kiely. photography: Malcolm Richards. composer: John McCubbery. design: Ian McWha. editors: Barry Peake and Ray Pond. cast: Gary Adams, Michael Bishop, Tracey Callender, Maryanne Fahey, Deborah Force, Tiriel Mora, Simon Thorpe.

GALLIPOLI
Released 1981. Eastman colour, 35 mm, 105 minutes. director: Peter Weir, producer: Patricia Lovell for Associated A and R Films. screenplay: David Williamson. photography: Russell Boyd. designer: Wendy Weir. editor: Bill Anderson. cast: David Argue, Mel Gibson, Robert Grubb, Harold Hopkins, Bill Hunter, Mark Lee, Tim McKenzie.

GETTING OF WISDOM, THE
Released 1977, Melbourne. Colour, 35 mm, 100 minutes. director: Bruce Beresford. producer: Phillip Adams for Southern Cross Films. screenplay: Eleanor Witcombe, from novel by Henry Handel Richardson. photography: Don McAlpine. design: Richard Kent. pianist: Sarah Grunstein. editor: William Anderson. cast: Terence Donovan, Susannah Fowle, Sheila Helpmann, Barry Humphries, Patricia Kennedy, Candy Raymond, Hilary Ryan, Sigrid Thornton, John Waters.

GINGER MEGGS
Released 1982. Eastman colour, 35 mm, 95 minutes. director: Jonathon Dawson. producer: John Sexton. screenplay: Michael Latimer, from comic strip by J. C. Bancks. photography: John Seale. composers: John Stuart, Kim Thraves. design: Larry Eastwood. editor: Phillip Howe. cast: Terry Camilleri, Paul Daniel, Harold Hopkins, Hugh Keays-Byrne, Coral Kelly, Garry McDonald, Gwen Plumb.

GOING DOWN
Released 1982. Eastman colour, 35 mm, 90 minutes. director: Haydn Keenan. producer: Haydn Keenan for X-Productions. screenplay: Julie Barry, Moira MacLaine-Cross and Melissa Woods. photography: Malcolm Richards. composer: Lloyd Carrick. design: Melody Cooper. editor: Paul Healey. cast: David Argue, Julie Barry, Mercia Deane-Johns, Hugh Keays-Byrne, Moira Maclaine-Cross, Tracy Mann, Richard Moir, Vera Plevnik, Esben Storm.

GOLDEN CAGE, THE
Released 1975. Colour. director: Ayteñ Kuyululu. producer: Ilhan Kuyululu. screenplay: Ayten Kuyululu and Ismet Soydan. photography: Russell Boyd. designer: Sonia Hofmann. composer: Mary Vanderby. cast: Michelle Fawdon, Ron Haddrick, Ilhan Kuyululu, Sayit Memisoglu, Kate Sheil.

GOODBYE PARADISE
Released 1982. Eastman colour, 35 mm, 110 minutes. director: Carl Schultz. producer: Jane Scott for Petersham Pictures. screenplay: Bob Ellis and Denny Lawrence. photography: Danny Batterham. composer: Peter Best. design: George Liddle. editor: Richard Francis-Bruce. cast: Ray Barrett, John Clayton, Kate Fitzpatrick, Lex Marinos, Robyn Nevin, Janet Scrivener, Charles Tingwell.

GREAT MacARTHY, THE
Released 1975. Colour, 35 mm, 93 minutes. director: David Baker. producer: David Baker for Stoney Creek Films. screenplay: David Baker and John Romeril, from A Salute to the Great McCarthy, novel by Barry Oakley. photography: Bruce McNaughton. design: David Copping. composer: Bruce Smeaton. editor: John Scott. cast: Sally Conabere, Cul Cullen, Peter Cummins, John Derum, Maurie Fields, Jon Finlayson, Kate Fitzpatrick, Max Gillies, Chris Haywood, Barry Humphries, John Jarratt, Sandy Macgregor, Max Meldrum, Dennis Miller, Judy Morris, Tim Robertson, Bruce Spence.

HARD KNOCKS
Released 1980. Eastman colour, 35 mm from 16mm, 90 minutes. director: Don McLennan. producers: Hilton Bonner and Don McLennan for Andromeda Productions. screenplay: Hilton Bonner and Don McLennan. photography: Peter Friedrich. editor: Peter Friedrich. cast: Tony Barry, Max Cullen, Bill Hunter, Tracy Mann.

A Select Filmography

HARLEQUIN
Released 1980. Eastman colour, 35 mm, 94 minutes. director: Simon Wincer. producer: Antony I. Ginnane for F. G. Film Productions. screenplay: Everett DeRoche. photography: Gary Hansen. composer: Brian May. design: Bernard Hides. editor: Adrian Carr. cast: Broderick Crawford, Carmen Duncan, David Hemmings, Gus Mercurio, Robert Powell.

HEATWAVE
Released 1981. Eastman colour, 35 mm, 90 minutes. director: Phillip Noyce. producers: Hilary Linstead and Ross Matthews for Heatwave Films. screenplay: Phillip Noyce and Marc Rosenberg, from original screenplay by Tim Gooding and Mark Stiles. photography: Vincent Monton. composer: Cameron Allan. designer: Ross Major. editor: John Scott. cast: Judy Davis, John Gregg, Chris Haywood, Bill Hunter, Anna Jemison, Richard Moir, John Meillon.

HOMESDALE
Released 1971. B & W, 16 mm, 50 minutes. director: Peter Weir. producers: Grahame Bond and Richard Brennan. screenplay: Piers Davies and Peter Weir. photography: Anthony Wallis. composers: Grahame Bond and Rory O'Donoghue. editor: Wayne Le Clos. cast: Grahame Bond, Barry Donnelly, Kate Fitzpatrick, Geoff Malone, Phil Noyce, Doreen Warburton, Peter Weir.

HOODWINK
Released 1981. Eastman colour, 35 mm, 90 minutes. director: Claude Whatham. producer: Errol Sullivan for CB Films. screenplay: Ken Quinnell. photography: Dean Semler. composer: Cameron Allen. editor: Nicholas Beauman. cast: Max Cullen, Judy Davis, John Hargreaves, Wendy Hughes, Dennis Miller.

HOSTAGE
Released 1983. Eastman colour, 35 mm Panavision, 90 minutes. director: Frank Shields. producers: Basil Appleby and Frank Shields for Frontier Films. screenplay: Frank Shields, John Lind, from a true story. photography: Vincent Monton. composer: Davood Tabrizi. designer: Phillip McLaren. editor: Don Saunders. cast: Gabriella Barraket Clare Binney, Bert Cooper Hank Johannes, Kerry Mack, Judy Nunn. Ralph Schicha

HOW WILLINGLY YOU SING
Released 1975, Melbourne. Colour, 16 mm, 89 minutes. director: Garry Patterson. producer: Garry Patterson for Inch Films. screenplay: Garry Patterson and cast. photography: Peter Tammer. cast: Isaac Gerson, Braham Glass, Morris Gradman, Allan Levy, Garry Patterson, Jerry Powderly, Jim Robertson.

ILLUMINATIONS
Released 1976, Melbourne. Colour, 16 mm, 74 minutes. director: Paul Cox. producer: Tibor Markus. screenplay: Paul Cox. photography: Paul Cox and Brian Gracey. design: Alan Stubenrauch. editors: Paul Cox and Russell Hurley. cast: Sheila Florance, Norman Kaye, Tony Llewellyn-Jones, Gabriella Trsek.

IN SEARCH OF ANNA
Released 1979. Eastman colour, 35 mm, 91 minutes. director: Esben Storm. producer: Esben Storm. screenplay: Esben Storm. photography: Michael Edols. composer: John Martyn. design: Alan Stivell. editor: Dusan Werner. cast: Chris Haywood, Bill Hunter, Richard Moir, Judy Morris, Gerda Nicholson, Martin Sharp, Garry Waddell.

INN OF THE DAMNED
Released 1975, Sydney. Colour, 35 mm, 118 minutes. director: Terry Bourke. producer: Terry Bourke and Rod Hay for Terryrod Productions. screenplay: Terry Bourke. photography: Brian Probyn. design: Gary Hansen. composer: Bob Young. editor: Rod Hay. cast: Dame Judith Anderson, Tony Bonner, Alex Cord, Michael Craig, Joseph Furst, Reg Gorman, Lionel Long, John Meillon, John Morris, Robert Quilter.

INSIDE LOOKING OUT
Released 1977, Sydney. Colour, 35 mm, 88 minutes. director: Paul Cox. producer: Bernard Eddy for Illumination Films. screenplay: Paul Cox and Susan Holly Jones. photography: Paul Cox. design: Alan Stubenrauch. composer: Norman Kaye. editor: Paul Cox. cast: Juliet Bacskai, Briony Behets, Tony Llewellyn-Jones, Norman Kaye, Elke Neidhardt.

IRISHMAN, THE
Released 1978. Gevacolor, 35 mm, 110 minutes. director: Donald Crombie. producer: Anthony Buckley for Forest Home Films. screenplay: Donald Crombie from the novel by Elizabeth O'Conner. photography: Peter James. composer: Charles Marawood. design: Graham Walker. editor: Tim Wellburn. cast: Vincent Ball, Tony Barry, Bryan Brown, Lou Brown, Simon Burke, Michael Craig, Gerard Kennedy, Robyn Nevin.

JACK AND JILL: A POSTCRIPT
Released 1970, Melbourne. Colour, 16 mm, 67 minutes. directors: Phillip Adams and Brian Robinson. producers: Phillip Adams and Brian Robinson. screenplay: Phillip Adams and Brian Robinson. photography: Phillip Adams and Brian Robinson. composer: Peter Best. cast: Lindsay Howatt, Judy Leech, Anthony Ward.

JOURNALIST, THE
Released 1979. Eastman colour, 35 mm, 95 minutes. director: Michael Thornhill. producer: Pom Oliver for Edgecliff Films. screenplay: Michael Thornhill, Edna Wilson. photography: Don McAlpine. design: Jenny Green. editor: Tim Wellburn. cast: Elizabeth Alexander, Penne Hackforth-Jones, Jane Harders, Sam Neill, Carol Raye, Jack Thompson, Charles Tingwell.

JOURNEY AMONG WOMEN
Released 1977, Sydney. Colour, 35 mm, 93 minutes. director: Tom Cowan. producer: John Weilley. screenplay: Tom Cowan, John Weiley, Dorothy Hewett and cast. photography: Tom Cowan. composer: Roy Ritchie. editor: John Scott. cast: Nell Campbell, Diane Fuller, Jude Kuring, Rose Lilly, Lisa Peers, Jeune Pritchard.

JUST OUT OF REACH
Released 1979. Eastman colour, 16 mm, 62 minutes. director: Linda Blagg. producer: Ross Mathews for Portrait Films. screenplay: Linda Blagg. photography: Russell Boyd. editor: Ted Otton. cast: Lou Brown, Jackie Dalton, Judi Farr, Ian Gilmour, Lorna Lesley, Sam Neill, Martin Vaughan.

KANGAROO
Released 1986. Eastman colour, 35 mm, wide-screen, 120 minutes. director: Tim Burstall. producer: Ross Dimsey for Naked Country Productions. screenplay: Evan Jones, from novel by D. H. Lawrence. photography: Dan Burstall. design: Tracy Watt. editor: Edward McQueen-Mason. cast: Judy Davis, Colin Friels, Peter Hehir, Hugh Keays-Byrne, Gerard Kennedy, Julie Nihill, John Walton.

KILLING OF ANGEL STREET, THE
Released 1981. Eastman colour, 35 mm, 100 minutes. director: Donald Crombie. producer: Anthony Buckley for Forest Home Films. screenplay: Michael Craig, Cecil Holmes and Evan Jones. photography: Peter James. composer: Brian May. design: David Copping. editor: Tim Wellburn. cast: Elizabeth Alexander, Alexander Archdale, David Downer, John Hargreaves, Reg Lye.

KITTY AND THE BAGMAN
Released 1982. Colour, Panavision, 35 mm, 98 minutes. director: Donald Crombie producer: Anthony Buckley for Forest Home Films for Adams Packer Film Productions. screenplay: John Burnie, Phillip Cornford. photography: Dean Semler. composer: Brian May. designer: Owen Williams. editor: Timothy Wellburn. cast: Liddy Clark, Reg Evans, John Ewart, Val Lehman, Colette Mann, Gerard McGuire, John Stanton.

KOSTAS
Released 1979. Eastman colour, 35 mm, 100 minutes. director: Paul Cox. producer: Bernard Eddy for Kostas Film Productions. screenplay: Linda Aronson, from an idea by Paul Cox. photography: Vittorio Bernini. composer: Mikis Theodorakis. design: Alan Stubenrauch. editor: John Scott. cast: Takis Emmanuel, Chris Haywood, Wendy Hughes, Kris McQuade, Tony Lewellyn-Jones, John Waters.

LADY, STAY DEAD
Released 1980. Eastman colour, 35 mm, 92 minutes. director: Terry Bourke. producer: Terry Bourke for Ryntare Productions. screenplay: Terry Bourke. photography: Ray Henman. composer: Bob Young. design: Bob Hill. editor: Ron Williams. cast: Deborah Coulls, James Elliott, Les Foxcroft, Chard Haywood, Louise Howitt, Roger Ward.

LAST OF THE KNUCKLEMEN, THE
Released 1979. Colour, 35 mm, 92 minutes. director: Tim Burstall. producer: Tim Burstall for Hexagon Productions. screenplay: Tim Burstall. photography: Dan Burstall. composer: Bruce Smeaton. design: Leslie Binns. editor: Edward McQueen-Mason. cast: Stephen Bisley, Michael Caton, Michael Duffield, Peter Hehir, Gerard Kennedy, Dennis Miller, Michael Preston.

LAST WAVE, THE
Released 1977. Eastman colour, 35 mm, 104 minutes. director: Peter Weir. producers: Hal McElroy, Jim McElroy. screenplay: Peter Weir, Tony Morphett, Petru Popescu. photography: Russell Boyd. production design: Goran Warff. editor: Max Lemon. music: Charles Wain. sound: Don Connolly. cast: Richard Chamberlain, Olivia Hamnett, David Gulpilil.

LET THE BALLOON GO
Released 1976, Sydney. Colour, 35 mm, 78 minutes. director: Oliver Howes. producer: Richard Mason for Film Australia. screenplay: Oliver Howes, Richard Mason and Ivan Southall, from novel by Ivan Southall. photography: Dean Semler. design: David Copping. composer: George Dreyfus. editor: Max Lemon. cast: Ray Barrett, Robert Bettles, John Ewart, Ben Gabriel, Ken Goodlet, Jan Kingsbury, Nigel Lovell, Charles Metcalfe, Grant Page, Goff Vockler.

LIBIDO
Released 1973, Melbourne. Colour, 35 mm, 118 minutes. producers: Christopher Muir and John B. Murray for Producers and Directors Guild of Australia. *The Husband.* director: John B. Murray. screenplay: Craig McGregor. photography: Eric Lomas. composers: Tim Healy and Billy Green. editor: Tim Lewis.

cast: Mark Albiston, Elke Neidhardt, Bryon Williams. *The Child*. director: Tim Burstall. screenplay: Hal Porter. photography: Robin Copping. design: Leslie Binns. composer: Peter Best. editor: David Bilcock. cast: Bruce Barry, Jill Forster, Judy Morris, John Williams.
The Priest. director: Fred Schepisi. screenplay: Thomas Keneally. photography: Ian Baker. design: Trevor Ling. composer: Bruce Smeaton. editor: Brian Kavanagh. cast: Arthur Dignam, Penne Hackforth-Jones, Robyn Nevin. *The Family Man*. director: David Baker. screenplay: David Williamson. photography: Bruce McNaughton. composer: Bruce Smeaton. editor: Edward McQueen-Mason. cast: Suzanne Brady, Max Gillies, Debbie Nankervis, Jack Thompson.

LISTEN TO THE LION
Released 1977, Sydney. Colour, 16 mm, 52 minutes. director: Henri Safran. producer: Robert Hill for Stockton Ferri Films. screenplay: Robert Hill. photography: Malcolm Richards. composer: Michael Carlos. editor: Mervyn LLoyd. cast: John Derum, Les Foxcroft, Barry Lovett, Wyn Roberts.

LONELY HEARTS
Released 1982. Eastman colour, 35 mm, 95 minutes. director: Paul Cox. producer: John B. Murray for Adams Packer Film Productions. screenplay: John Clarke and Paul Cox. photography: Yuri Sokol. composer: Norman Kaye. designer: Neil Angwin. editor: Tim Lewis.

LONG WEEKEND, THE
Released 1977. Eastman colour, 35 mm widescreen, 102 minutes. director: Colin Eggleston. producer: Colin Eggleston for Dugong Films. screenplay: Everett DeRoche. photography: Vincent Monton. composer: Michael Carlos. design: Larry Eastwood. editor: Brian Kavanagh. cast: Briony Behets, John Hargreaves.

LOST IN THE BUSH
Released 1973, Horsham, Vic. Colour, 16 mm, 64 minutes. director: Peter Dodds. producer: Audio-Visual Education Centre, Education Department of Victoria. screenplay: Peter Dodds, from story by Les Blake. photography: Lee Wright. composer: Geoff D'Ombrau. editor: Peter Dodds. cast: Gabrielle Bulle, Colin Freckleton, Richard McClelland.

LOVE EPIDEMIC, THE
Released 1975, Melbourne and Sydney. Colour, 35 mm from 16 mm, 83 minutes. director: Brian Trenchard Smith. producer: Brian Trenchard Smith for Hexagon Productions. screenplay: Brian Trenchard Smith. photography: Ross Blake, Russell Boyd, Stuart Fist, Greg Hunter. editor: Ronda McGregor. cast: John Ewart, Michael Laurence, Grant Page, Ros Spiers, Roger Ward.

LOVE-LETTERS FROM TERALBA ROAD, THE
Released 1977, Sydney. Colour, 16 mm, 50 minutes. director: Stephen Wallace. producer: Richard Brennan. screenplay: Stephen Wallace. photography: Tom Cowan. composer: Ralph Schneider. editor: Henry Dangar. cast: Bryan Brown, Kris McQuade.

MAD DOG MORGAN
Released 1976, Sydney. Colour, wide-screen, 102 minutes. director: Philippe Mora. producer: Jeremy Thomas for Motion Picture Productions. screenplay: Philippe Mora, from Morgan, the Bold Bushranger, book by Margaret Carnegie. photography: Mike Molloy. design: Robert Hilditch. composer: Patrick Flynn. editor: John Scott. cast: Graeme Blundell, Liddy Clark, John Derum, Wallas Eaton, David Gulpilil, John Hargreaves, Dennis Hopper, Bill Hunter, Norman Kaye, Hugh Keays-Byrne, Robert McDarra, Grant Page, Michael Pate, Robin Ramsay, Bruce Spence, Jack Thompson, Peter Thompson, Frank Thring, Roger Ward.

MAD MAX
Released 1979. Eastman colour, 35 mm, 90 minutes. director: George Miller. producer: Byron Kennedy for Mad Max Pty Ltd. screenplay: James McAusland and George Miller. photography: David Eggby. composer: Brian May. design: Jon Dowding. editors: Tony Patterson and Cliff Hayes. cast: Steve Bisley, Mel Gibson, Vince Gil, Hugh Keays-Byrne, Nick Lathouris, Lulu Pinkus, Joanne Samuel.

MAD MAX II
Released 1982. Eastman colour, 35 mm, 96 minutes. director: George Miller. producer: Byron Kennedy for Kennedy Miller. screenplay: Brian Hannant, Terry Hayes and George Miller. photography: Dean Semler. cmposer: Brian May. design: Graham Walker. editor: Michael Chirgwin. cast: Mel Gibson, Emil Minty, Kjell Nilsson, Max Phipps, Mike Preston, Bruce Spence, Vern Wells.

MAD MAX: BEYOND THUNDERDOME
Released 1985. Eastman colour, 70 mm and 35 mm, 106 minutes. director: George Miller, George Ogilvie. producers: George Miller, Doug Mitchess, Terry Hayes. screenplay: Terry Hayes, George Miller. photography: Dean Semler. visual design: Ed Verraux. production design: Graham Walker. Costume design: Norma Moriceau. music: Maurice Jarre. sound: Roger Savage. cast: Mel Gibson, Tina Turner, Helen Buday, Frank Thring, Bruce Spence.

MALCOLM
Released 1986. Eastman colour, 35 mm, 90 minutes. director: Nadia Tass. producer: Nadia Tass and David Parker for Cascade Films. screenplay: David Parker. photography: David Parker. composer: Paul Coppens. editor: Ken Sallows. cast: Lindy Davies, Colin Friels, John Hargreaves, Chris Haywood, Heather Mitchell, Beverley Phillips, Bud Tingwell.

MAN FROM HONG KONG, THE
Released 1975, USA. Colour, wide-screen, 103 minutes. director: Brian Trenchard Smith. producers: Raymond Chow and John Fraser for The Movie Company and Golden Harvest. screenplay: Brian Trenchard Smith. photography: Russell Boyd. design: David Copping and Chien Shun. composer: Noel Quinlan. editors: Ron Williams and Alan Lake. cast: Deryck Barnes, Rebecca Gilling, Bill Hunter, Hugh Keays-Byrne, George Lazenby, Grant Page, Ros Spiers, Frank Thring, Jimmy Wang Yu, Roger Ward.

MAN FROM SNOWY RIVER, THE
Released 1982. Eastman colour, 35 mm, widescreen, 100 minutes. director: George Miller. producer: Geoff Burrowes for Michael Edgley International and Cambridge Films. screenplay: John Dixon and Fred 'Cul' Cullen, from poem by 'Banjo' Paterson. photography: Keith Wagstaff. composer: Bruce Rowland. design: Leslie Binns. editor: Adrian Carr. cast: Lorraine Bayly, Tony Bonner, Tom Burlinson, Chris Haywood, Kirk Douglas, Gus Mercurio, Jack Thompson, Sigrid Thornton.

MAN OF FLOWERS
Released 1983. Fuji colour, 35 mm, 91 minutes. director: Paul Cox. producers: Jane Ballantyne and Paul Cox for Flowers International. screenplay: Paul Cox and Bob Ellis. photography: Yuri Sokol. design: Asher Bilu. editor: Tim Lewis. cast: Alison Best, Chris Haywood, Werner Herzog, Norman Kaye, Sarah Walker.

MANGANNINIE
Released 1980. Eastman colour, 35 mm, 90 minutes. director: John Honey. producer: Gilda Baracchi for Tasmanian Film Corporation. screenplay: Ken Kelso. photography: Gary Hansen. design: Neil Angwin. editor: Mike Woolveridge. cast: Buruminy Dhamarrandji, Jonathon Elliott, Reg Evans, Philip Hinton

MANGO TREE, THE
Released 1977, Bundaberg, Qld. Colour, widescreen, 104 minutes. director: Kevin Dobson. producer: Michael Pate for Pisces Productions. screenplay: Michael Pate, from novel by Ronald McKie. photography: Brian Probyn. design: Leslie Binns. composer: Marc Wilkinson. editor: JohnScott. cast: Tony Barry, Carol Burns, Diane Craig, Gloria Dawn, Geraldine Fitzgerald, Ben Gabriel, Robert Helpmann, Gerard Kennedy, Christopher Pate, Charles Tingwell.

MATCHLESS
Released 1974, Sydney. B & W, 16 mm, 55 minutes. director: John Papadopoulos. producer: John Papadopoulos. screenplay: Sally Blake. photography: Russell Boyd. composer: Charles Pileso. editor: Kit Guyatt. cast: Sally Blake, Denise Otto, Alan Penney.

MAYBE THIS TIME
Released 1980. Eastman colour, 35 mm, 100 minutes. director: Chris McGill. producer: Brian Kavanagh for Cherrywood Film Productions. screenplay: Anne Brooksbank and Bob Ellis. photography: Russell Boyd. designer: Chris Webster. editor: Wayne le Closs. cast: Michele Fawdon, Bill Hunter, Judy Morris, Jill Perryman, Mike Preston, Ken Shorter, Leonard Teale.

MELVIN, SON OF ALVIN
Released 1985. Kodak colour, 35 mm, 90 minutes. director: John Eastway. producer: Jim McElroy for Memorelle. screenplay: Morris Gleitzman. photography: John Eastway. composer: Colin Stead. design: Jon Dowding. editor: John Hollands. cast: Abigail, David Argue, Graeme Blundell, Tina Bursill, Jon Finlayson, Lenita Sillakis, Gerry Sont.

MIDNITE SPARES
Released 1982. Eastman colour, 35 mm, 97 minutes. director: Quentin Masters. producer: Tom Burstall for Wednesday Investments. screenplay: Terry Larsen. photography: Geoff Burton. composer: Cameron Allen. design: George Liddle. editor: Andrew Prowse. cast: David Argue, Tony Barry, Gia Carides, John Clayton, Max Cullen, James Laurie, Bruce Spence, Graeme Blundell.

MOLLY
Released 1983. Eastman colour, 35 mm, 90 minutes. director: Ned Lander. producer: Hilary Linstead for Troplisa. screenplay: Ned Lander, Phillip Roope and Mark Thomas. photography: Vincent Monton. composer: Graeme Isaac. musical performers: Mick Conway, Jim Conway. design: Robert Dein. editor: Stewart Young. cast: Ruth Cracknell, Slim de Grey, Melissa Jaffer, Claudia Karvan, Reg Lye, Garry McDonald, Flying Fruit Fly Circus.

MONEY MOVERS
Released 1979. Eastman colour, 35 mm, 100 minutes. director: Bruce Beresford. producer: Matt Carroll for South Australian Film Corporation. screenplay: Bruce Beresford from novel by Devon Minchin. photography: Don McAlpine. design: David Copping.

editor: Bill Anderson. cast: Tony Bonner, Ed Devereaux, Terence Donovan, Candy Raymond, Bud Tingwell, Frank Wilson.
MONKEY GRIP
Released 1981. Eastman colour, 35 mm, 105 minutes. director: Ken Cameron. producer: Patricia Lovell for Pavilion Films. screenplay: Ken Cameron with Helen Garner, from the novel by Helen Garner. photography: David Gribble. composer: Bruce Smeaton. musicians: Divinyls. design: Clark Munro. editor: David Huggett. cast: Tim Burns, Michael Caton, Colin Friels, Alice Garner, Noni Hazlehurst, Harold Hopkins, Candy Raymond.
MORE THINGS CHANGE, THE
Released 1985. Eastman colour, 35 mm, widescreen, 94 minutes. director: Robyn Nevin. producer: Jill C. Robb for Syme International Productions. screenplay: Moya Wood. photography: Dan Burstall. composer: Peter Best. design: Jo Ford. editor: Jill Billcock. cast: Peter Carroll, Lewis Fitz-Gerald, Owen Johnson, Victoria Longley, Judy Morris, Barry Otto.
MOUTH TO MOUTH
Released 1978. Eastman colour, 35mm, 96 minutes. director: John Duigan. producers: John Duigan and Jon Sainken for Vega Film Productions. screenplay: John Duigan. photography: Tom Cowan. composer: Roy Ritchie. design: Tracy Watt. editor: Tony Patterson. cast: Serge Frazetto, Ian Gilmour, Kim Krejus, Sonia Peat.
MOVING OUT
Released 1982. Kodak colour, super 16 mm, 92 minutes. director: Michael Pattinson. producers: Jane Ballantyne and Michael Pattinson for Pattinson Ballantyne. screenplay: Jan Sardi. photography: Vincent Monton. musicians: Danny Beckerman, Umberto Tozzi. design: Neil Angwin. editor: Robert Martin. cast: Vince Colosimo, Kate Jason, Peter Sardi, Ivor Kants, Sandy Gore, Sally Cooper.
MY BRILLIANT CAREER
Released 1979. Eastman colour, 35 mm, 100 minutes. director: Gillian Armstrong. producer: Margaret Fink. screenplay: Eleanor Witcombe from novel by Miles Franklin. photography: Don McAlpine. musical director: Nathan Waks. design: Luciana Arrighi. editor: Nick Beauman. cast: Aileen Britton, Max Cullen, Judy Davis, Robert Grubb, Wendy Hughes, Patricia Kennedy, Sam Neill.
MY FIRST WIFE
Released 1984. Fuji colour, 35 mm, 100 minutes. director: Paul Cox. producers: Jane Ballantyne and Paul Cox. screenplay: Paul Cox and Bob Ellis. photography: Yuri Sokol. design: Asher Biln. editor: Tim Lewis. cast: Lucy Charlotte Angwin, David Cameron, John Hargreaves, Wendy Hughes, Robin Lovejoy, Betty Lucan, Charles Tingwell, Lucy Uralon.
NAKED BUNYIP, THE
Released 1970, Melbourne. B & W and colour, 16 mm, 136 minutes. director: John B. Murray. producer: Phillip Adams for Southern Cross Films. screenplay: John B. Murray and Ray Taylor. photography: Bruce McNaughton. editor: Brian Kavanagh. cast: Graeme Blundell, Barry Humphries, Jacki Weaver.
NAKED COUNTRY
Released 1984. Colour, 35 mm, 90 minutes. director: Tim Burstall. producer: Ross Dimsey for Naked Country Productions. screenplay: Tim Burstall and Ross Dimsey, from novel by Morris West. photography: David Eggby. composer: Bruce Smeaton. design: Philip Warner. editor: Tony Patterson. cast: Rebecca Gilling, Ivar Kants, Tommy Lewis, John Stanton.
NEWSFRONT
Released 1978. Eastman colour, 35 mm, 110 minutes. director: Phil Noyce. producer: David Elfick for Palm Beach Pictures. screenplay: Phil Noyce after Bob Ellis, from original idea by David Elfick. photography: Vincent Monton. design: Lisa Coote. editor: John Scott. cast: Chris Haywood, Wendy Hughes, Bill Hunter, Gerard Kennedy.
NEXT OF KIN
Released 1982. Eastman colour, 35 mm, 95 minutes. director: Tony Williams. producers: Robert le Tet and Timothy White for The Film House and SIS Productions. screenplay: Michael Heath and Tony Williams. photography: Gary Hansen. design: Richard Francis and Nick Hepworth. editor: Max Lemon. cast: John Jarratt, Jackie Kerin, Charles McCallum, Gerda Nicholson, Alex Stitt.
NICKEL QUEEN
Released 1971, Perth. Colour, 35 mm, 89 minutes. director: John McCallum. producers: Joy Cavill and John McCallum. screenplay: Joy Cavill, Henry C. James and John McCallum, from story by Anneke and Henry James. photography: John Williams. design: Bernard Hides. composer: Sven Libaek. editor: Don Saunders. cast: Ed Devereaux, Peter Gwynne, John Laws, Tom Oliver, Alfred Sandor, Ross Thompson, Doreen Warburton, Googie Withers.
NIGHT THE PROWLER, THE
Released 1978. Eastman colour, 35 mm, 90 minutes. director: Jim Sharman. producer: Anthony Buckley for Chariot Films. screenplay: Patrick White, from his own short story. photography: David Sanderson. design: Luciana Arrighi. editor: Sara Bennett. cast: Terry Camilleri, Ruth Cracknell, John Derum,

John Frawley, Maggie Kirkpatrick, Kerry Walker.
NIGHTMARES
Released 1980. Eastman colour, 35 mm, 90 minutes. director: John Lamond. producers: John Lamond and Colin Eggleston for John Lamond Motion Picture Enterprises. screenplay: Colin Eggleston. photography: Gary Wapshott. composer: Brian May. design: Paul Jones.
NORMAN LOVES ROSE
Released 1982. Eastman colour, 35 mm, 98 minutes. director: Henri Safran. producers: Basil Appleby and Henri Safran for Norman Films. screenplay: Henri Safran. photography: Vincent Monton. design: Darrell Lass. editor: Don Saunders. cast: Myra de Groot. David Downer. Sandy Gore. Carole Kane. Warren Mitchell. Barry Otto. Tony Owen.
NOW AND FOREVER
Released 1982. Eastman colour, 35 mm, 102 minutes. director: Adrian Carr. producer: Treisha Ghent for Now and Forever Film Partnership. screenplay: Richard Cassidy from novel by Danielle Steel. photography: Don McAlpine. composer: Bruce Rowland. design: Rene and Rochford. editor: Adrian Carr. cast: Christine Amor, Aileen Britton, Robert Coleby, Carmen Duncan, Cheryl Ladd, Kris McQuade, Henri Szeps.

ODD ANGRY SHOT, THE
Released 1979. Eastman colour, 35 mm, 90 minutes. director: Tom Jeffrey. producers: Sue Milliken and Tom Jeffrey for Samson Film Services. screenplay: Tom Jeffrey, from a novel by William Nagel. photography: Don McAlpine. design: Bernard Hides. editor: Brian Kavanagh. cast: Graeme Blundell, Bryan Brown, Ian Gilmour, John Hargreaves, John Jarratt, Graham Kennedy, Richard Moir.
OFFICE, PICNIC, THE
First shown 1972, Melbourne. B & W, 35 mm, 83 minutes. director: Tom Cowan. producer: Tom Cowan for Child's Play Moving Picture Company. screenplay: Tom Cowan. photography: Michael Edols. composer: Don Mori. editor: Kit Guyatt. cast: Max Cullen, Philip Deamer, Ben Gabriel, Kate Fitzpatrick, Gay Steel, John Wood.
ONE NIGHT STAND
Released 1984. Eastman colour, 35 mm, 93 minutes. director: John Duigan. producer: Richard Mason for Astra Film Productions. screenplay: John Duigan. photography: Tom Cowan. composer: William Motzing. design: Ross Major. editor: John Scott. cast: Tyler Copping, Cassandra Delaney, Jay Hackett, David Pledger, Saskia Post.

ON GUARD
Released 1983. colour, 16 mm, 52 minutes. director: Susan Lambert. producer: Digby (Janice) Duncan for RedHeart Pictures. screenplay: Sarah Gibson, Susan Lambert. photography: Laurie McInnes. editor: Catherine Murphy. sound: Pat Fiske and Sue Kerr. cast: Liddy Clark, Jan Cornall, Kerry Dwyer, Mystery Carnage.
ON OUR SELECTION
Released 1932, Sydney. B & W, 35 mm, 99 minutes. director: Ken G. Hall. producer: Cinesound Productions. screenplay: Bert Bailey and Ken G. Hall, from stories by Steele Rudd. photography: Walter Sully. editor: George Malcolm. cast: Bert Bailey, Alfreda Bevan, Dorothy Dunkley, Dick Fair, Fred Kerry, Fred Macdonald, Jack McGowan, Molly Raynor, John Warwick.
ON THE LOOSE
Released 1985. colour, 35 mm, 83 minutes. director: Jane Oehr. prodcuer: Lyn Norfor for Health Media Productions. screenplay: Ken Cameron, Jane Oehr, Tim Gooding, Mark Shles, Tom McPartland. photography: Tom Cowan. production design: David Trethewey. music: Todd Hunter. sound: John Franks. cast: Steve Bergan, Jim Filipovski, Tamsin Hardman, John Hamblin, Carole Skinner, Ray Meagher.
OZ
Released 1976, Melbourne. Colour, 35 mm, 103 minutes. Shorter version released in USA as 20th Century Oz. director: Chris L fven. producers: Lyne Helms and Chris L fven. screenplay: Chris L fven. photography: Dan Burstall. design: Robbie Perkins. editor: Les Luxford. cast: Michael Carman, Joy Dunstan, Graham Matters, Robin Ramsay, Bruce Spence, Gary Waddell.

PACIFIC BANANA
Released 1981. Eastman colour, 35 mm wide screen, 80 minutes. director: John Lamond. producer: John Lamond for Pacific Banana. screenplay: Alan Hopgood. photography: Gary Wapshott. design: Herbert Pinter. editor: Ray Daley. cast: Alyson Best, Graeme Blundell, Deborah Gray, Helen Hemmingway, Luane Peters, Robin Stewart, Manuia Taie.
PALM BEACH
Released 1979. Eastman colour, 35 mm, 88 minutes. director: Albie Thoms. producer: Albie Thoms. screenplay: Albie Thoms. photography: Oscar Scherl. composer: Terry Hannigan. design: Dave Fennell, Ace Follington. editor: Albie Thoms. cast: Amanda Berry, Bryan Brown, Ken Brown, Lyn Collingwood, John Flaus, Julie McGregor, Nat Young.

A Select Filmography 265

PATRICK
Released 1978. Agfa colour, 35 mm, 120 minutes. director: Richard Franklin. producers: Antony I. Ginnane and Richard Franklin for Patrick Productions for Australian International Film Corporation. screenplay: Everett de Roche. photography: Don McAlpine. composer: Brian May. design: Leslie Binns. editor: Edward McQueen-Mason. cast: Bruce Barry, Julia Blake, Robert Helpmann, Rod Mullinar, Susan Penhaligon, Frank Wilson.
PETERSEN
Released 1974, Sydney. Colour, 35 mm, 107 minutes. director: Tim Burstall. producer: Tim Burstall for Hexagon Productions. screenplay: David Williamson. photography: Robin Copping. composer: Peter Best. design: Bill Hutchinson. editor: David Bilcock. cast: Christine Amor, Arthur Dignam, Cliff Ellen, John Ewart, Belinda Giblin, Wendy Hughes, Sandy Macgregor, George Mallaby, Dina Mann, Helen Morse, Anne Pendlebury, Tim Robertson, Lindsay Smith, Jack Thompson, Charles Tingwell, Jacki Weaver.
PHAR LAP
Released 1983. Eastman colour, 35 mm, 118 minutes. director: Simon Wincer. producer: John Sexton for John Sexton Productions and Michael Edgley International. screenplay: David Williamson. photography: Russell Boyd. editor: Tony Paterson. composer: Bruce Rowland. design: Larry Eastwood. editor: Tony Paterson. cast: Vincent Ball, Tom Burlinson, Celia de Burgh, Ron Leibman, Judy Morris, John Stanton, Martin Vaughan.
PICNIC AT HANGING ROCK
Released 1975, Adelaide. Colour, 35 mm, 115 minutes. director: Peter Weir. producer: Patricia Lovell. screenplay: Cliff Green from novel by Joan Lindsay. photography: Russell Boyd. composer: Bruce Smeaton. design: David Copping. editor: Max Lemon. cast: Kirsty Child, John Fegan, Vivean Gray, Dominic Guard, John Jarratt, Anne Lambert, Tony Llewellyn-Jones, Ingrid Mason, Garry McDonald, Helen Morse, Rachel Roberts, Martin Vaughan, Jacki Weaver.
PICTURE SHOW MAN, THE
Released 1977, Melbourne. Colour, 35 mm, 98 minutes. director: John Power. producer: Joan Long for Limelight Productions. screenplay: Joan Long, from Penn's Pictures on Tour by Lyle Penn. photography: Geoff Burton. composer: Peter Best. design: David Copping. cast: Tony Barry, Patrick Cargill, Sally Conabere, Jeanie Drynan, John Ewart, Harold Hopkins, Garry McDonald, John Meillon, Judy Morris, Grant Page, Rod Taylor.

PIRATE MOVIE, THE
Released 1982. Eastman colour, 35 mm, 100 minutes. director: Ken Annakin. producer: David Joseph for JHI Productions. screenplay: Trevor Farrant. photography: Robin Copping. editor: Ken Zemke. composer: Terry Britten. design: John Dowding. editor: Ken Zemke. cast: Christopher Aitkens, Ted Hamilton, Bill Kerr, Maggie Kirkpatrick, Garry McDonald, Kristy McNicholl, Roger Ward.
PLAINS OF HEAVEN, THE
Released 1982. Fuji colour, 16 mm, 80 minutes. director: Ian Pringle. producer: John Cruthers for Seon Films. screenplay: Ian Pringle, Doug Ling and Elizabeth Parsons. photography: Ray Argall. composer: Andrew Duffield. design: Elizabeth Stirling. editor: Ray Argall. cast: Adam Briscombe, Jenny Cartwright, Reg Evans, John Flaus, Gerard Kennedy, Richard Moir.
PLUGG
Released 1975, Perth. Colour. director: Terry Bourke. producer: Ninki Maslansky for Romac Productions. screenplay: Terry Bourke. photography: Brian Probyn. design: Barry Adler. composer: Bob Young. editor: Rod Hay. cast: Reg Gorman, Cheryl Rixon, Peter Thompson, Norman Yemm.
PRIVATE COLLECTION
Released 1972, Sydney. Colour, 16 mm, 92 minutes. director: Keith Salvat. producer: Keith Salvat for Keisal/Bonza Films. screenplay: Keith Salvat and Sandy Sharp. photography: David Gribble. composer: Mike Perjanik. editor: G. Turney-Smith. cast: Brian Blain, Grahame Bond, Noel Ferrier, Les Foxcroft, Peter Reynolds, Pamela Stephenson.
PROMISED WOMAN
Released 1976, Sydney. Colour, 35 mm, 84 minutes. director: Tom Cowan. producers: Richard Brennan and Tom Cowan for BC Productions. screenplay: Tom Cowan, from Throw Away Your Harmonica, play by Theo Patrikareas. photography: Tom Cowan. design: Gillian Armstrong. composer: Vassili Daramaras. editor: David Stiven. cast: Gillian Armstrong, Takis Emmanuel, Kate Fitzpatrick, Nikos Gerissimou, Yelena Zigon.
PUBERTY BLUES
Released 1981. Eastman colour, 35 mm, 90 minutes. director: Bruce Beresford. producer: Joan Long for Limelight Productions. screenplay: Margaret Kelly, from book by Kathy Lette and Gabrielle Carey. photography: Don McAlpine. composers: Les Gock and Tim Finn. design: David Copping. editor: William Anderson. cast: Jad Capelja, Jay Hackett, Ned Lander, Tony Nogaes, Sandy Paul, Geoff Rhoe, Nell Schofield.

PURE S
Released 1976, Melbourne. Colour, 35 mm, 83 minutes. director: Bert Deling. producer: Bob Weis. screenplay: Bert Deling and the cast. photography: Tom Cowan. editor: John Scott. cast: Helen Garner, Max Gillies, Anne Hetherington, John Laurie, Phil Motherwell, Carol Porter, Tim Robertson, Gary Waddell.

QUEENSLAND
Released 1976, Melbourne. Colour, 16 mm, 52 minutes. director: John Ruane. producer: Chris Fitchett. screenplay: John Ruane and Ellery Ryan. photography: Ellery Ryan. editor: Mark Norfolk. cast: Alison Bird, Patricia Condon, John Flaus, Bob Karl.

RACE TO THE YANKEE ZEPHYR
Released 1981. Eastman colour, 35 mm, 100 minutes. director: David Hemmings. producers: John Barnett, Antony I. Ginnane and David Hemmings for F. G. H. Film Consortium, Zephyr Films and First City Films. screenplay: Everett DeRoche. photography: David Monton. composer: Brian May. editor: John Laing. design: Bernard Hides. cast: Bruno Lawrence, George Peppard, Donald Pleasance, Ken Wahl, Lesley Ann Warren, Donald Pleasance.

RAW DEAL
Released 1977, Melbourne and Sydney. Colour, 94 minutes. director: Russell Hagg. producers: Russell Hagg and Patrick Edgeworth. screenplay: Patrick Edgeworth. photography: Vincent Monton. composer: Ronald Edgeworth. design: Jon Dowding. editor: Tony Patterson. cast: Gerard Kennedy, Bethany Lee, Gus Mercurio, Rod Mullinar, Christopher Pate, Anne Pendelbury, Norman Yemm.

RAZORBACK
Released 1984. Kodak colour, 35 mm, 95 minutes. director: Russell Mulcahy. producer: Hal McElroy for McElroy and McElroy. screenplay: Everett de Roche from novel by Peter Brennan. photography: Dean Semler. composer: Ivar Davies. design: Neil Angwin. editor: Bill Anderson. cast: David Argue, John Ewart, Gregory Harrison, Chris Haywood, Bill Kerr, Judy Morris, Arkie Whiteley.

REBEL
Released 1985. Kodak colour, 35 mm, 105 minutes. director: Michael Jenkins. producer: Phillip Emanuel. screenplay: Bob Herbert and Michael Jenkins, from play by Bob Herbert. photography: Peter James. composer: Ray Cook. designer: Brian Thompson. editor: Michael Honey. cast: Ray Barrett, Bryan Brown, Debbie Byrne, Kim Deacon, Matt Dillon, Bill Hunter, Julie Nihill.

RELATIVES
Released 1985. Eastman colour, 90 minutes, 16 mm. director: Anthony Bowman. producer: Basil Appleby and Henri Safran for Archer Films. screenplay: Anthony Bowman. photography: Tom Cowan. designer: Darrel Lass. editor: Colin Greive. cast: Michael Atkins, Ray Barrett, Robin Bowring, Jeannie Drynan, Norman Kaye, Bill Kerr, Ray Meagher, Carol Raye, Rowena Wallace.

REMOVALISTS, THE
Released 1975, Sydney. Colour, 35 mm, 93 minutes. director: Tom Jeffrey. producer: Margaret Fink. screenplay: David Williamson, from his own play. photography: Graham Lind. design: Margaret Fink. musicians: Galapagos Duck. editor: Anthony Buckley. cast: Peter Cummins, John Hargreaves, Martin Harris, Chris Haywood, Kate Fitzpatrick, Jacki Weaver.

RETURN OF CAPTAIN INVINCIBLE, THE
Released 1982. Eastman colour, 35 mm, 92 minutes. director: Philippe Mora. producer: Andrew Gaty for Seven Keys. screenplay: Andrew Gaty and Steven de Souza. photography: Mike Molloy. designer: David Copping. editor: John Scott. cast: Alan Arkin, Noel Ferrier, Kate Fitzpatrick, Hayes Gordon, Chris Haywood, Bill Hunter, Graham Kennedy, Christopher Lee, Michael Pate, Max Phipps, Bruce Spence.

ROADGAMES
Released 1981. Eastman colour, 35 mm, 110 minutes. director: Richard Franklin. producer: Richard Franklin for Quest Films. screenplay: Everett DeRoche, from short story by Richard Franklin and Everett DeRoche. photography: Vincent Monton. composer: Brian May. designer: John Dowding. editor: Edward McQueen-Mason. cast: Stacy Keach, Jamie-Lee Curtis, Marion Edward, Grant Page, Bill Stacey, Thaddeus Smith, Stephen Millichamp.

RUN CHRISSIE RUN
Released 1984. Kodak colour, 35 mm, 98 minutes. director: Chris Langman. producer: Harley Manners for South Australian Film Corporation. screenplay: Graham Hartley, from the novel When We Run by Keith Leopold. photography: Bernie Clark. designer: Andrew Livingstone. editor: Andrew Prowse. cast: Michael Aitkens, Shane Briant, Carmen Duncan, Nicholas Eadie, Annie Jones, Redmond Symons.

A Select Filmography

RUNNING ON EMPTY
Released 1982. Kodak colour, 35 mm, 104 minutes. director: John Clark. producer: Pom Oliver for Film Corporation of Western Australia. screenplay: Barry Tomblin. photography: David Gribble. design: Greg Brown. editor: Stuart Butterworth. cast: Grahame Bond, Debbie Conway, Max Cullen, Penne Hackforth-Jones, Richard Moir, Vangeliz Mourikis, Terry Serio.

SCOBIE MALONE
Released 1975, Brisbane. Colour, 35 mm, 98 minutes. director: Terry Ohlsson. producer: Casey Robinson for Kingcroft Productions. screenplay: Casey Robinson, from Helga's Web, novel by Jon Cleary. photography: Keith Lambert. composer: Peter Clarke. editor: Bill Stacey. cast: James Condon, Cul Cullen, Noel Ferrier, Ken Goodlet, Joe James, Jacqueline Kott, Max Meldrum, Judy Morris, Shane Porteous, Rod Taylor, Jack Thompson.

SETTLEMENT, THE
Released 1983. Eastman colour, 35 mm, 95 minutes. director: Howard Rubie. producer: Robert Bruning. screenplay: Ted Roberts. photography: Ernest Clark. production designer: John Watson. editor: Henry Dangar. composer: Sven Libaek. design: John Watson. editor: Henry Dangar. cast: Tony Barry, Allen Cassell, John Jarratt, Bill Kerr, Lorna Lesley, Katy Wild, Babette Stephens, David Downer.

SHIRLEY THOMPSON VERSUS THE ALIENS
Released 1972. Colour, 16 mm, 104 minutes. director: Jim Sharman. producer: Jim Sharman for Kolossal Pictures. screenplay: Helmut Bakaitis and Jim Sharman. photography: David Sanderson. design: Brian Thomson. editor: Malcolm Smith. cast: Helmut Bakaitis, June Collis, Tim Elliott, Kate Fitzpatrick, Ron Haddrick, Jane Harders, Alexander Hay, Max Hess, John Ivkovitch, Phil Kitamura, Marion Johns, John Llewellyn, Sue Moir, Marie Nicholas, Candy Raymond, Julie Rodgers, Georgina West.

SHORT CHANGED
Released 1986. Eastman colour, super 16 mm, 104 minutes. director: George Ogilvie. producer: Ross Matthews for Magpie Films. screenplay: Robert J. Merritt. photography: Peter Levy. design: Kristian Fredrikson. editor: Richard Francis-Bruce. cast: Jamie Aquis, David Kennedy, Susan Leith, Mark Little, Ray Meagher.

SIDECAR RACERS
Released 1975, Sydney. Colour, 35 mm, 100 minutes. director: Earl Bellamy. producer: Richard Irving for Universal Pictures. screenplay: Jon Cleary. photography: Paul Onorato. composer: Tom Scott. editor: Robert Kimble. cast: Liddy Clark, John Clayton, John Derum, Peter Graves, Peter Gwynne, Wendy Hughes, Serge Lazareff, John Meillon, Ben Murphy, Arna-Maria Winchester.

SILVER CITY
Released 1984. Eastman colour, 35 mm. director: Sophia Turkiewicz. producer: Joan Long for Limelight Productions. screenplay: Thomas Keneally and Sophie Turkiewicz. photography: John Seale. composer: William Motzing. design: Igor Nay. editor: Don Saunders. cast: Steve Bisley, Ewa Brok, Annie Byron, Gosia Dobrowolska, Jan Hurley, Anna Jemison, Ivar Kants, Debra Lawrence, Igor Nay, Don Saunders.

SINGER AND THE DANCER, THE
Released 1977, Melbourne. Colour, 35 mm from 16 mm, 52 minutes. director: Gillian Armstrong. producer: Gillian Armstrong. screenplay: Gillian Armstrong, John Pfeffer, from Old Mrs Bilson, short story by Alan Marshall. composer: Robert Murphy. photography: Russell Boyd. design: Sue Armstrong. editor: Nicholas Beauman. cast: Ruth Cracknell, Elizabeth Crosby, Jude Kuring, Kate Sheil, Rob Steele.

SLICE OF LIFE
Released 1982. Eastman colour, 35 mm, 100 minutes. director: John Lamond. producer: John Lamond. screenplay: Alan Hopgood. photography: Ross Berryman. composer: Brian May. design: Paul Jones. editor: Jill Rice. cast: Jane Clifton, John Ewart, Juliet Jordan, Caz Lederman, Dina Mann, Amanda Muggleton, Robin Nedwell.

SNAPSHOT
Released 1978. Colour, 35 mm, Panavision, 90 minutes. director: Simon Wincer. producer: Antony I. Ginnane for Australian International Film Corporation. screenplay: Chris DeRoche and Everett DeRoche. photography: Vincent Monton. composer: Brian May. design: Jon Dowding. editor: Philip Reid. cast: Chantal Contouri, Sigrid Thornton, Robert Bruning, Hugh Keays-Byrne, Denise Drysdale, Vincent Gill, Lulu Pinkus.

SOLO
Released 1978. Eastman colour, 35 mm, 95 minutes. director: Tony Williams. producers: David Hannay and Tony

Williams. screenplay: Martyn Sanderson and Tony Williams. photography: John Blick. composers: Marion Arts, Dave Fraser, Robbie Laven. design: Paul Carvel. editor: Tony Williams. cast: Perry Armstrong, Maxwell Fernie, Vincent Gil, Lisa Peers, Martyn Sanderson, Davina Whitehouse.

SQUATTER'S DAUGHTER, THE
Released 1933, Sydney. B & W, 35 mm, 104 minutes. director: Ken G. Hall. producer: Ken G. Hall for Cinesound Productions. screenplay: Gayne Dexter and E. V. Timms, from play by 'Albert Edmunds' (Bert Bailey and Edmund Duggan). photography: Frank Hurley and George Malcolm. composers: Frank Chapple and Tom King. design: Fred Finlay. editors: George Malcolm and William Shepherd. cast: Owen Ainley, W. Lane Bayliff, Dorothy Dunkley, Jocelyn Howarth, George Lloyd, Grant Lyndsay, Fred Macdonald, Claude Turton, Katie Towers, Les Warton, John Warwick.

SQUIZZY TAYLOR
Released 1982. Eastman colour, 35 mm, 105 minutes. director: Kevin Dobson. producer: Roger le Mesurier for Simpson le Mesurier Films. screenplay: Roger Simpson. photography: Dan Burstall. composer: Bruce Smeaton. design: Logan Brewer. editor: David Pulbrook. cast: David Atkins, Allen Cassell, Cul Cullen, Robert Hughes, Michael Long, Kim Lewis, Jacki Weaver.

STANLEY
Released 1983. Eastman colour, 35 mm, 93 minutes. director: Esben Storm. producer: Andrew Gaty for Seven Keys. screenplay: Esben Storm, from story by Esben Storm and Andrew Gaty. photography: Russell Boyd. design: Owen Paterson. editor: Bill Anderson. cast: David Argue, Peter Bensley, Nell Campbell, Jonathan Coleman, Michael Craig, Max Cullen, Graham Kennedy, Lorna Lesley.

STARSTRUCK
Released 1982. Eastman colour, 35 mm, 105 minutes. director: Gillian Armstrong. producers: David Elfick and Richard Brennan for Palm Beach Pictures. screenplay: Stephen Maclean. photography: Russell Boyd. design: Brian Thomson. editor: Nicholas Beauman. cast: Max Cullen, Pat Evison, Melissa Jaffer, Jo Kennedy, Ned Lander, Margo Lee, Ross O'Donovan.

STILL POINT, THE
Released 1986. Eastman colour, 16 mm, 81 minutes. director: Barbara Boyd-Anderson. producer: Rosa Colosimo for Colosimo Film Productions. screenplay: Barbara Boyd-Anderson, Rosa Colosimo. photography: Kevin Anderson. composer: Pierre Pierre. design: Patrick Reardon. editor: Zbigniew Friedrich. cast: Steve Bastoni, Robin Cuming, Nadine Garner, Lyn Semmler, Alex Mengler.

STIR!
Released 1980. Eastman colour, 35 mm, 100 minutes. director: Stephen Wallace. producer: Richard Brennan for Smiley Films. screenplay: Bob Jewson. photography: Geoff Burton. composer: Cameron Allen. design: Lee Whitmore. editor: Henry Dangar. cast: Bryan Brown, Michael Gow, Ray Marshall, Dennis Miller, Phil Motherwell, Max Phipps, Gary Waddell.

STONE
Released 1974, Sydney. Colour, 35 mm, 126 minutes. director: Sandy Harbutt. producer: Sandy Harbutt for Hedon Productions. screenplay: Sandy Harbutt and Michael Robinson. photography: Graham Lind. design: Tim Storrier. composer: Billy Green. editor: Ian Barry. cast: Deryck Barnes, Slim de Grey, Vincent Gill, Rebecca Gilling, Sandy Harbutt, Bill Hunter, Hugh Keays-Byrne, Harry Lawrence, Sue Lloyd, Gary McDonald, Helen Morse, Ken Shorter, Ros Spiers, Roger Ward, Owen Weingott.

STORK
Released 1971, Melbourne. Colour, 35 mm, 90 minutes. director: Tim Burstall. producer: Tim Burstall for Tim Burstall and Associates and Bilcock and Copping Film Productions. screenplay: David Williamson, from his play The Coming of Stork. photography: Robin Copping. design: Leslie Binns. editor: Edward McQueen-Mason. composer: Hans Poulsen. cast: Helmut Bakaitis, Graeme Blundell, Peter Cummins, Sean McEuan, Max Gillies, Dennis Miller, Bruce Spence, Jacki Weaver.

STORM BOY
Released 1976, Adelaide. Colour, 87 minutes. director: Henri Safran. producer: Matt Carroll for South Australian Film Corporation. screenplay: Sonia Borg, from novel by Colin Thiele. photography: Geoff Burton. composer: Michael Carlos. design: David Copping. editor: G. Turney-Smith. cast: Peter Cummins, Judy Dick, David Gulpilil, Grant Page, Greg Rowe.

STREET HERO
Released 1984. Eastman colour, 35 mm, 100 minutes. director: Michael Pattinson. producer: Julie Monton for Paul Dainty Films. screenplay: Jan Sardi. photography: Vincent Monton. composer: Red Symons. design: Brian Thomson. editor: David Pulbrook. cast: Vince Colombo, Sandy Gore, Bill Hunter, Ray Marshall, Amanda Muggleton, Peter Sardi, Sigrid Thornton.

STREET TO DIE, A
Released 1985. Colour, 35 mm, 91 minutes. director: Bill Bennett. producer: Bill Bennett. screenplay: Bill Bennett. photography: Geoff Burton. production design: Igor Nay. costume design: Magie Beswick. music: Michael Atkinson, Michael Spicer. editor: Denise Hunter. cast: Chris Haywood, Jennifer Cluff, Robin Ramsay, Pat Evison, Arianthe Galani, Peter Hehir.

STRIKEBOUND
Released 1984. Eastman colour, 35 mm, 100 minutes. director: Richard Lowenstein, producers: Miranda Bain and Timothy White for TRM Productions, screenplay: Richard Lowenstein, photography: Andrew de Groot. design: Tracy Watt, editor: Jill Billcock. cast: Carol Burns, Reg Evans, Nik Forster, Chris Haywood, Hugh Keays-Byrne, David Kendall, Rob Steele.

SUMMER CITY
Released 1977, Sydney. Colour, 35 mm. director: Chris Fraser. producer: Phillip Avalon for Avalon Films and Summer City Productions. screenplay: Phillip Avalon. photography: Jerry Marek. design: Jann Harris. composer: Phil Birkis. editor: David Stiven.

SUMMER OF SECRETS
Released 1976. Colour, 35 mm, 102 minutes. director: Jim Sharman. producer: Michael Thornhill. screenplay: John Aitken. photography: Russell Boyd. design: Jane Norris. composer: Cameron Allan. editor: Sara Bennett. cast: Nell Campbell, Rufus Collins, Arthur Dignam, Kate Fitzpatrick, Jude Kuring, Andrew Sharp.

SUMMERFIELD
Released 1977, Sydney. Colour, 35 mm, 91 minutes. director: Ken Hannam. producer: Patricia Lovell. screenplay: Cliff Green. photography: Mike Molloy. design: Graham Walker. composer: Bruce Smeaton. editor: Sara Bennett. cast: Elizabeth Alexander, Max Cullen, Barry Donnelly, Sheila Florance, Michelle Jarman, Nick Tate, Charles Tingwell, Geraldine Turner, John Waters.

SUNDAY TOO FAR AWAY
Released 1975, Adelaide. Colour, 35 mm, 94 minutes. director: Ken Hannam. producer: Gil Brealey and Matt Carroll for South Australian Film Corporation. screenplay: John Dingwall. photography: Geoff Burton. composer: Patrick Flynn (arr. Michael Carlos). design: David Copping. editor: Rod Adamson. cast: Robert Bruning, Max Cullen, Peter Cummins, John Ewart, Reg Lye, Lisa Peers, Sean Scully, Ken Shorter, Jack Thompson.

SUNSHINE SALLY
Released 1922. B & W, 35 mm, silent, 5000 ft. Fragments in National Film and Sound Archive. director: Lawson Harris. producers: Lawson Harris and Yvonne Pavis for Austral Super Films. screenplay: John Cosgrove. photography: Arthur Higgins. cast: John Cosgrove, J. P. O'Neill, Dinks Patterson, Yvonne Pavis, Joy Revelle.

SURRENDER IN PARADISE
Released 1976, Brisbane. Colour, 16 mm, 92 minutes. director: Peter Cox. producer: Peter Cox for Paradise Pictures. screenplay: Peter Cox. photography: Don McAlpine. composer: Ralph Tyrell. editors: Bob Blasdall and Peter Cox. cast: Ross Gilbert, Carolyn Howard, Erroll O'Neill, Rod Wissler.

SURVIVOR, THE
Released 1980. Eastman colour, 35 mm, 94 minutes. director: David Hemmings. producer: Antony I. Ginnane for Riaci Investments and Tuesday Film Productions. screenplay: David Ambrose and James Herbert. photography: John Seale. composer: Brian May design: Bernard Hides. editor: Tony Paterson. cast: Joseph Cotten, Ralph Cotterill, Lorna Lesley, Robert Powell, Angela Punch-McGregor, Peter Sumner.

SWEET DREAMERS
Released 1982. Eastman colour, 16 mm, 96 minutes. director: Tom Cowan. producer: Lesley Tucker for TC Productions. screenplay: Tom Cowan and Lesley Tucker. photography: Brian Probyn. composer: Brett Cabot. design: Lesley Tucker. editor: Tom Cowan. cast: Adam Brown, Richard Moir, Frankie Raymond, Sue Smithers, Richard Tipping, Maisie Turner.

TALL TIMBERS
Released 1937, Brisbane. B & W, 35 mm, 89 minutes. director: Ken G. Hall. producer: Ken G. Hall for Cinesound Productions. screenplay: Frank Harvey from story by Frank Hurley. photography: George Heath. musical director: Lindley Evans. design: Eric Thompson. special effects: J. Alan Kenyon. cast: Aileen Britton, Campbell Copelin, Letty Craydon, Peter Dunstan, Frank Harvey, Frank Leighton, George Lloyd, Shirley Ann Richards, Joe Valli, Ronald Whelan.

THIRD PERSON PLURAL
Released 1978. Kodak colour reversal, 16 mm, 90 minutes. director: James Ricketson. producers: Gill Eatherley, Greg Ricketson and John Weiley for Abraxas Films. screenplay: James Ricketson. photography:

Tom Cowan. composer: Greg McLean. editor: Christopher Cordeaux. cast: Bryan Brown, Margaret Cameron, George Shevstov, Linden Wilkinson.

THIRST
Released 1979. Eastman colour, 35 mm Panavision, 98 minutes. director: William Fayman. producer: Antony I Ginnane for F. G. Film Productions. screenplay: John Pinkney. photography: Vincent Monton. composer: Brian May. design: Jon Dowding and Jill Eden. editor: Phil Reid. cast: Shirley Cameron, Chantal Contouri, David Hemmings, Max Phipps, Lulu Pinkus, Walter Pym, Henry Silva.

THREE TO GO
Released 1971. B & W, 35 mm, 89 minutes. producer: Gil Brealey for Commonwealth Film Unit. photography: Kerry Brown. editor: Wayne Le Clos. *Michael*. director: Peter Weir. screenplay: Peter Weir. cast: Grahame Bond, Matthew Burton, Peter Colville, Betty Lucas, Judy McBurney, Georgina West. *Judy*. director: Brian Hannant. screenplay: Brian Hannant. composers: Grahame Bond and Rory O'Donoghue. cast: Brian Anderson, Gary Day, Serge Lazareff, Judy Morris, Cliff Neate, Wendy Playfair, Penny Ramsay, Mary Ann Severne. *Toula*. director: Oliver Howes. screenplay: Oliver Howes. cast: Gabrial Battikha, Erica Crown, Joe Hasham, Rina Ioannou, Andrew Pappas.

TIM
Released 1979. Eastman colour, 35 mm, 100 minutes. director: Michael Pate. producer: Michael Pate for Pisces Productions. screenplay: Michael Pate. photography: Paul Onorato. composer: Eric Jupp. design: John Carroll. editor: David Stiven. cast: Pat Evison, Mel Gibson, Deborah Kennedy, Alwyn Kurts, Piper Laurie.

TOUCH AND GO
Released 1980. Eastman colour, 35 mm, 92 minutes. director: Peter Maxwell. producer: John Pellat for Mutiny Pictures. screenplay: Peter Yeldham. photography: John McLean. design: David Copping. editor: Sara Bennett. cast: Brian Blain, John Bluthal, Chantal Contouri, Jeannie Drynan, Carmen Duncan, Jon English, Wendy Hughes.

TRAPS
Released 1985. Colour, 16 mm, 96 minutes. director: John Hughes. producer: John Hughes. screenplay: John Hughes, Paul Davies. photography: Jaems Grant, Erika Addis. editor: Zbigniew Friedrich. cast: Carolyn Howard, Paul Davies, John Flaus, Gwenda Wiseman.

TRESPASSERS, THE
Released 1976, Melbourne. Colour, 35 mm, 91 minutes. director: John Duigan. producer: John Duigan. screenplay: John Duigan. photography: Vincent Monton. design: Gillian Armstrong. composer: Bruce Smeaton. editor: Tony Patterson. cast: Briony Behets, Peter Carmody, Sydney Conabere, John Derum, Cliff Ellen, Max Gillies, Chris Haywood, Hugh Keays-Byrne, Judy Morris, Peter Thompson, Ross Thompson.

TRUE STORY OF ESKIMO NELL, THE
Released 1975, Melbourne. Colour, 35 mm, 103 minutes. director: Richard Franklin. producers: Ron Baneth and Richard Franklin for Quest Films and Filmways. screenplay: Richard Franklin and Alan Hopgood. photography: Vincent Monton. design: Josephine Ford. composer Brian May. editor: Andrew London. cast: Abigail, Grahame Bond, Max Gillies, Serge Lazareff, Kris McQuade.

TURKEY SHOOT
Released 1982. Kodak colour, 35 mm, 94 minutes. director: Brian Trenchard-Smith. producers: Antony I. Ginnane and William Fayman for Second FGH Film Consortium. screenplay: Jon George, Neill Hicks. photography: John McLean. composer: Brian May. design: Bernard Hides. editor: Alan Lake. cast: Michael Craig, Carmen Duncan, Noel Ferrier, Olivia Hussey, Steve Railsback, Lynda Stoner, Roger Ward, Peter Gwynne, David Foster, Margo Lee, James Condon.

27A
Released 1974, Melbourne. Colour, 16 mm, 86 minutes. director: Esben Storm. producer: Hayden Keenan for Smart Street Films. screenplay: Esben Storm. photography: Michael Edols. design: Peter Minnett. editor: Richard Moir. cast: Graham Corry, Bill Hunter, James Kemp, Robert McDarra, Richard Moir, Max Osbiston.

TWO FRIENDS
Released for television 1986. Colour, 16 mm, 80 minutes. director: Jane Campion. producer: Jan Chapman for the ABC. screenplay: Helen Garner. photography: Julian Penney. cast: Emma Coles, Kris Bidenko, Kris McQuade, Peter Hehir.

TWO THOUSAND WEEKS
Released 1969, Melbourne. B & W, 35 mm, 89 minutes. director: Tim Burstall. producers: David Bilcock snr and Patrick Ryan for Eltham Film Productions and Senior Film Productions. screenplay: Tim Burstall and Patrick Ryan. photography: Robin Copping. editor: David Bilcock jnr. design: Rosemary

Ryan. music: Don Burrows. cast: Graeme Blundell, Eileen Chapman, Michael Duffield, Jeanie Drynan, Will Gardiner, David Turnbull.commentary [200]

UNDERCOVER
Released 1983. Eastman colour, 35 mm, wide-screen, 100 minutes. director: David Stevens. producer: David Elfick for Palm Beach Pictures. screenplay: Miranda Downes. photography: Dean Semler. designer: Herbert Pinter. editor: Tim Wellburn. cast: Sandy Gore, Caz Lederman, Michael Pate, Peter Phelps, Genevieve Picot, Andrew Sharp, John Walton.

UNFINISHED BUSINESS
Released 1985. Colour, 16 mm, 75 minutes. director: Bob Ellis. producer: Rebel Penfold-Russell for Unfinished Business Productions and Lipsync Productions. screenplay: Bob Ellis. photography: Andrew Lesnie. design: Jane Jonson. composer: Norman Kaye. editor: Amanda Robson. cast: John Clayton, Michele Fawdon, Norman Kaye, Bob Ellis.

WAKE IN FRIGHT
Released 1971, Paris, as Outback. Colour, 35 mm, 109 minutes. director: Ted Kotcheff. producer: George Willoughby. screenplay: Evan Jones from novel by Kenneth Cook. photography: Brian West. design: Dennis Gentle. composer: John Scott. editor: Anthony Buckley. cast: Gary Bond, Slim de Gray, Sylvia Kay, Dawn Lake, Harry Lawrence, Robert McDarra, John Meillon, Donald Pleasance, Chips Rafferty, Al Thomas, Jack Thompson, Peter Whittle.

WALKABOUT
Released 1971, USA. Colour, 35 mm, 100 minutes. director: Nicolas Roeg. producer: Si Litvinoff for Max L. Raab and Si Litvinoff Films. screenplay: Edward Bond, from novel by James Vance Marshall. photography: Nicolas Roeg. composer: John Barry. design: Terry Gough. editors: Anthony Gibbs, Alan Patillo. cast: Jenny Agutter, Noelene Brown, Peter Carver, Barry Donnelly, David Gulpilil, Lucien John, John Meillon.

WARMING UP
Released 1983. Eastman colour, 35 mm, 93 minutes. director: Bruce Best. producer: James Davern for Film Rep. screenplay: James Davern. photography: Joseph Pickering. design: Michael Ralph. editor: Zsolt Kollanyi. cast: Queenie Ashton, Adam Fernance, Kim Grogan, Lloyd Morris, Barbara Stephens, Henri Szeps.

WE OF THE NEVER-NEVER
Released 1982. Eastman colour, 35 mm, 90 minutes. director: Igor Auzins. producer: Greg Tepper for Adams Packer Productions and Film Corporation of Western Australia. screenplay: Peter Schreck from novel by Mrs Aeneas Gunn. photography: Gary Hansen. design: Josephine Ford. editor: Cliff Hayes. cast: Tony Barry, Arthur Dignam, Lewis Fitz-Gerald, John Jarratt, Tommy Lewis, Angela Punch-McGregor, Martin Vaughan.

WEEKEND OF SHADOWS
Released 1978. Eastman colour, 35 mm, 95 minutes. director: Tom Jeffrey. producers: Tom Jeffrey and Matt Carroll for Samson Film Services and South Australian Film Corporation. screenplay: Peter Yeldham, from The Reckoning, novel by (?). photography: Richard Wallace. design: Christopher Webster. editor: Rod Adamson. cast: Graeme Blundell, Bill Hunter, Melissa Jaffer, Wyn Roberts, Graham Rouse, John Waters.

WILLS AND BURKE
Released 1987. Eastman colour, 35 mm, 100 minutes. director: Bob Weis producer: Bob Weis and Margot McDonald for Stony Desert. screenplay: Philip Dalkin. photography: Gaetano Nino Martinetti. composer: Fred Symons. design: Tracy Watt. editor: Edward McQueen-Mason. cast: Roy Baldwin, Peter Collingwood, Kim Gyngell, Jonathon Hardy, Mark Little, Garry McDonald, Rod Williams.

WINDS OF JARRAH
Released 1983. Eastman colour, 35 mm, wide screen, 94 minutes. director: Mark Egerton. producers: Mark Egerton and Marj Pearson for Film Corporation of Western Australia. screenplay: Mark Egerton, based on a storyline, characters and screenplay by Anne Brooksbank and Bob Ellis, which is based on the novel The House in the Timber Woods by Joyce Dingwell. photography: Geoff Burton. composer: Bruce Smeaton. design: Graham Walker. editor: Sarah Bennett. cast: Isabelle Anderson, Steve Bisley, Terence Donovan, Harold Hopkins, Susan Lyons, Emil Minty, Martin Vaughan, Dorothy Alison, Nikki Gemmell, Steven Grives, Mark Kounnas.

WINTER OF OUR DREAMS
Released 1981. Eastman colour, 35 mm, 90 minutes. director: John Duigan. producer: Richard Mason for Vega Film Productions. screenplay: John Duigan. photography: Tom Cowan. design: Lee Whitmore. editor: Henry Dangar. cast: Bryan Brown, Judy Davis, Cathy Downes, Mervyn Drake, Zoe Lake, Mark Luhrman, Peter Mochrie.

WRONG SIDE OF THE ROAD
Released 1981. Eastman colour, 35 mm, 80 minutes. director: Ned Lander. producer: Ned Lander for Inma Productions. screenplay: Graeme Isaac and Ned Lander. photography: Louis Irving. musical performers: No Fixed Address, Us Mob. design: Jan Mackay. editor: John Scott. cast: Veronica Brodie, Donna Drover, Chris Haywood, Gayle Rankine, Leila Rankine

WRONG WORLD
Released 1985. Fuji colour, 35 mm, 100 minutes. director: Ian Pringle. producers: Bryce Menzies and Ian Pringle for Seon Film Productions. screenplay: Ian Pringle and Doug Ling. photography: Ray Argall. composer: Eric Gradman. design: Christine Johnson. editor: Ray Argall. cast: Jo Kennedy, Nick Lathouris, Robbie McGregor, Richard Moir, Esben Storm.

WRONSKY
Released 1980. Eastman colour, 16 mm, 70 minutes. director: Ian Pringle. producer: Ian Pringle for Seon Film Productions. screenplay: Ian Pringle, Doug Ling. photography: Ray Argall. editor: Tony Paterson. cast: Miranda Brown, Phil Dagg, John Flaus, Rob Jordan, Doug Ling, Lisa Parish, Ross Thompson, Frank Walsh.

YACKETY YACK
Released 1974, Melbourne. Colour, 16 mm, 86 minutes. director: Dave Jones. producer: Dave Jones. screenplay: Dave Jones. photography: Gordon Glenn. cast: John Flaus, Dave Jones, Jerzy Toeplitz.

YEAR OF LIVING DANGEROUSLY, THE
Released 1982. Eastman colour, 35 mm, 105 minutes. director: Peter Weir. producer: Jim McElroy for Wayan Productions. screenplay: David Williamson, from novel by C. J. Koch. design: Herbert Pinter. editor: Bill Anderson. cast: Peter Collingwood, Noel Ferrier, Mel Gibson, Linda Hunt, Bill Kerr, Sigourney Weaver.

INDEX

A page reference in **bold** type is the principal reference to a topic.

Aborigines, 19, 41, 81-82, 116-119, 125, 126, 207-208
Abramovicz, Halina, 228
action films, 47, 48
actors, 63-66; overseas, 15
Actors' Equity, 15
actresses, 65-66
adultery, 125
adventure films, 47, 48
Adventures of Barry Mackenzie, The, 52, 55, 86, **87-89**, 91, 112, 237
AFC, *see* Australian Film Commission
AFDC, *see* Australian Film Development Corporation
Agutter, Jenny, 82
Alexander, Liz, 193
All the Rivers Run, 62, 65
Allen, Cameron, 195
Allies, 242
Alvin Purple, 54, 86, **90-92**
American culture: influence on Australian films, 13-14
American distribution and exhibition, 13
American films, 23-25; made in Australia, 15
Annie's Coming Out, 40
anti-Britishness, 87-88, 151-157, 162
Anzacs, The, 32, 233
Apps, Gregory, 60, 100
Argue, David, 198, 230
Armstrong, Gillian, 135-136, 196

Arrighi, Luciana, 136
'art' films, 33-34, 69-71, 116, 144-145, 214; *see also* Australian Film Commission genre films
Asian politics, 189-193
audience: creation of, 244; search for, 79; sophistication, 73
Australia After Dark, 47
Australian Council for the Arts: Film and Television Committee, 11
Australian culture, 11, 15
Australian Film Commission, 12, 14, 31, 43; genre films, 23, **28-38**, 63, 66, 70, 98, 111, 153, 158, 223, 229, 233; Creative Development Branch, 40; *see also earlier name* Australian Film Development Corporation
Australian Film Commission Act, 34
Australian Film Development Corporation, 14, 31, 88; *see also later name* Australian Film Corporation
Australian Gothic, 40, 47, **49-52**, 83, 94, 128-129, 140, 217, 230, 237-239
Australianness, 13, 19, 22, 25, 33-34, 36-37, 62-63, *examples are given throughout Part II; see also* Australian culture; male

Australianness; nationalism
Auzins, Igor, 205

Backroads, 37, 41, 42, **115-116**
Baker, David, 55, 84, 85
Barrett, Ray, 113, 117, 202, 204, 206
Barry, Julie, 198
Barry, Tony, 208, 234
Barry Mackenzie, see Adventures of Barry Mackenzie, The
Behets, Briony, 125
Bell, John, 189, 193
Beresford, Bruce, 54, 55, 113, 151
Berry, Amanda, 142
Between Wars, **92-94**
bikie films, 137
Binney, Clare, 113
Bird, Alison, 122
Bishop, Pat, 113
Bisley, Steve, 139, 228, 229, 234
blacks, *see* Aborigines
Bliss, 51, **237-239**
Blood Money, 41
Blundell, Graeme, 90, 113, 150
Bodyline, 32, 62, 63, 222, 225, 233
Boer War, 153
Bond, Gary, 80
bourgeoisie, 23
Bourke, Terry, 48
Box, The, 54
box office receipts, 232-233
Break of Day, 36
Breaker Morant, **151-157**; AFC genre film, 32, 55; Australianness, 36, 62, 149, 233; male ensemble film, 32, 61, 63, 147, 161-162, 222
Breakfast in Paris, 48
Brennan, Richard, 40
British: antagonism toward, 87-88, 151-157, 162
Brooksbank, Anne, 145
Brown, Bryan, 60, 63, 64; 1976-80, 124, 133, 142, 147, 148, 150; 1980-81, 152, 153, 155, 164, 165, 168, 170-171; 1981 to date, 189, 191-193, 233
Brown, Ken, 142
Bruning, Robert, 45, 100
Buckley, Anthony, 193
Buddies, 62, **219-221**
buddy films 62, 157-161, 174, 220
budgets, 12
Burke, Simon, 111
Burlinson, Tom, 63, 64, 180, 181, 188, 223
Burns, Carol, 228
Burns, Tim, 200
Burrowes, Geoff, 181
Burstall, Tim, 46-47, 54, 55, 79, 84, 85, 86, 90, 146
Buzo, Alexander, 78
Byron, Annie, 228

cable television: influence on film-making, 47
Caddie, 30, **111-112**
Cameron, Ken, 41, 199-200, 227
Cameron, Margaret, 141
Camilleri, Terry, 95, 130
Campion, Jane, 241
Canadian film industry, 36-37
Capelja, Jad, 152, 171
car-crash films, 47, 94-96, 137
Careful, He Might Hear You, 188, 192, **210-214**, 241
Carman, Michael, 115
Cars That Ate Paris, The, 50, **94-96**
Catholicism, 110-111, 132
Cathy's Child, 40, 41
censorship laws, 78

Chain Reaction, 74
Chamberlain, Richard, 123, 126
Chant of Jimmie Blacksmith, The, **116-119**, 205
characterisation, 33
children's films, 126
Chilvers, Simon, 221
City's Edge, The, 41, 57
Clancy, Jack, 204
Clark, Liddy, 66
Clarke, John, 215
class differences, 106-109, 196-214
Clinic, The, **221-222**
Club, The, 55, 86
colonialism, 19-20
Colossimo, Vince, 64, 229
comedy, 56, 86-92, 215-217, 220-222; *see also* ocker comedy; sex comedies
comedy of manners, 84
comic-porn films, 92
commercialism, 43-49, 70 232-234
Cool Change, 241
Couzens, Paul, 119
Cowan, Tom, 41, 57, 124
Cox, Paul, 69, 192, 214-215, 227, 241
Cracknell, Ruth, 128
Crawford, Henry, 164
Creative Development Branch (AFC), 40
critics, 79
Crocker, Barry, 87-88, 91
Crocodile Dundee, 12, 14, **234-237**
Crombie, Don, 193
Cruthers, John, 210
Cullen, Max, 35, 60, 100, 104, 234
cultural nationalism, 11, 15
culture versus industry, 11-13; *see also* Industry-1

and Industry -2
Cummins, Peter, 100-101, 126

Dark Room, The, 48
Darra, Robert, 199
Davis, Judy, 30, 65, 136, 138, 168, 170-171, 191-193, 195
Dawn!, 40
Dead Kids, 45
de Burgh, Celia, 225
defeat, 21-22
de Laurentiis, Dino, 15
Deling, Bert, 199
dependency theory, 20, 232
derelicts, 41, 121
detective films, 203-205
Devil's Playground, The, 58, **110-111**
Dickinson, Eva, 119
Dignam, Arthur, 85, 111, 207
Dingwall, John, 61, 62, 98-99, 220
Dismissal, The, 32, 62, 209, 222, **225-227**
distribution: American, 13; on TV and video, 244
Dobrowolska, Gosia, 228, 229
documentary treatment, 41
Don's Party, 54, 55, 62, 86, **112-114**
double bind, 20, **23-26**, 232, 234
Douglas, Kirk, 182
Downes, Cathy, 169
drug addiction, 121, 169
Drynan, Jeannie, 113, 230
Duet for Four, 55
Duigan, John, 40-41, 121, 168, 189, 191
Dunstan, Joy, 115

Economic conditions, 18
Edgley, Michael, 181, 222
Eklund, Kay, 103

Eliza Fraser, 54, 92
Elliott, Sumner Locke, 210
Ellis, Bob, 131, 145, 202, 215, 217
Elsaesser, Thomas, 16-17
Emery, John, 115
Emmanuel, Takis, 111
Emma's War, 32
End Play, 48
Essay in Pornography, 47
Evans, Reg, 210
Everage, Edna (film character), 88-89
Evison, Pat, 66, 197, 221
Ewart, John, 100
Exits, 227, 242
experimental films, 143

family, 217-219
fantasy films, 97
Fantasy Man, 57, **230**
Far East, 188, **189-193**
Fast Talking, 41, 42, **227-229**
female characters, 32, 33, 55-57, 65-68; 1970-75, 86, 102; 1976-80, 111-112, 129, 135-137; 1980-81, 172, 177-178; 1981 to date, 197, 198, 202, 207-208, 221
femaleness, 86, 105-109
feminism, 112, 135-137, 184-185
fifties' subculture, 83
Fighting Back, 41, 121
Final Cut, 48
Finch, Peter, 234
Fink, Margaret, 136
Fitz-Gerald, Lewis, 152, 156, 207, 208
F. J. Holden, 41, 42, 55, **119-122**
Flaus, John, 103, 122, 123, 141, 240
Foley, Gary, 115
For Love Alone, 32, 192

Franklin, Miles, 135
Frawley, John, 128
Frazetto, Serge, 121
Friels, Colin, 64, 201, 220-221
Fringe Dwellers, The, 38
funding, private, 137

Gallipoli, 50, 55, 59, 126, **157-163**, 168; Australianness, 36, 63, 149, 153-154; male ensemble film, 32, 62, 147, 222, 233
Garner, Alice, 201
gay characters, 197, 222
'genre' films, 31-32, 47-48; *see also* Australian Film Commission genre films
German films, 16-27
Gibson, Mel, 64, 139, 140, 159, 160, 174, 190-191, 200, 233
Gillies, Max, 227
Gilmour, Ian, 121, 150
Ginnane, Tony, 48, 205
Gledhill, Nicholas, 212
Going Down, 36, 37, 41-42, 51, 74, **198-199**
Goodbye Paradise, 37, 74, **202-205**, 206
Gothic films, *see* Australian Gothic
government funding, 12
Grubb, Robert, 136
Guard, Dominic, 106, 126
guilt, 82, 126
Gulpilil, David, 81, 126

Hall, Ken, 241
Hancock, W.K., 62
Hanna, Pat, 234
Hannam, Ken, 61
Hansen, Gary, 205
Hard Knocks, 35, 36, 41, 42
Harders, Jane, 66, 83

Index

Hargreaves, John, 60, 64, 113, 125, 150, 214, 215, 219
Harlequin, 48
Haywood, Chris, 127, 133, 145, 217, 221-222, 228, 230
Hazlehurst, Noni, 66, 200, 201
Heatwave, **193-196**
Herzog, Werner, 217
Hinde, John, 79
historical films, *see* period films
Hogan, Paul, 64, 78, 233, 234-236
Hollywood films, *see* American films
Homesdale, 50, 94
homo-eroticism, 156; *see also* gay characters
Hoodwink, 41
Hopkins, Harold, 113, 220, 230
horror films, 48-51-52, 97-125
horses, 182-185, 222-225
Hughes, Wendy, 66, 132, 212, 213, 215-216, 219
Humphries, Barry, 87-88, 91, 92
Hunt, Linda, 190-191
Hunter, Bill, 103, 115-116, 127, 131, 145-146, 162, 209, 234

icons, **62-64**, 233
ideas films, 67-70
I'll Be Home for Christmas, 41
In Search of Anna, **144-145**, 148
Industry-1 and Industry-2, 13, 37, 43, 47, 151, 179, 233; *see also Vol. 1 pp. 197-201*
industry versus art, 11-13; *see also* Industry-1 and Industry-2
insanity, 51, 83-84, 128-129
interior films, 67-70
'international' films, 14, 23-24
Irishman, The, 32, 36

issue films, *see* social realism

Jack and Jill: a Postscript, 50
Jackson, Gordon, 164
Jarrett, John, 106, 150, 208
Jeffrey, Tom, 150
Jemison, Anna, 229
Journey Among Women, 55, 57, 82
Just Out of Reach, 57

kammerspiel, 110
Kants, Ivar, 228, 229
Karl, Bob, 122, 123
Kaye, Norman, 215-218, 220
Keays-Byrne, Hugh, 139
Keenan, Haydn, 198, 199
Kelly, Margaret, 173
Keneally, Thomas, 85, 116
Kennedy, Byron, 137, 173
Kennedy, Gerard, 132
Kennedy, Graham, 60, 113, 150
Kennedy, Jo, 66, 180, 196, 245
Kerr, Bill, 162
Killing of Angel Street, The, 40, **193-196**
Killing Time, 48
Kitty and the Bagman, 32
Koch, Christopher, 190
Kostas, 40, 41
Kotcheff, Ted, 80
Kozlowski, Linda, 236
Kracauer, Siegfried, 16
Krajus, Kim, 121

Lambert, Anne, 106
Lamond, John, 48
Lander, Ned, 180
Lang, Veronica, 113
larrikinism, 33, 61, 164, 219
Last Bastion, The, 32, 162, 222, 225, 233
Last Wave, The, 50, 123, **124**, 126

Laurentiis, Dino de, 15
Laurie, John, 71
Lawrence, Denny, 202
Laws, John, 81
Lawson, Sylvia, 19
Lee, Margo, 197
Lee, Mark, 126, 159, 160
Leibman, Ron, 225
Les Patterson Saves the World, 92
Lesley, Lorna, 66
Let the Balloon Go, 32
Lewis, Tommy, 117, 118
Libido, 31, 55, **84-86**, 211
Lighthorsemen, The, 66
Listen to the Lion, 41
literariness, 32-33, 106
Lonely Hearts, 37, 51, **214-215**
loners, 149
Long, Joan, 229
Long Weekend, The 82, **124-126**
Love Letters from Teralba Road, 41, **122-124**, 192
Lowenstein, Richard, 227
Lye, Reg, 100

McGregor, Craig, 84
McGregor, Julie, 142
McKeon, Raina, 193
Maclaine-Cross, Moira, 198
McQuade, Kris, 66, 124, 192, 204, 220-221
Mad Max films, 47, 50, 73
Mad Max, 36, **137-140**, 188
Mad Max 2, 63, 137, 140, 168, **173-178**, 188, 200, 241
Mad Max: Beyond Thunderdome, 14, 238, 239, 243
madness, 51, 83-84, 128, 129
male actors, 63-65
male Australianness, 65, 97-105, 144-145, 154, 156

male couple films, 62, 157-161, 174, 220
male ensemble films, 32, 52-58, **58-62**, 62-63, 233; 1970-75, 80, 86, 97, 98; 1976-80, 112-114, 147-150; 1980-81, 157, 162
male ritual, 81, 113
maleness, 86, 115, 180, 184-85; *see also* male Australianness
Man from Hong Kong, The, 48
Man from Snowy River, The, 65, 168, **179-188**, 192, 222, 234; male ensemble film, 32, 62; melodrama, 211, 241; nationalism and Australianness, 12, 36, 63, 233
Man of Flowers, 51, **214-217**, 218, 227
Mann, Tracy, 35, 66, 198
marketing: overseas, 14-15
masculine ritual, 81, 113
Maxwell, John, 148
Maybe This Time, 55, 57-58, 86, **145-147**
Meagher, John, 230
Meillon, John, 80, 209
melancholy, 21-22
melodrama, 121, 185-186, 211-212, 239-240; *see also* Australian Gothic
Melvin, Son of Alvin, 92
Midnite Spares, 50, 74
migrants, 41
Miller, Dennis, 228
Miller, George (maker of the *Mad Max* films), 137, 173
Miller, George (maker of *The Man from Snowy River*), 181
Millins, Greg, 221
Minty, Emil, 174
Moir, Richard, 144, 148, 150,

194, 209, 210, 245
Money Movers, The, 48
Monkey Grip, 37, 55, 58, 66, 73, 192, **199-202**
Moorhouse, Frank, 92
More Things Change, The, 57-58
Morris, Judy, 66, 144-145, 148, 225
Morse, Helen, 30, 66, 111, 164, 165, 189, 191-193
Motherwell, Phil, 148
Mouth to Mouth, 41, 42, **121-122**, 199
Moving Out, 41
Mulcahy, Russell, 230
Murray, John, 84
musical comedy, 196; see also rock musicals
My Brilliant Career, 30, 32, 33, 65, **135-137**, 138, 192
My First Wife, **214-219**, 227

Naked Bunyip, The, 47
Naked Country, The, 57
national cinema, **15-17**
national culturalism, 11, 15
national identity, 21, 22-23, 24, 25-26; see also Australian culture; Australianness
national psyche, **15-17**
nationalism, 12-13, 36, 63, 154, 164, 219, 233; see also Australian culture; Australianness; patriotism; populism
Nehm, Kristina, 38
Neidhard, Elke, 91
Neill, Sam, 64, 136-137, 192
Neilson, Juanita: films about, 193-196
Nelson, Margaret, 108
Nevin, Robyn, 85, 204, 212
New South Wales Film Corporation, 31, 147
Newsfront, 33, 37, 73, 74, 93, 103, 127, **129-135**, 154, 242
Next of Kin, 48
Nickel Queen, 81
Night the Prowler, The, 50, **128-129**, 130
nostalgia films, see period films
Noyce, Phillip, 115, 132, 193
nudity in films, 90
No. 96, 54

obscene language, 78
'ocker comedy', 33, 52, 55, 56, 112-113, 146
ockerism, 59, 77-78, 197
Odd Angry Shot, The, 55, 60, 86, 147, **149-150**, 154
O'Donovan, Ross, 180, 196
Office Picnic, The, 57
O'May, John, 180
One Night Stand, 40, 121
oppression, 41
Ordell, Tal, 234
Otto, Barry, 238
overseas actors, 15
Oz, **114-115**

Palm Beach, 36, 73, 140, **141-144**, 199, 203
Paterson, A.B. 'Banjo', 181
Patrick, 48
patriotism, 153, 162; see also nationalism
Pattinson, Michael, 229
Peat, Sonia, 121
period films, 31, 32, 33-36, 92-94, 97, 118, 135, 158, 205; see also Australian Film Commission genre films
Petersen, 54, 55, 61, 86, 145, 146
Phar Lap, 36, 62, 162, 188, **222-225**

Phipps, Max, 209
Picnic at Hanging Rock, 31, 33, 50, 97, **105-109**, 124, 126
Picture Show Man, The, 32
Plains of Heaven, The, 209, 210
Plevnik, Vera, 198
Plumber, The, 50
police corruption, 193
political corruption as film subject, 193
political environment, 18-19
political films, 241-242
politics as film subject, 189-193, 224-227
populism, 223-234, 236-237
pornography, 47; *see also* comic-porn films; sexploitation films
Porter, Hal, 85
poverty, 111
Prescott, Mike, 146
Pringle, Ian, 210
prisoners, 41
Prisoners' Action Group, 147
private funding, 137
privatisation, 12
'problem' films, *see* social realism
Producers' and Directors' Guild of Australia, 84
Promised Woman, 41
prostitution, 168-169
psychoanalysis, 16
Puberty Blues, 41-42, 55, 57, 111, 152, 168, **171-173**, 203
Punch McGregor, Angela, 66, 103, 118, 133, 206, 207-209
Pure Shit, 42, 71, 199
Pym, Walter, 121

Queensland, 41, **122**, 123

R-certificate, 54, 78

racial tension, 116-119
racism, 207-209
Rafferty, Chips, 80, 234
Raw Deal, 48, 205
Raymond, Candy, 113
Razorback, 51, 74, 188, **230**
Redgrave, Corin, 93
Removalists, The, 61
repression, 110; *see also* sexual repression
Return of Captain Invincible, The, 51
Reynolds, Freddy, 118
Ricketson, James, 140
rite of passage, 182, 234
road films, 42, 115-116, 117, 119, 144
Road Warrior, The, 168
Roadgames, 48
Roberts, Rachel, 106
rock musicals, 42, 115
romances, 48, 56
romantic Australianness, 36-37
Ronin Films, 215, 244
Rooted, 78
Ross, Philip, 100
Rowe, Greg, 126
Ruane, John, 122
Runnin' on Empty, 50, 74

Samuel, Joanne, 139
satire, 61
Saunders, Justine, 38
Scacchi, Greta, 66
Scales of Justice, 195
Schepisi, Fred, 110
Schepisi, John, 84, 85
Schofield, Nell, 152, 171
Schuler, Christine, 106
Schultz, Carl, 202-203, 210
Seale, John, 210
second cinema, **11-26**
settlers, 19, 21
sex comedies, 54, 56

Index

sexism, 56, 86, 102, 184; see *also* male Australianness
sexploitation films, 48, 57; see *also* pornography
Sexton, John, 222
sexual mores films, **52-58**, 70, 84
sexual politics, 61
sexual repression, 55, 107-109
sexuality: 1970-75, 81, 82, 86-92, 107-109; 1976-80, 115, 121, 124; 1981 to date, 210-211, 217-219
Sharman, Jim, 50, 51, 82, 128
shearing, 100-105
Shevtsov, George, 141
Shirley Thompson Versus the Aliens, 37, 50, **82-84**, 197, 199
Shorter, Ken, 145
Side Car Racers, 81
Silver City, 32, 228, **229**
Singer and the Dancer, The, 57
single mothers, 121
Skinner, Carole, 66
Snapshot, 45, 48, 205
social comment, 87
social imaginary, 16-17, **17-23**, 24-25, 232, 234
social realism, **39-43**, 121, 144, 147, 227-229, 244-245
Sokol, Yuri, 217
Spence, Bruce, 86-87, 115, 140, 174, 176
Squatter's Daughter, The, 241
Stacey, Tom, 88
Stanley, 51
Stanton, John, 209
stars, 63-64
Starstruck, 51, 66, 74, 180, **196-198**
Stevens, Carl, 119
Stevens, David, 164, 221
Stir, 41, 147-150

Stork, 54, 55, 61, **86-87**
Storm, Esben, 199
Storm Boy, **126**
Street Hero, 42, 65, 229
Strikebound, 227, 228, 242
strikes as film subject, 104-105, 227
suburbia, 119-120, 128
Summer of Secrets, 50
Summerfield, 48
Sunday Too Far Away, 60, 61, 63, 86, **97-105**, 112, 155, 225, 227
Sunshine Sally, 111
surf films, 144
Survivor, The, 48
Sweet, Gary, 63, 64, 225
Sweet and Sour, 42
Sweet Dreamers, 40

Tall Timbers, 241
Tauchert, Arthur, 234
tax concession incentives, 12, 14
Taylor, Kit, 113
television, 64; docu-drama, 226; films on, 244; mini-series, 32, 164-167
10B(A), 12, 14
theatre: influence on film 77, 86
Third Person Plural, 37, **140-141**, 171, 192
Thirst, 48
Thomas, Jerry, 100
Thompson, Jack, 63, 64, 233; 1970-75, 80, 85, 98, 99; 1976 to date, 146, 152, 156, 187
Thoms, Albie, 140
Thornhill, Mike, 92
Thornton, Sigrid, 45, 65, 192, 229
Three to Go, 41
thrillers, 31, 48
Town Like Alice, A, 62, 63,

164-169, 192
Traps, 240, 242
*True Story of Eskimo Nell,
The*, 54
Turkey Shoot, 48, 205
Turkiewicz, Sophia, 229
27A, 41, 199

Undercover, 219
underground films, 52
unemployment, 121
unions, 15; as film subject, 104-105; *see also* Actors' Equity
*Unknown Industrial Prisoner,
The*, 36

Vallis, Jane, 106
vampire films, 48
Vaughan, Martin, 208, 223
vernacular, *see* ockerism
videos: films on, 244; influence on film-making, 47; threat to cinema, 232-234
violence, 81, 116-118

Waddell, Gary, 71, 115
Wake in Fright, 50, **80-81**, 188
Walkabout, 81, 124
Walker, Kerry, 128-130, 238
Wallace, Stephen, 122, 192
war, 151-163, 164
Ward, Russel, 62
Waterfront, 222, 227
We of the Never-Never, 32, 133, **205-210**
Weaver, Jacki, 30, 66
Weaver, Sigourney, 190-191
Weaving, Hugo, 64, 225
Weekend of Shadows, 36
Weimar cinema, 16-17
Weir, Peter, 50, 51, 69-70, 241; 1970-75, 94, 107; 1976-80, 123, 124, 126; 1980 to date,

159, 190
Westerns, 48
White, Patrick, 128
Whittle, Peter, 80
Wilkinson, Linden, 141
Williamson, David, 54, 58-61, 233; 1970-75, 85, 86-87, 98; 1976-80, 113, 146; 1980 to date, 162, 163, 188, 222
Wincer, Simon, 222
Winchester, Jone, 103
Winds of Jarrah, 48
winning, 22
Winter of Our Dreams, 37, 74, **168-171**, 191
Witcombe, Eleanor, 136
women: actors, 65-66; as sexual prey, 155; characters, *see* female characters; femaleness, 86, 105-109; in the film industry, 136; point of view, 55, 145
Women of the Sun, 41
Woodward, Edward, 152, 156
working class, 41, 59, 77, 124
Wrong Side of the Road, 35, 36, 41, 42, 116
Wrong World, 245

*Year of Living Dangerously,
The*, **190-193**
Young, Nat, 142
youth, 41, 42, 121

Zuanick, Rod, 227

FILM BOOKS FROM CURRENCY PRESS
The performing arts publishers

AN AUSTRALIAN FILM READER — Albert Moran and Tom O'Regan, eds.

Divided into four parts covering Early Cinema, Documentary Hopes, Renaissance of the Feature and Alternative Cinema, the *Reader* provides some of the most lucid commentary on this area of our national culture with fifty extended articles, some contemporary with their subject and others written with an historical perspective, from the most authoritative writers in their field. A fascinating overview of Australian film history, the *Reader* is of interest to both the general reader for its reflection of social attitudes, and to the student of film history.

LEGENDS ON THE SCREEN: The Narrative Film in Australia — John Tulloch

A richly illustrated and documented study of the silent feature film and the social climate in which it was made. Through the works of Raymond Longford, Franklyn Barrett, Beaumont Smith and others, Tulloch examines the professional, economic and ideological constraints on production and the complex operation of the Australian bush legend.

GOVERNMENT AND FILM IN AUSTRALIA — Ina Bertrand and Diane Collins

Clashes between film-makers and government have challenged the existence of the Australian film industry: from the battles against the Hollywood Goliath in the 20s to the moralists' lobby of the 30s and the Vincent Report in the 60s, the authors trace the patterns of intervention and non-intervention by State and Federal Governments. This study, by two film historians, analyses successive changes in the political control of film.

Complete list available on application to Currency Press, 330 Oxford Street, Paddington 2021 NSW, Australia.